ADVANCED
READING POWER

**Extensive Reading • Vocabulary Building
Comprehension Skills • Reading Faster**

PEARSON
Longman
www.longman.com

Beatrice S. Mikulecky
Linda Jeffries

Acknowledgments

The authors thank Laura Le Dréan, executive editor, whose feedback was invaluable as we developed *Advanced Reading Power*, and Gosia Jaros-White, associate development editor, who helped us clarify our ideas and stay on schedule.

We gratefully acknowledge the gentle pressure from the many teachers who have wanted us to write an advanced level book for the Reading Power series. We have made every effort to respond to their concerns.

We would also like to thank friends and colleagues, including Anita Belt and Jane Stevenson, for their helpful input and encouragement.

We acknowledge the influence of Tom Cobb, Averil Coxhead, and I. S. Paul Nation, whose work was essential in planning the new vocabulary development units.

Finally, we wish to thank Richard M. Ravin for his outstanding work in researching and drafting the reading passages in Part 4.

The publisher would like to extend special thanks to the following individuals who reviewed *Advanced Reading Power* and whose comments were instrumental in developing the book.

Jennifer Altman, University of Washington English Language Program, Seattle, WA; **Mary Hill**, North Shore Community College, Danvers, MA; **Helen Kallenbach**, Sonoma State American Language Institute, Rohnert Park, CA; **Alessandro Massaro**, Bunker Hill Community College, Boston, MA; **Susan Reynolds**, Seminole Community College, Oviedo, FL; **Ishida Saori**, University of Hawaii at Manoa, NICE Program Outreach College, Honolulu, HI

Advanced Reading Power:
Extensive Reading, Vocabulary Building, Comprehension Skills, Reading Faster

Pearson Education, 10 Bank Street, White Plains, NY 10606

Staff credits: The people who made up the *Advanced Reading Power* team, representing editorial, production, design, and manufacturing, are Christine Edmonds, Ann France, Gosia Jaros-White, Laura Le Dréan, Edith Pullman, Jennifer Stem, and Paula Van Ells.

Text composition: Rainbow Graphics
Text font: 10/14 Stone Serif
Text, Illustration, and Photo credits: See page 311

Library of Congress Cataloging-in-Publication Data

Mikulecky, Beatrice S.
  Advanced reading power : extensive reading, vocabulary building, comprehension skills, reading faster / Beatrice S. Mikulecky, Linda Jeffries.
      p. cm.
  ISBN 0-13-199027-6 (pbk.)
  1. Reading (Higher education) 2. College reading improvement programs. 3. Vocabulary—Study and teaching. 4. Reading comprehension. I. Jeffries, Linda. II. Title.
  LB2395.3.M53 2007
  428.4'3—dc22
                                     2006032213

ISBN - 13: 978-0-13-199027-2
ISBN - 10: 0-13-199027-6

Printed in the United States of America
    11–V001–13

Contents

Introduction

To the Teacher

Advanced Reading Power is unlike most other reading textbooks. First, the focus is different. This book directs students' attention to their own reading processes, while most other books focus primarily on the content. Second, *Advanced Reading Power* is organized in a different way. It contains four separate sections that correspond to four important aspects of proficient reading, and therefore it is like four books in one. *Teachers should assign work on all four parts of the book concurrently.*

The four parts of *Advanced Reading Power* are:

- Part 1: Extensive Reading

- Part 2: Vocabulary Building

- Part 3: Comprehension Skills

- Part 4: Reading Faster

Advanced Reading Power was designed to meet the needs of students who are enrolled in pre-college programs, college bridge programs, or advanced reading classes at the post-secondary level. Consequently, emphasis has been placed on the development of skills necessary for academic success, including building academic vocabulary.

The purpose of *Advanced Reading Power* is to develop students' awareness of their own reading and thinking processes so that they can be successful in reading college-level texts. To accomplish this, the book addresses the various reading skills in a direct manner, calling students' attention to how they think as they read.

Many students have a conceptualization of reading as translating, and that can interfere with their ability to read well in English. In *Advanced Reading Power,* students acquire an accurate understanding of what it means to read in English and gain confidence in their ability to deal with college-level reading assignments.

In order to allow students to focus on the process of reading, the lexical and syntactic content of some exercises has been controlled. In other exercises, however, students practice working with authentic texts of different types, including excerpts from college textbooks.

Student awareness of reading and thinking processes is further encouraged in many parts of the book by exercises that require them to work in pairs or small groups. In discussions with others, students formulate and articulate their ideas more precisely and thus acquire new ways of talking and thinking about a text. When students are asked to write sentences or paragraphs, they are also asked to exchange their work with others and discuss it so they can experience the connections between reading and writing.

The success of a reading class depends to a large extent on the teacher. You can enhance your students' learning while working with *Advanced Reading Power* by providing the following:

- an anxiety-free environment in which students feel comfortable taking risks and trying new ways of reading.

- enough practice so the students can master new strategies.
- friendly pressure in the form of persuasion and timing.
- positive examples of how to approach a text.
- a model for the kind of thinking that good reading requires.
- an inspiring example of an enthusiastic reader.

Note: A rationale for the approach taken in *Advanced Reading Power,* specific suggestions for using it in the classroom, and a Sample Syllabus can be found in the *Answer Key* booklet. For a more complete explanation of the theory and methodology see *A Short Course in Teaching Reading Skills* by Beatrice S. Mikulecky (Addison-Wesley, 1990).

To the Student

Using *Advanced Reading Power*

Since this book is different from other reading textbooks, it must be used in a different way. *Advanced Reading Power* is divided into four parts. Instead of working on one part at a time, as you would in most books, you **should work regularly on all four parts of the book.**

Part 1: Extensive Reading. The more you read, the better you read. In Part 1, you will have an opportunity to develop the habit of reading extensively—that is, reading many books that you choose for yourself. This will help improve your reading fluency, increase your comprehension and expand your vocabulary.

Part 2: Vocabulary Building. Research has shown that a strong vocabulary is an essential aspect of reading ability. In this part, you will develop strategies for expanding your knowledge of vocabulary, particularly words used often in academic texts.

Part 3: Comprehension Skills. Reading is a complex activity that involves a wide variety of skills. Your ability to understand and remember what you read depends in large part on your ability to apply these skills to your reading. Each unit in Part 3 focuses on an essential reading skill for you to explore and practice. In the Focus on Vocabulary section at the end of each skills unit, you will also have the opportunity to learn some of the academic words from the unit.

Part 4: Reading Faster. Reading rate (speed) is a crucial factor in academic performance, but one that is often overlooked. Reading faster allows you to save time on reading assignments. It also makes reading more enjoyable so you are likely to read more, and it leads to better comprehension. In this part of the book, you will work on improving your reading rate.

Reading questionnaires

What is your experience as a reader? What do you know about reading?

Questionnaire 1

Reading in your native language (_____)

For each statement, write **T** *(true) or* **F** *(false).*

1. It is always necessary to read every word of a passage.   _____

2. It is a good idea to say the words aloud when you read.   _____

3. Reading more slowly improves comprehension.   _____

4. Knowing every word is necessary for comprehension.   _____

5. As you read, you should always look up the meaning of words you do not know.   _____

6. To read well, you need to know the pronunciation of every word.   _____

7. Learning vocabulary is the only way to improve reading ability.   _____

8. Learning grammar is the only way to improve reading ability.   _____

9. You can read all kinds of texts (books, newspapers, etc.) the same way.   _____

10. Reading in different languages requires some different reading methods.   _____

Questionnaire 2

Reading in English

For each statement, write **T** *(true) or* **F** *(false).*

1. It is always necessary to read every word of a passage   _____

2. It is a good idea to say the words aloud when you read.   _____

3. Reading more slowly improves comprehension.   _____

4. Knowing every word is necessary for comprehension.   _____

5. As you read, you should always look up the meaning of words you do not know.   _____

6. To read well, you need to know the pronunciation of every word.   _____

7. Learning vocabulary is the only way to improve reading ability.   _____

8. Learning grammar is the only way to improve reading ability.   _____

9. You can read all kinds of texts (books, newspapers, etc.) the same way.   _____

10. Reading in different languages requires some different reading methods.   _____

Were your answers the same in both questionnaires? Compare your answers with those of another student. Do you agree?

You should have written **F** for every question in both questionnaires! If you marked some answers **T**, then you may need to learn more about reading. In *Advanced Reading Power*, you will discover more about the reading process and will have opportunities to re-evaluate your ideas about reading.

PART 1

Extensive Reading

Introduction to Extensive Reading

Answer the questions below on your own. Then form a group of two to four students and compare your answers.

1. Looking back at your childhood, what do you remember as your first reading experiences?

2. What kinds of reading material did your parents have in the house when you were young?

3. Do you remember having books or other materials read to you as a child? If so, what did you like best?

4. When you were able to read on your own, what did you enjoy reading?

5. Did your parents or other members of the family like to read? If so, what did they read?

6. What kind of reading is important in your life today? For example, do you read a lot for school or for your job?

7. About how many hours a week do you usually read materials of your own choice (magazines, newspapers, novels, nonfiction)?

8. Do you have a favorite writer in your first language? A favorite book?

9. What books have you read in English?

10. If you could easily read anything in English, what would you like to read?

Would you like to . . .

. . . read English faster with good comprehension?
. . . increase your vocabulary in English?
. . . improve your grammar in English?
. . . improve your writing skills in English?
. . . succeed in academic courses in English?
. . . gain broad knowledge of the world?

If you answered yes to these questions, then extensive reading is for you.

What is extensive reading?

- reading **a lot**—at least one book every two or three weeks;
- choosing a book that is interesting to you;
- no tests on comprehension or vocabulary;
- reading at your own pace.

You will benefit most from extensive reading if you follow these three essential rules:

Rule 1: Enjoy!
Rule 2: Enjoy!
Rule 3: Enjoy!

(Source: "Rules" adapted from J. Bamford and R. Day, *Extensive Reading Activities for Teaching Language.* Cambridge: Cambridge University Press, 2004, p. 5)

Because extensive reading is enjoyable, you will read faster and more, which makes it more enjoyable, so you will read even faster and more. This is the cycle of positive reinforcement that leads to the positive effects on comprehension and general language skills listed on page 2.

What the experts say about extensive reading

"Extensive reading is the most efficient way to help students change old habits and become confident second language readers." Prof. Mary Lee Field, Wayne State University, Michigan

". . . reading for pleasure [extensive reading] is the major source of our reading competence, our vocabulary and our ability to handle complex grammatical constructions." Prof. Stephen Krashen, University of Southern California

"Extensive reading may play a role in developing the capacity for critical thinking so important for success in higher education." Prof. Richard R. Day, University of Hawaii and Prof. Julian Bamford, Bunkyo University, Japan

"It is clear from these studies that extensive reading can be a major factor in success in learning another language." Prof. I. S. P. Nation, Victoria University of Wellington, New Zealand

---

UNIT 1 — Choosing a Book for Extensive Reading

Where to Find a Book

Ask your teacher, classmates, or friends for suggestions, or look on best-seller lists or the Internet (*http://www.NYTimes.com* or *http://www.Amazon.com*, for example) for titles that might interest you. Then go to a bookstore or library to see what is available.

How to Choose a Book

1. Choose a book that interests *you*. Your teacher and classmates may have good suggestions, but choose the book that is best for you, not for them.

2. Choose a full-length book, not a collection of articles or stories. Reading a whole book by a single author allows you to become comfortable with the writer's style and vocabulary.

3. Avoid a book whose story you are already familiar with because you have read it in another language or have seen the movie made from it. Knowing what will happen may make it less interesting for you.

4. Evaluate the book. To find out about the author and the genre (type of book), read the front and back covers. Read the first few pages, to find out about the style and subject.

5. Check the level of difficulty. If a book is too easy, it may be boring; if it is too difficult, you may become discouraged and stop reading. To find out how difficult the book is for you, count the number of unknown key words on a typical page. (A key word is a word you must know in order to follow the general meaning.) Five unknown key words on one page means the book is difficult for you. No unknown key words means the book is easy.

Hints for success in extensive reading

- Set a goal for yourself. Decide how many books you would like to read during the semester.

- Make reading a part of your daily routine. Set a time and place for reading. Read for at least thirty minutes at a time so that you can become involved in your book.

- Carry your book wherever you go and read it whenever you have time.

- Keep a journal. Write about your reactions to the book or any thoughts that are stimulated by your reading.

- When you finish a book, complete a Book Response Form, following the form on page 24. Then make an appointment with your teacher for a book conference to share your thoughts and reactions to it.

List of Recommended Titles

The books on this list have been read and enjoyed by students around the world, but you may choose a title that is not on the list. What matters most is that you find a book at an appropriate level that interests you.

(*) This author has written other books that might be of interest.
(**) This book may be easier to read.

Note: The number of pages is included to give you an idea of the approximate length. Other editions may be of slightly different length.

Book List

Fiction

Things Fall Apart. Achebe, Chinua. A classic African novel about how a Nigerian faces conflict within his society, as well as the effects of British colonialism. (215 pages)

Little Women. Alcott, Louisa May.* The classic novel of the joys and sorrows of the four March sisters and their mother in New England in the 1800s. (561 pages)

*If Beale Street Could Talk.*** Baldwin, James. A talented New York musician is falsely accused of a crime and put in prison. His girlfriend is determined to free him. (213 pages)

Sacajawea. Bruchac, Joseph. A novel about a young Native American woman in the early nineteenth century who helped two explorers find a safe route across North America to the Pacific Ocean. (199 pages)

*My Antonia.*** Cather, Willa.* A young woman who is the daughter of an immigrant from Bohemia faces loneliness and other challenges as an early settler in the American West. (175 pages)

Disgrace. Coetzee, J. M.* A brilliant tale of loneliness and violence in post-apartheid South Africa. (220 pages)

The Chocolate War. Cormier, Robert.* A high school student fights against a secret society of other students and becomes a hero in the school. (191 pages)

Bridget Jones's Diary. Fielding, Helen.* A funny and realistic novel (in the form of a diary) of the life of a single young woman today in search of self-improvement. (267 pages)

Tender Is the Night. Fitzgerald, F. Scott.* Set in the 1920s on the French Riviera, this is the story of a psychiatrist and his wealthy wife, who is also his patient. (315 pages)

*Johnny Tremaine.*** Forbes, Esther. The American Revolution and life in Boston in the 1770s, as seen through the experiences of a youth. (269 pages)

A Lesson Before Dying. Gaines, Ernest J. The moving story of an unusual friendship between a young teacher and a man in prison for murder, waiting to be executed. (256 pages)

Father Melancholy's Daughter. Godwin, Gail. A young woman's search for an understanding of the mother who left her when she was six years old and died soon after. (404 pages)

Snow Falling on Cedars. Guterson, David. During World War II, the Japanese-American community on an island near Seattle is sent to a prison camp in Montana, and after the war, a young Japanese-American is accused of murder. (460 pages)

*The Friends.*** Guy, Rosa.* A family moves to the United States from the West Indies and finds love and friendship. (185 pages)

For Whom the Bell Tolls. Hemingway, Ernest.* This famous romantic novel is set during the Spanish Civil War, when a young American volunteer falls in love with a Spanish girl. (471 pages)

Jazz Country. Hentoff, Nat.* A white youth in New York plays his trumpet in a jazz club in Harlem. (146 pages)

About a Boy. Hornby, Nick. The hilarious account of a friendship between an adolescent and a thirty-six-year-old man. Through their relationship, they both grow up and learn to cope with their lives. (307 pages)

The Kite Runner. Hosseini, Khalid. Narrated by a young Afghani, this novel gives a vivid picture of contemporary Afghanistan and the conflict and hardships endured by the Afghan people. (371 pages)

A Pale View of Hills. Ishiguro, Kazuo. A novel that reflects the author's own experience as a Japanese person in England. The story shifts from Nagasaki and the atomic bomb during World War II to England twenty years later. (183 pages)

The Metamorphosis. Kafka, Franz. The story of a young man who wakes up one morning to discover that he has turned into a beetle-like insect. (55 pages)

Flowers for Algernon. Keyes, Daniel. A sad tale of a mentally challenged man who is given an experimental drug. For a short time, he becomes normal. (216 pages)

*Annie John.*** Kincaid, Jamaica.* A young girl growing up on the Caribbean island of Antigua tries to escape from her close emotional ties to her mother. (148 pages)

The Bean Trees. Kingsolver, Barbara.* Driving west to start a new life, Taylor stops for gas. A woman gives her a little girl. The touching story of how they grow to love each other. (323 pages)

*A Separate Peace.*** Knowles, John. Friendship and tragedy in a private boys' school in New Hampshire during World War II. (186 pages)

Being There. Kosinski, Jerzy. A simple gardener inherits a fortune, becomes adviser to the U.S. president and a popular TV personality. (140 pages)

The Namesake. Lahiri, Jhumpa.* A sensitive and vivid account of how the son of a family from Bombay deals with the difficulties of being both Indian and American. (291 pages)

To Kill a Mockingbird. Lee, Harper. Racism in the southern United States in the 1960s, as viewed by a young white girl, whose lawyer father defends a black man unjustly accused of a crime. (323 pages)

The Grass Is Singing. Lessing, Doris. A novel about racism and the inability to accept another culture in white South Africa during the 1950s. (245 pages)

*The Call of the Wild.*** London, Jack.* In this classic account of life in the Alaskan wilderness, Buck, a family pet, is kidnapped and taken to work as a sled dog. (143 pages)

*The Daydreamer.*** McEwan, Ian. In his daydreams, a boy becomes a cat and then the dreams seem to become real. (137 pages)

The Secret Life of Bees. Monk, Sue Ellen.* Lily Owens, a fourteen-year-old white girl from South Carolina, and Rosaleen, her family's black housekeeper, run away and are taken in by a family of beekeepers. (302 pages)

*Anne of Green Gables.*** Montgomery, Lucy Maud. An orphan girl is accepted into a loving family and small community on Prince Edward Island, Canada. (309 pages)

The Glory Field. Myers, Walter Dean. An African-American family's history from the time of slavery. Their farm unites them in this story of pride, determination, struggle, and love. (196 pages)

*Chain of Fire.*** Naidoo, Beverley. The story of two young people who struggled against racist policies in South Africa under apartheid. (242 pages)

Bel Canto. Patchett, Ann.* The complex relations that develop among a group of hostages, including illustrious foreign guests, and their terrorist captors in a South American country. (318 pages)

The Bell Jar. Plath, Sylvia. In a semiautobiographical novel, a brilliant young woman slides into a depression that almost takes her life. (264 pages)

All Quiet on the Western Front. Remarque, Erich Maria. A classic antiwar novel that describes the horrors of trench warfare in Europe during World War I. (236 pages)

A Tree Grows in Brooklyn. Smith, Betty. The dreams and trials of a girl growing up in Brooklyn, New York, in a poor, but proud family. (483 pages)

*The Pearl.*** Steinbeck, John.* A poor man finds a big pearl in the sea and hopes to get rich by selling it. Can a pearl bring happiness to his family? (118 pages)

The Grapes of Wrath. Steinbeck, John.* A poor farming family is forced in the 1930s to leave Oklahoma and move to California, where they face hardship and more poverty. (455 pages)

The Kitchen God's Wife. Tan, Amy.* An immigrant from China tells her American daughter about her past, painting a vivid picture of Chinese life and tradition. (530 pages)

Dinner at the Homesick Restaurant. Tyler, Anne.* Three siblings return home as their mother is dying, and they try to make sense of their past. (303 pages)

The House of Mirth. Wharton, Edith.* Lily Bart, a poor relative, lives with rich New Yorkers at the end of the nineteenth century and learns to love luxury, but not the vulgar social values she finds. (354 pages)

The Picture of Dorian Gray. Wilde, Oscar. Dorian Gray remains handsome and young, but his portrait, hidden in the attic, shows his age and the effects of his evil. (165 pages)

Mystery and Suspense

The Da Vinci Code. Brown, Dan.* A murder in a museum and a mysterious symbol lead Robert Langdon and Sophie Neveu on a hunt to find a secret before it is lost forever. (467 pages)

And Then There Were None. Christie, Agatha.* Ten weekend guests who don't know one another meet on a private island. All they have in common is a secret, evil past. One by one, they die. (275 pages)

Whiteout. Follett, Ken.* Samples of a deadly virus are missing, and scientists meet at a lonely cottage during a fierce snowstorm to find a cure amid jealousy, distrust, and attractions. (474 pages)

*A is for Alibi.*** Grafton, Sue.* After serving a jail sentence for a crime she didn't commit, Nikki hires Kinsey Mulhone to find out who was really her husband's killer. (214 pages)

The Tenth Man. Greene, Graham.* During World War II, men held prisoner by the Germans are told that three of them must die. One man trades his wealth for his life—and then has to pay. (149 pages)

The Broker. Grisham, John.* A master of finance knows too many secrets. Released from prison by the American president, he flees to Europe and begins a new life in order to stay alive. (357 pages)

Night Shift. King, Stephen.* Twenty short stories guaranteed to scare the reader: Hidden rats in deep lower cellars, a beautiful girl hanging by a thread above a hellish fate. (326 pages)

The Night Manager. Le Carré, John.* After the end of the cold war, spy Jonathon Pine is enlisted to help bring down Roper, a notorious kingpin in the world of arms smuggling and drug dealing. (474 pages)

Tunnel Vision. Paretsky, Sara.* Chicago private detective V. I. Warshawsky finds a prominent attorney's wife dead in her office while a homeless family disappears. She finds that these events are connected. (470 pages)

The Rottweiler. Rendell, Ruth.* The killer is called "The Rottweiler" because he bites his victims when he murders them. A victim's belongings are found in an antiques shop and everyone who knew her is a suspect. (339 pages)

*The Sky Is Falling.*** Sheldon, Sidney.* This thriller is about the mysterious death of Gary Winthrop, the last of five people in his family to die in a single year. (398 pages)

*The No.1 Ladies' Detective Agency.*** Smith, Alexander McCall.* As the first woman to run a detective agency in Botswana, Africa, Precious Ramatswe solves delicate and complicated mysteries. (235 pages)

The Secret History. Tartt, Donna. As a new student at Hampden College, Richard is accepted by a circle of friends who share a terrible secret. (559 pages)

Science Fiction and Fantasy

I, Robot. Asimov, Isaac.* Tales about how robots can be developed and taught not to harm humans. Includes the "three laws of robotics." A classic. (224 pages)

Fahrenheit 451. Bradbury, Ray.* A classic of science fiction about a society in which books are prohibited and television dominates people's lives. (180 pages)

*Island of the Aunts.*** Ibbotson, Eva.* Two children are snatched by three elderly aunts and taken to a distant island populated by mermaids and strange creatures whose mission is to swim the world humming and healing the oceans. (281 pages)

The Left Hand of Darkness. LeGuin, Ursula K.* On a strange planet called Gethen, people do not see each other as men or women. This poses a challenge to an explorer from planet Earth. (304 pages)

*Animal Farm.*** Orwell, George.* The story of what happens when overworked, mistreated animals take over a farm. A story that reflects any place where freedom is attacked. (139 pages)

Harry Potter and the Sorcerer's Stone. Rowling, J. K.* This book tells of the beginning of the many adventures of a young boy who goes to a school for wizards. (312 pages)

Lord of the Rings: The Fellowship of the Ring. Tolkien, J. R. R.* This is the first of three books in an epic tale about good against evil. A small creature with hairy feet has a gold ring that belongs to a creature called Gollum. (400 pages)

Nonfiction

Nonfiction books are factual. Books about history, biography, and science are examples of nonfiction. Reading nonfiction can help develop your vocabulary and knowledge in a specialized area.

Biography and Autobiography

I Know Why the Caged Bird Sings. Angelou, Maya. A prize-winning American poet writes about her childhood experiences and how she survived violence and racism. (246 pages)

*Go Ask Alice.*** Anonymous. The true story in diary form of how a fifteen-year-old girl became addicted to drugs. (188 pages)

Growing Up. Baker, Russell. The memoir of a journalist and humorist growing up in America during the Depression and World War II. (278 pages)

*J. R. R. Tolkien: The Man Who Created the Lord of the Rings.*** Coren, Michael. Tolkien's life experiences as an orphan, a scholar, a soldier, and a professor and how they helped him to create his famous trilogy. (125 pages)

*Boy.*** Dahl, Roald. The funny and sometimes shocking childhood and school experiences of this famous writer of children's books. (160 pages)

An American Childhood. Dillard, Annie.* The author's childhood in 1950s Pittsburgh, Pennsylvania, described in fond detail. (255 pages)

Out of Africa. Dinesen, Isak. The author's experiences from 1914 to 1931 running a coffee plantation in Kenya, first with her husband and later alone. (288 pages)

The Spirit Catches You and You Fall Down. Fadinan, Ann. A Hmong family settles in California and comes into conflict with American doctors. (300 pages)

*Anne Frank: The Diary of a Young Girl.*** Frank, Anne. The diary kept by a thirteen-year-old Jewish girl hidden in an apartment with her family for two years in Amsterdam, Holland, during World War II. (308 pages)

*Homesick.*** Fritz, Jean. The author's childhood in China and the dramatic escape of her family at the time of the Chinese Cultural Revolution. (140 pages)

Seabiscuit: An American Legend. Hillenbrand, Laura. The story of a racehorse named Seabiscuit who became a winner, and the people who believed in him. (377 pages)

Mountains Beyond Mountains. Kidder, Tracy.* The inspiring life and work of Dr. Paul Farmer, who has dedicated himself to the idea that "the only real nation is humanity." (304 pages)

Into the Wild. Krakauer, Jon.* How and why a young man walked into the Alaskan wilderness alone and died there. (207 pages)

The Autobiography of Malcolm X. Malcolm X with Alex Haley. The dramatic life story of an important figure in African-American history, as told by Malcolm X himself. (350 pages)

Long Walk to Freedom. Mandela, Nelson. Mandela's life story, written while he was in a South African prison. (544 pages)

Rosa Parks: My Story. Parks, Rosa, with Jim Haskins. A key figure in the civil rights movement tells how she refused to give up her seat to a white man on a bus. (188 pages)

*J. K. Rowling: The Wizard Behind Harry Potter.*** Shapiro, Marc. This is the life story of one of the most successful writers of our time. (163 pages)

Nisa: The Life and Words of a !Kung Woman. Shostak, Marjorie. The remarkable story of an African woman and her people in the Kalahari Desert, as told by an anthropologist. (402 pages)

Almost Lost. Sparks, Beatrice.* The true story of an anonymous teenager's life on the streets of a big city. (239 pages)

Stephen Hawking: A Life in Science. White, M., and G. Gribbin. A biography of Stephen Hawking, the English scientist who is often considered the smartest man alive. (304 pages)

*Helen Keller: From Tragedy to Triumph.*** Wilkie, Katherine E. Helen Keller became deaf and blind when she was a small child. This is the story of her success as a student, a writer, and a lecturer. (192 pages)

Other Nonfiction

*How Did We Find Out About Outer Space?*** Asimov, Isaac. Clear explanations of scientific principles, with references to mythology and literature by this famous writer. (59 pages)

Bury Me Standing: The Gypsies and Their Journey. Fonseca, Isabel. A striking portrait of the life and history of the Roma (Gypsies) in Eastern Europe. (316 pages)

An Inconvenient Truth. Gore, Al. Pictures and text showing the consequences of climate change are accompanied by personal essays. Gore makes a complex and serious issue easy to understand. (327 pages)

October Sky. Hickham, Homer. How Hickham and his friends were inspired in 1957 by *Sputnik,* the Russian satellite, to spend their lives working on rockets for space launches. (428 pages)

Field Notes from a Catastrophe. Kolbert, Elizabeth. This book brings the science of climate change to life. The author describes how global warming threatens the traditional way of life in a small Alaskan village. (210 pages)

Never Cry Wolf. Mowat, Farley.* How a young scientist in northern Canada learns to respect and understand wolves. (242 pages)

Homage to Catalonia. Orwell, George.* In 1937, Orwell joined the fight against Fascism in the Spanish Civil War and wrote this classic report of the ridiculous, pathetic, and, above all, tragic aspects of war. (232 pages)

The Omnivore's Dilemma. Pollan, Michael. Pollan follows the journey of four meals from farm to table, weaving together literature, science, and hands-on investigation. This book shows the serious consequences of the way we eat. (464 pages)

Why Birds Sing. Rothenberg, David. This book explores the tweets, squawks, and flute-like songs of birds to investigate the scientific mysteries of bird song and how it sparks the human imagination. (256 pages)

Reading and Discussing Nonfiction

In this unit, you will practice reading and discussing nonfiction with an article from the *New York Times*, "Why the Internet Isn't the Death of the Post Office."

Before you read the article, preview it.

1. Read the first paragraph. Can you tell what the article will be about?

2. Scan the article for names, dates, numbers, and **boldface** type.

3. Read the last paragraph on the next page.

Now read the article all the way to the end. As you read, underline any unfamiliar words with a pencil but do not look them up in a dictionary now. (You can do that later.)

Why the Internet Isn't the Death of the Post Office

by James Fallows

Millions of people now rent their movies the **Netflix** way. They fill out a wish list from the 50,009 titles on the company's web site and receive the first few DVD's in the mail; when they mail each one back, the next one on the list is sent.

The Netflix model has been exhaustively analyzed for its disruptive, new-economy implications. What will it mean for video stores like **Blockbuster,** which has, in fact, started a similar service? What will it mean for movie studios and theaters? What does it show about "long tail" businesses—ones that amalgamate many niche markets, like those for Dutch movies or classic musicals, into a single target audience?

But one other major implication has barely been mentioned: what this and similar Internet-based businesses mean for that stalwart of the old economy, the **United States Postal Service.**

Every day, some two million Netflix envelopes come and go as first-class mail. They are joined by millions of other shipments from online pharmacies, **eBay** vendors, **Amazon.com** and other businesses that did not exist before the Internet.

The eclipse of "snail mail" in the age of instant electronic communication has been predicted at least as often as the coming of the paperless office. But the consumption of paper keeps rising. (It has roughly doubled since 1980, with less use of newsprint and much more of ordinary office paper.) And so, with some nuances and internal changes, does the flow of material carried by mail. On average, an American household receives twice as many pieces of mail a day as it did in the 1970's.

"Is the Internet hurting the mail, or helping?" asks Michael J. Critelli, a co-chairman of the public-private Mail Industry Task Force. "It's doing both." Mr. Critelli's day job is chief executive of **Pitney Bowes**—yes, that Pitney Bowes, once known for its postage meters and now a "mail and document management" company. In the last few years, it has also functioned as a research group for the mail industry, commissioning a series of studies, available free at PostInsight@PB.com, that contain startling findings about the economic, technological and cultural forces that affect use of mail.

The harmful side of the Internet's impact is obvious but statistically less important than many would guess. People naturally write fewer letters when they can send e-mail messages. To leaf through a box of old paper correspondence is to know what has been lost in this shift: the pretty stamps, the varying look and feel of handwritten and typed correspondence, the tangible object that was once in the sender's hands. To stay in instant touch with parents, children and colleagues around the world is to know what's been gained.

But even before e-mail, personal letters had shrunk to a tiny share of the flow. As a consultant, Fouad H. Nader, wrote in a Pitney Bowes study, personal mail had "long ago been reduced to a minimum with the proliferation of telephone services in the last 50 years."

Personal letters of all sorts, called "household to household" correspondence, account for less than 1 percent of the 100 billion pieces of first-class mail that the Postal Service handles each year. Most of that personal mail consists of greeting cards, invitations, announcements, and other mail with "emotional content," a category that is generally holding its own.

The same higher-income households that rely the most on e-mail correspondence also send and receive the most letters. Whatever shrinkage e-mail has caused in personal correspondence, it is not likely to do much more.

The Internet and allied technologies, meanwhile, are increasing the volume of old-fashioned mail in three ways.

The first follows the Netflix example: Postal Service fulfillment of transactions made on the Internet. About two million prescriptions a day—roughly one-fifth of the total—are delivered by first-class mail. EBay's vendors list five million new items daily, and those that are sold ship mainly by mail. One Pitney Bowes study found that online retailers were increasingly using paper catalogs sent through the mail to steer people to their sites.

The second force also involves finance. Many studies conclude that people are more and more willing to make payments online, but that they strongly prefer to receive the original bills on paper, by mail.

Since the late 1980's, mail to households from credit card companies has risen about 10 percent a year. Americans' financial lives have become more complicated, in part because of choices created by the Internet. In turn, banks, telecommunication companies, insurance companies and investment houses send more mail.

Third is the sleeper: the increasing sophistication of the Postal Service's own technology. Everyone takes for granted that **FedEx** and the **United Parcel Service** can track the movement of each item through their systems. The Postal Service has now installed similar scanning equipment, and in principle it can bar-code and scan every envelope or postcard and know where it is at any time. In reality, it does this mainly for a fee, for businesses that want to know their material has reached the right audience at the right time—for instance, the Thursday before a weekend sale at a local store.

In Internet terms, this and related improvements are intended to make advertising mail less like spam—unwanted and discarded—and more like embedded ads, tied to the content of a particular web site.

"Over time, there is an increasing ability to send you only what's interesting to you, at a time when you're interested in it," Mr. Critelli says. If you have just moved, for example, that may mean mail from your new area's window-cleaning or handyman services. He says response rates to these targeted mailings are better than the dismal rates for the usual direct-mail campaigns.

The most touching artifact among these e-mail studies is a survey conducted by the Postal Service called "The Mail Moment."

"Two thirds of all consumers do not expect to receive personal mail, but when they do, it makes their day," it concluded. "This 'hope' keeps them coming back each day." Even in this age of technology, according to the survey, 55 percent of Americans said they looked forward to discovering what each day's mail might hold.

Now I'll confess my bias. My first real job was at the post office. On the day when I was paroled from the sorting floor to substitute for an absent letter carrier, I felt as if I were bringing "the mail moment" to people along the route. It's nice to think that such moments will survive the Internet.

(Source: *The New York Times*. September 4, 2005)

A. *Write any unfamiliar words that made comprehension difficult and write their dictionary definitions. Compare your words with those of another student. Do you have any of the same words?*

B. *Discuss the article with another student. Consider these questions.*

1. Where does the writer tell you what this article is about?

2. What do you already know about this?

3. Were there any parts of the article that you did not understand?

C. *Read the article again. Then discuss these questions with a group of three or four students.*

1. Why does the writer believe that the Internet is not the death of the Post Office?

2. Do you agree with the writer? Why or why not?

3. What evidence does the writer give to support his ideas?

4. How do you use the post office?

5. Do you ever buy things over the Internet?

In this unit you will practice reading and discussing fiction with a short story titled "All Summer in a Day," by Ray Bradbury.

Before you read, discuss these questions with another student.

1. Have you ever heard of this author? Have you read any of his stories or books or seen movies made from them?

2. Ray Bradbury's other books include *Fahrenheit 451* and *The Martian Chronicles*. Do these titles help you to guess what kind of fiction Bradbury writes?

3. Think about the title of this story, "All Summer in a Day," and try to imagine what the title might refer to. Guess what type of story this will be.

Read the story all the way to the end. As you read, underline any unfamiliar words with a pencil but do not look them up in a dictionary now. Mark any confusing parts of the story with a question mark (?). Make notes in the margin about your reactions. Then complete the exercises that follow.

All Summer in a Day

 "Ready?"

"Ready."
"Now?"
"Soon."
"Do the scientists really know? Will it happen today, will it?"
"Look, look; see for yourself!"

The children pressed to each other like so many roses, so many weeds, intermixed, peering out for a look at the hidden sun.

It rained.

It had been raining for seven years; thousands upon thousands of days compounded and filled from one end to the other with rain, with the drum and gush of water, with the sweet crystal fall of showers and the concussion of storms so heavy they were tidal waves come over the islands. A thousand forests had been crushed under the rain and grown up a thousand times to be crushed again. And this was the way life was forever on the planet Venus, and this was the schoolroom of the children of the rocket men and women who had come to a raining world to set up civilization and live out their lives.

"It's stopping, it's stopping!"
"Yes, yes!"

Margot stood apart from them, from these children who could never remember a time when there wasn't rain and rain and rain. They were all nine years old, and if there had been a day, seven years ago, when the sun came out for an hour and showed its face to the stunned world, they could not recall.

Sometimes, at night, she heard them stir, in remembrance, and she knew they were dreaming and remembering gold or a yellow crayon or a coin large enough to buy the world with. She knew they thought they remembered a warmness, like a blushing in the face, in the body, in the arms and legs and trembling hands. But then they always awoke to the tatting drum, the endless shaking down of clear bead necklaces upon the roof, the walk, the gardens, the forests, and their dreams were gone.

All day yesterday they had read in class about the sun. About how like a lemon it was, and how hot. And they had written small stories or essays or poems about it:

> I think the sun is a flower,
> That blooms for just one hour.

That was Margot's poem, read in a quiet voice in the still classroom while the rain was falling outside.

"Aw, you didn't write that!" protested one of the boys. "I did," said Margot. "I did."

"William!" said the teacher.

But that was yesterday. Now the rain was slackening, and the children were crushed in the great thick windows.

"Where's teacher?"

"She'll be back."

"She'd better hurry, we'll miss it!"

They turned on themselves, like a feverish wheel, all tumbling spokes.

Margot stood alone. She was a very frail girl who looked as if she had been lost in the rain for years and the rain had washed out the blue from her eyes and the red from her mouth and the yellow from her hair. She was an old photograph dusted from an album, whitened away, and if she spoke at all her voice would be a ghost. Now she stood, separate, staring at the rain and the loud wet world beyond the huge glass.

"What're *you* looking at?" said William.

Margot said nothing.

"Speak when you're spoken to." He gave her a shove. But she did not move; rather she let herself be moved only by him and nothing else.

They edged away from her, they would not look at her. She felt them go away. And this was because she would play no games with them in the echoing tunnels of the underground city. If they tagged her and ran, she stood blinking after them and did not follow. When the class sang songs about happiness and life and games her lips barely moved. Only when they sang about the sun and the summer did her lips move as she watched the drenched windows.

And then, of course, the biggest crime of all was that she had come here only five years ago from Earth, and she remembered the sun and the way the sun was and the sky was when she was four in Ohio. And they, they had been on Venus all their lives, and they had been only two years old when last the sun came out and had long since forgotten the color and heat of it and the way it really was. But Margot remembered.

"It's like a penny," she said once, eyes closed.

"No, it's not!" the children cried.

"It's like a fire," she said, "in the stove."

"You're lying, you don't remember!" cried the children.

But she remembered and stood quietly apart from all of them and watched the patterning windows. And once, a month ago, she had refused to shower in the school shower rooms, had clutched her hands to her ears and over her head, screaming the water mustn't touch her head. So after that, dimly, dimly, she sensed it, she was different and they knew her difference and kept away.

There was talk that her father and mother were taking her back to Earth next year; it seemed vital to her that they do so, though it would mean the loss of thousands of dollars to her family. And so, the children hated her for all these reasons of big and little consequence. They hated her pale snow face, her waiting silence, her thinness, and her possible future.

"Get away!" The boy gave her another push. "What're you waiting for?"

Then, for the first time, she turned and looked at him. And what she was waiting for was in her eyes.

"Well, don't wait around here!" cried the boy savagely. "You won't see nothing!"

Her lips moved.

"Nothing!" he cried. "It was all a joke, wasn't it?" He turned to the other children. "Nothing's happening today. Is it?"

They all blinked at him and then, understanding, laughed and shook their heads. "Nothing, nothing!"

"Oh, but," Margot whispered, her eyes helpless. "But this is the day, the scientists predict, they say, they *know*, the sun . . ."

"All a joke!" said the boy, and seized her roughly. "Hey, everyone, let's put her in a closet before teacher comes!"

"No," said Margot, falling back.

They surged about her, caught her up and bore her, protesting, and then pleading, and then crying, back into a tunnel, a room, a closet, where they slammed and locked the door. They stood looking at the door and saw it tremble from her beating and throwing herself against it. They heard her muffled cries. Then, smiling, they turned and went out and back down the tunnel, just as the teacher arrived.

"Ready, children?" She glanced at her watch.

"Yes!" said everyone.

"Are we all here?"

"Yes!"

The rain slackened still more.

They crowded to the huge door.

The rain stopped.

It was as if, in the midst of a film concerning an avalanche, a tornado, a hurricane, a volcanic eruption, something had, first, gone wrong with the sound apparatus, thus muffling and finally cutting off all noise, all of the blasts and repercussions and thunders, and then, second, ripped the film from the projector and inserted in its place a peaceful tropical slide which did not move or tremor. The world ground to a standstill. The silence was so immense and unbelievable that you felt your ears had been stuffed or you had lost your hearing altogether. The children put their hands to their ears. They stood apart. The door slid back and the smell of the silent, waiting world came in to them.

The sun came out.

It was the color of flaming bronze and it was very large. And the sky around it was a blazing blue tile color. And the jungle burned with sunlight as the children, released from their spell, rushed out, yelling, into the springtime.

"Now, don't go too far," called the teacher after them. "You've only two hours, you know. You wouldn't want to get caught out!"

But they were running and turning their faces up to the sky and feeling the sun on their cheeks like a warm iron; they were taking off their jackets and letting the sun burn their arms.

"Oh, it's better than the sun lamps, isn't it?"

"Much, much better!"

They stopped running and stood in the great jungle that covered Venus, that grew and never

stopped growing, tumultuously, even as you watched it. It was a nest of octopi, clustering up great arms of flesh-like weed, wavering, flowering in this brief spring. It was the color of rubber and ash, this jungle, from the many years without sun. It was the color of stones and white cheeses and ink, and it was the color of the moon.

The children lay out, laughing, on the jungle mattress, and heard it sigh and squeak under them, resilient and alive. They ran among the trees, they slipped and fell, they pushed each other, they played hide-and-seek and tag, but most of all they squinted at the sun until tears ran down their faces, they put their hands up to that yellowness and that amazing blueness and they breathed of the fresh, fresh air and listened and listened to the silence which suspended them in a blessed sea of no sound and no motion. They looked at everything and savored everything. Then, wildly, like animals escaped from their caves, they ran and ran in shouting circles. They ran for an hour and did not stop running.

And then—

In the midst of their running one of the girls wailed. Everyone stopped.

The girl, standing in the open, held out her hand.

"Oh, look, look," she said, trembling.

They came slowly to look at her opened palm.

In the center of it, cupped and huge, was a single raindrop.

She began to cry, looking at it.

They glanced quietly at the sky.

"Oh. Oh."

A few cold drops fell on their noses and their cheeks and their mouths. The sun faded behind a stir of mist. A wind blew cool around them. They turned and started to walk back toward the underground house, their hands at their sides, their smiles vanishing away.

A boom of thunder startled them and like leaves before a new hurricane, they tumbled upon each other and ran. Lightning struck ten miles away, five miles away, a mile, a half mile. The sky darkened into midnight in a flash.

They stood in the doorway of the underground for a moment until it was raining hard. Then they closed the door and heard the gigantic sound of the rain falling in tons and avalanches, everywhere and forever.

"Will it be seven more years?"

"Yes. Seven."

Then one of them gave a little cry.

"Margot!"

"What?"

"She's still in the closet where we locked her."

"Margot."

They stood as if someone had driven them, like so many stakes, into the floor. They looked at each other and then looked away. They glanced out at the world that was raining now and raining and raining steadily. They could not meet each other's glances. Their faces were solemn and pale. They looked at their hands and feet, their faces down.

"Margot."

One of the girls said, "Well . . . ?"

No one moved.

"Go on," whispered the girl.

They walked slowly down the hall in the sound of cold rain. They turned through the doorway to the room in the sound of the storm and thunder, lightning on their faces, blue and terrible. They walked over to the closet door slowly and stood by it.

Behind the closet door was only silence.

They unlocked the door, even more slowly, and let Margot out.

A. Write any unfamiliar words that made comprehension difficult and write their dictionary definitions. Compare your words with those of another student. Do you have any of the same words?

B. Discuss these questions with another student. You may look back at the story if necessary.

1. Did you enjoy reading the story? Explain your answer.

2. Were there any parts of the story that you did not understand? Which ones?

3. Were there any unfamiliar words that you need to look up in order to understand the story?

4. Why do you think the author decided to call this story "All Summer in a Day"?

C. Read the story a second time. Then, working with two or three other students, retell the story to each other in your own words.

EXERCISE 2

A. In this exercise you will analyze the story for the way the writer sets the scene and tells us "who," "when," and "where." (This is called the "exposition.") Working with another student, look back at the first part of "All Summer in a Day" and fill in the table.

Main characters (list and describe):
Setting (time):
Setting (place):

B. Compare your work with that of another pair of students. If you disagree, look back at the story to check your answers.

EXERCISE 3

A. *Listed below are the events that make up the plot of "All Summer in a Day." Working with another student, put the events in chronological order by numbering them from 1 to 11.*

____ a. They let Margot out of the closet.

____ b. The children stood at the window waiting for the sun.

____ c. The children remembered that Margot was in the closet.

____ d. All day the children read and wrote about the sun in class.

____ e. The teacher left the classroom.

____ f. The children put Margot in the closet.

____ g. William and the children began to mistreat Margot.

____ h. The whole world seemed silent and the sun came out.

____ i. Raindrops began to fall and a boom of thunder startled the children.

____ j. The children went inside.

____ k. The children ran and played in the sunlight.

B. *Compare your answers with those of another pair of students. If you disagree, look back at the story to check your answers.*

EXERCISE 4

A. *In the chart below you will find the terms that are often used to discuss the main elements of the plot in a work of literature. Look again at the events listed in Exercise 3 and decide where they belong in the chart. Write the letters (a–k) of the events in the appropriate box. The first one has been done for you.*

Note: Like many other stories, this story can be interpreted in several different ways, depending on the reader's point of view. Therefore, a variety of different answers is possible in this chart. Be prepared to explain your choices.

Exposition (Where the writer provides essential information about the story: "who," "where," "when," and "what.")	*b*
Complicating action (Often involving a conflict between two characters.)	
Climax (The moment of greatest tension, usually also the turning point in the story.)	
Resolution (The ending, which may or may not be happy, and may even be left open for the reader to imagine.)	

B. Compare your answers in the chart with those of two or three other students. If the answers are different, explain them to each other.

C. Discuss these questions with two or three other students.

1. Did the children have any doubts about whether or not they should be locking Margot in the closet? How can you tell?

2. How do you think Margot feels being locked in the closet?

3. Was the author trying to teach a lesson to the readers of the story? If so, what was the lesson?

4. How would you describe the ending of this story? Happy, sad, or inconclusive (incomplete)? Explain.

5. Could this story have an alternate ending? Try to imagine one and describe it.

EXERCISE 5

A. In "All Summer in a Day" Bradbury used rich descriptive language. Working with another student, look back at the story to find examples of the way he used words to create images and tell the story.

1. The setting (when and where)

   a. *a raining world*

   b.

   c.

   d.

2. Margot

   a. *pale snow face*

   b.

   c.

   d.

3. The children

   a. *running and turning their faces up to the sky*

   b.

   c.

   d.

4. William

   a. *cried savagely*

   b.

   c.

   d.

5. The sun
   a. *flaming bronze*
   b.
   c.
   d.

6. The rain
   a. *the drum and gush of water*
   b.
   c.
   d.

7. The sky
   a. *stir of mist*
   b.
   c.
   d.

B. *Compare your answers with those of another pair of students. If you disagree, look back at the story and explain your choices.*

UNIT 4

Responding to and Reporting on Your Extensive Reading Books

Sharing your experience of reading with others can benefit you in several ways. First of all, your reading comprehension improves when you talk about what you read. And second, sharing ideas and information about your book with others is enjoyable, and this enjoyment can motivate you to read more. This unit gives you suggestions for how to share books with your classmates and teacher.

Book Conferences

A book conference is a one-on-one conversation about your book with the teacher. Since a book conference is not a test, you will not need to remember details from the book. There is no need to prepare notes in advance of the conference. Your teacher may ask various questions, including: Why did you choose this book? What was your reaction? Did you enjoy it? What do you already know about the subject? Does the book relate in any way to your own life? If so, how? What are your favorite characters in the book? What was your favorite part?

Reading Circles

A reading circle is a small group of four to six students who meet regularly to talk about their extensive reading books and compare reading experiences.

Instructions for Reading Circles

1. Form a group with about four other students.

2. Take turns telling the other students in your group briefly about your book (not more than five minutes). Include the following: Title, author and genre (fiction, non-fiction, biography, etc.); Publication date; Number of pages; Reaction so far (Does it seem interesting or involving?); Level of difficulty for you (Are there many new words? Is the subject familiar or new for you?); Predictions about the book (What might happen next?).

3. One student in the group should time the student who is talking.

4. While each student is talking, the others should listen carefully, take brief notes, and ask questions afterward.

5. Follow the same procedure for each meeting of your group. Include the following in your talk: number of pages read so far; your reaction at this point (Are you enjoying it so far?); difficulties or problems in reading. Read aloud to your reading circle a short passage (about half a page) that you especially like or that you find surprising.

6. When you finish a book, tell your teacher and schedule a book conference.

Book Presentations

A book presentation is a brief (about five minutes) oral report to the class about a book that you have finished reading. To prepare a presentation, make five note cards, one for each of the following points.

1. About the book and the author: Title, author, and year first published; information about the author (from the back of the book or the Internet); genre and number of pages

2. Difficulty: Language (use of technical or unusual vocabulary, use of dialect, complicated sentences); plot or point of view (multiple points of view or multiple time frames)

3. Key elements of the plot (*very* briefly)

4. Your reaction to the book: Did you enjoy it? Why or why not? Would you read another book by the same author? Would you recommend this book to your classmates?

5. One or two of the following topics: A part of the book or one of the characters that interests you particularly; one of the characters that you like and identify with; personal experiences or thoughts related to the book; larger issues that are dealt with in the book (e.g., racism, poverty, war, etc.)

Here is an example of a note card for the first point.

Title: <u>Mountains Beyond Mountains</u>, by Tracy Kidder (2004)

Tracy Kidder graduated from Harvard and studied at the University of Iowa.
. . . served in the army during the Vietnam War
. . . has won many prizes including the Pulitzer and the National Book Award
. . . lives in Massachusetts and in Maine

Other books include <u>The Soul of a New Machine</u> and <u>Home Town</u>

Genre: Biography (of Dr. Paul Farmer)
301 pages

When you have completed the note cards, try out your presentation aloud several times to practice the way you will present your ideas.

Time yourself to see how long the presentation takes. If it takes more than five minutes, cut out some parts and try again. If it takes less than five minutes, think of more information to add to some of your note cards.

Book Response Form

When you finish reading a book, complete a copy of this form and give it to your teacher.

Book Response Form

Book title: _____

Author: _____

Publisher: _____

Date published: _____ Number of pages: _____

Genre (Type of book)—Circle one:

    novel   mystery   science fiction   romance   biography

    history   science/technology   other: _____

Why did you decide to read this book?

_____

_____

_____

Were you glad that you decided to read it? Explain.

_____

_____

_____

What did you like best about this book?

_____

_____

_____

What did you like least?

_____

_____

_____

Would you recommend this book to a friend? Explain.

_____

_____

_____

On a scale of 1–10, how difficult was this book for you? (1 = easy, 10 = difficult) Why?

_____

_____

_____

PART 2

Vocabulary Building

Strategies for Building a Powerful Vocabulary

Good reading comprehension depends on understanding the words you are reading. The more words you recognize and understand in a text, the better your comprehension will be.

What do you do when you encounter (meet) a new word in your reading?

_____ Ask another student about the meaning.

_____ Try to guess the meaning of the word from the context.

_____ Look up the definition in a dictionary.

_____ Skip over the word and continue reading.

_____ Analyze the word for clues to its meaning.

Compare your answers with those of another student and discuss these questions:

• When do you use these strategies?

• What are the advantages or disadvantages of each?

In fact, a good reader does all of the above at different times, depending on the word, the text, and the reason for reading it.

In this unit you will learn and practice five important strategies for building your vocabulary.

Strategy 1: Check your knowledge of the words used most frequently in English

Advances in computer technology have made it possible for researchers to analyze thousands of English-language texts containing millions of words. From this research they have learned that a small percentage of words—about 2,000—are used much more frequently than all the other words. In fact, these 2,000 most frequent words account for almost 80 percent of most texts. If you know these words, you have a much better chance of understanding what you read.

EXERCISE 1

A. Before you look at the list of the 2,000 most frequent words in English, answer this question:

How many unfamiliar words do you think you will find on the list? (Make a guess.) _____

B. Now turn to the list of the 2,000 most frequent words in Appendix 1 on page 303. Read through the list and mark all the words you DO NOT recognize.

How many of these words did you mark? _____

Compare this number with your guess in Part A. Did you have a good idea of the extent of your vocabulary?

If you have marked many words on this list, you probably have some difficulty understanding what you read. You need to spend extra time working on your vocabulary.

Strategy 2: Focus on the words used in academic texts

Research on academic texts (textbooks and academic journals) has shown that certain words are used very frequently in these texts, regardless of the subject matter. These words allow academic writers to explain or generalize their ideas or research, and to compare them with the work of others. Learning these 570 academic words can improve your comprehension of academic materials.

EXERCISE 2

A. Before you look at the Academic Word List, answer this question:

How many of the words on the list do you think you will recognize? (Make a guess.) _____

B. Turn to the Academic Word List in Appendix 2 on page 308. Read through the list and mark the words that you DO recognize.

How many of these words did you mark? _____

If you have marked some of the words in the Academic Word List, you have a good start on building your academic vocabulary. In Part 2 and in the Focus on Vocabulary sections in the units in Part 3, you will work on learning more words from this list.

Strategy 3: Use the dictionary effectively

Along with the definition, a dictionary provides a great deal of other information about a word. It tells you the part of speech of the word (noun, verb, adjective, etc.), how to pronounce it, and how to divide it into syllables. An example sentence is often included as well.

A. Use this dictionary page to answer the questions.

1. How many syllables are there in *scrutinize*?

2. What part of speech is *scrupulous*?

3. When your teacher *scrutinizes* your work, how do you feel?

4. What else can you *scrunch* besides a napkin?

5. What food do you consider *scrumptious*?

6. When pronouncing the word *scrutinize*, where should you place the emphasis?

7. How do you spell the past tense of the verb *scrub*?

scrub¹ /skrʌb/ *v.* **1** [I,T] to rub something hard, especially with something rough, in order to clean it: *The kitchen floor needs to be scrubbed and waxed.* | *The children's freshly-scrubbed faces beamed up at us.* **2** [T usually passive] INFORMAL to decide not to do something that you had planned, especially because there is a problem: *Yesterday's shuttle launch was scrubbed just ten minutes before liftoff.*
   scrub up *phr. v.* [I] to wash your hands and arms before doing a medical operation

scrub² *n.* **1** [U] low bushes and trees that grow in very dry soil **2 scrubs** [plural] INFORMAL a loose green shirt and pants worn by doctors during medical operations

scrub·ber /'skrʌbɚ/ *n.* [C] a plastic or metal object or a brush that you use to clean pans or floors

scrub brush /'skrʌb-brʌʃ/ *n.* [C] a stiff brush that you use for cleaning things —see picture at BRUSH¹

scrub·by /'skrʌbi/ *adj.* covered by low bushes: *scrubby terrain*

scrub·land /'skrʌblænd/ *n.* [U] land that is covered with low bushes

scruff /skrʌf/ *n.* **by the scruff of the neck** if you hold a person or animal by the scruff of their neck, you hold the flesh, fur, or clothes at the back of the neck

scruff·y /'skrʌfi/ *adj.* **scruffier, scruffiest** dirty and messy and not taken care of very well: *a scruffy sweatshirt*

scrum /skrʌm/ *n.* [C] an arrangement of players in the game of RUGBY, in which they are pushing very close together

scrump·tious /'skrʌmpʃəs/ *adj.* INFORMAL food that is scrumptious tastes very good: *scrumptious cheesecake*

scrunch /skrʌntʃ/ *v.* [T always + adv./prep.] INFORMAL to crush and twist something into a small round shape: [scrunch sth up/into etc.] *She tore out the pages and scrunched them up into a ball.*

scrunch·ie /'skrʌntʃi/ *n.* [C] a circular rubber band that is covered with cloth, used for holding hair in place

scru·ple¹ /'skrupəl/ *n.* [C usually plural] a belief about right and wrong that prevents you from doing something bad: *He has absolutely no scruples about claiming other people's work as his own.*

scruple² *v.* **not scruple to do sth** FORMAL to be willing to do something, even though it may have harmful or bad effects: *They did not scruple to bomb innocent civilians.*

scru·pu·lous /'skrupyələs/ *adj.* **1** careful to be honest and fair, and making sure that every detail is correct: *The finance department is always scrupulous about their bookkeeping.* —opposite UNSCRUPULOUS **2** done very carefully so that every detail is correct: *This job requires scrupulous attention to detail.* —**scrupulously** *adv.*: *Employees' hands must be kept scrupulously clean.* —**scrupulousness** *n.* [U]

scru·ti·nize /'skrutʰn,aɪz/ *v.* [T] to examine someone or something very thoroughly and carefully: *Detectives scrutinized the area, looking for clues.*

(Source: *Longman Advanced American Dictionary.* White Plains, NY: Pearson Longman, 2005)

B. Compare your answers with those of another student.

Strategy 4: Keep a vocabulary notebook

When you encounter new words, write them in a notebook that you use only for vocabulary and not for other course work. (A small notebook is preferable so you can carry it around with you.) This notebook will help you study vocabulary more effectively. With all your words in one place in the notebook, you can easily check your knowledge of words you have studied before.

How to organize and use the notebook

1. Decide on a method for putting words in order. Many students prefer alphabetical order, though you may also order words according to other categories, such as topic or source (words from extensive reading books, words from *Advanced Reading Power,* and words from other course books).

2. Use two pages in the notebook. On the left-hand page, write a word, the part of speech, and the word in syllables. Under the word, write the sentence in which you found it. Then, on the right-hand page, write the meaning. (Note: If you can learn the words more quickly using definitions in your native language, and your teacher agrees, you may write the meanings in that language.)

3. Check your knowledge of the words by covering one of the pages and trying to remember the information on the other.

Example:

1. assumption—noun (as-sump-tion)	1. Something that you think is true
○ How could you make an assumption	although you have no proof
about their family without meeting them?	

Strategy 5: Use study cards

Study cards can help you review words and make them part of your permanent vocabulary. When you have made a set of cards, carry them with you and test yourself often. Add new words that you encounter and want to learn. You should not remove a word from your set until you are completely sure of the meaning and can recall it instantly.

To make study cards, you will need small, blank cards (3 × 5 inches or about 7 × 12 cm).

Example:

On one side of the card write a word, the part of speech, the word in syllables, and the phrase or sentence in which you found the word.

vary (verb)
va -ry
Ideas of beauty <u>vary</u> from one culture to another.

On the other side of the card, write the dictionary definition of the word as it was used in the passage.

> *to differ from other things of the same type*

EXERCISE 4

Choose five words that you have encountered in your reading (in this textbook or any other book). Fill in the information for five study cards, following the example.

Side A

> Word and part of speech:
>
> Word in syllables:
>
> Sentence:

Side B

> Dictionary definition:

Guidelines for Using Study Cards

- Go through all your cards twice on your own: Look at each word and say it aloud. If you remember the definition, say it aloud, too. If you do not remember the definition, look at the back of the card. Then say the word and the definition aloud.

- Go through the cards again with another student: Ask him/her to read each word to you. Tell him/her the definition. If you do not remember it, ask him/her to tell you. Then repeat it aloud.

- Rearrange your cards each time you use them, so they are in a different order. Put cards for especially difficult words in a separate group and quiz yourself on them. Then return the cards to the large group.

- Use the words on the study cards in conversation and in writing.

- Carry your cards with you and review your words whenever you have a few spare moments.

UNIT 2

Learning New Words from Your Reading

To learn words from your reading:

- Read a lot. Research has shown that in order to learn a word, you must encounter it many times. Each time you see the word in context, you build up a stronger sense of its meaning. The best way to increase the number of encounters with words and to learn how words are used is by reading extensively.

- Work with a new word in a way that requires active thinking. Simply noticing the word and looking up the meaning is not enough. You need to analyze the word and use it in speaking and writing.

- Note how a new word is used. If you look closely at the context and write down the sentence where you found the word, you are more likely to remember it.

Choosing Words to Learn

Since it would be impossible to learn all the new words you encounter in your reading, you should decide which ones would be the most useful for you and try to learn those.

A word will be useful for you if it is included in one of the word lists (Appendices 1 and 2), or if you have encountered it several times and think you will encounter it again.

In this unit you will practice selecting words from short passages.

Example:

A. Read the excerpt from a textbook and complete the tasks that follow.

Why Is Reading in a Second Language Sometimes Difficult?

Cross-cultural <u>research</u> shows that cultures have varying attitudes about language in general and that these differences are reflected in the printed word. As a result, the way ideas are organized in expository writing (e.g., in essays) <u>varies</u> across cultures. Originally called to our attention by Kaplan (1966), this suggestion has inspired research in several different languages. Ostler, for example, found that the patterns of expository writing in a language "reflect the patterns valued in the native culture." Researchers have found significant differences in text organization between English and the Korean, German, Japanese, Arabic, and Athabaskan languages. It is logical to conclude from this that when people read in a second language they comprehend best the texts that meet their beliefs and expectations about the patterns of written language. To the extent that the patterns in the text of a second language are different from those of the first language, the reader is likely to have difficulty comprehending.

*Mark each statement **T** (true) or **F** (false).*

1. Texts such as essays have the same form in every language.   *F*
2. Different cultures have different ways of organizing texts.   *T*
3. When you read in a second language, you can find the same patterns as in your first language.
4. It is easier to read in a language that has text patterns similar to those in your first language.

Compare your answers with those of another student.

B. Read the passage again and underline the words that are new to you.

C. Look at the word lists in Appendices 1 and 2 (pages 303 and 308) for the words you underlined. Choose two of your underlined words that are on the lists and write them below. Then write the part of speech and the dictionary definition that best fits each word as it is used in the passage.

Word	Definition
1. *research (noun)*	*serious study of a subject to learn new facts about it*
2. *varies (verb)*	*to change*
3. _____	_____
4. _____	_____

EXERCISE 1

A. Read the excerpt from a newspaper article and complete the tasks that follow.

How Culture Molds Habits of Thought

By Erica Goode

For more than a century, Western philosophers and psychologists have based their discussions of mental life on a cardinal assumption: that the same basic processes underlie all human thought, whether in the mountains of Tibet or the grasslands of the Serengeti.

Cultural differences might dictate what people thought about. Teenage boys in Botswana, for example, might discuss cows with the same passion that New York teenagers reserve for sports cars.

But the habits of thought—the strategies people adopted in processing information and making sense of the world around them—were, Western scholars assumed, the same for everyone, exemplified by, among other things, a devotion to logical reasoning, a penchant for cat-egorization and an urge to understand situations and events in linear terms of cause and effect.

Recent work by a social psychologist at the University of Michigan, however, is turning this long-held view of mental functioning upside down. In a series of studies comparing European Americans to East Asians, Dr. Richard Nisbett and his colleagues have found that people who grow up in different cultures do not just think about different things: they think differently.

"We used to think that everybody uses categories in the same way, that logic plays the same kind of role for everyone in the understanding of everyday life, that memory, perception, rule application and so on are the same," Dr. Nisbett said. "But we're now arguing that cognitive processes themselves are just far more malleable than mainstream psychology assumed."

(Source: *The New York Times*, August 8, 2000, excerpt, p. D1)

Mark each statement T *(true)* or F *(false)*.

1. People think about different things depending on where they live.

2. People all think in the same way.

3. A social psychologist has come up with a new idea about how we think.

4. Logic is the same in every culture.

Compare your answers with those of another student.

B. Read the passage again and underline the words that are new to you.

C. Look on the word lists in Appendices 1 and 2 (pages 303 and 308) for the words you underlined. Choose five of your underlined words that are on the lists and write them below. Then write the part of speech and the dictionary definition that best fits each word as it is used in the passage

Word   **Definition**

1. _____   _____

2. _____   _____

3. _____   _____

4. _____   _____

5. _____   _____

D. Write a new sentence for each word above. The sentences should show that you understand the meaning of each word as it is used in the passage.

1. _____

2. _____

3. _____

4. _____

5. _____

E. Ask another student to read your sentences. Then discuss these questions.

1. Do the sentences make sense?

2. Do the sentences show the meaning of the words?

A. Read the excerpt from a textbook and complete the tasks that follow.

Symbols

Reality for human beings is not action or feeling but meaning. Humans are symbolic creatures; a *symbol* is anything that carries a particular meaning recognized by the people who share culture. A whistle, a wall of graffiti, a flashing red light, a fist raised in the air—all serve as symbols. We see the human capacity to create and manipulate symbols in the various ways a simple wink of the eye can convey interest, understanding, or insult.

We are so dependent on our culture's symbols that we take them for granted. Often, however, we gain a heightened sense of the importance of a symbol when someone uses it in an unconventional way, say when a person in a political demonstration burns a U.S. flag. Entering an unfamiliar culture also reminds us of the power of symbols; culture shock is nothing more than the inability to "read" meaning in one's surroundings. We feel lost, unsure of how to act, and sometimes frightened—a consequence of slipping outside the symbolic web of culture.

Culture shock is both what travelers experience and what they *inflict* on others by acting in ways that may offend them. For example, because North Americans consider dogs to be beloved household pets, travelers to the People's Republic of China might well be appalled to discover people roasting dogs as a wintertime meal. On the other hand, a North American who orders a hamburger in India causes offense to Hindus, who hold cows to be sacred and thus unfit for human consumption.

(Source: John J. Macionis, *Society: The Basics,* 4th Edition. Upper Saddle River, NJ: Prentice Hall, 1998)

Mark each statement **T** *(true) or* **F** *(false).*

1. A symbol is usually written.

2. We always notice the symbols of our own culture.

3. In an unfamiliar culture, we feel confused by the symbols.

4. Culture shock is mostly about food.

Compare your answers with those of another student.

B. Read the passage again and underline the words that are new to you.

C. Look on the word lists in Appendices 1 and 2 (pages 303 and 308) for the words you underlined. Choose five of your underlined words that are on the lists and write them below. Then write the part of speech and the dictionary definition that best fits each word as it is used in the passage.

Word   **Definition**

1. _____   _____

2. _____   _____

3. _____   _____

4. _____   _____

5. _____   _____

D. Write a new sentence for each word above. The sentences should show that you understand the meaning of each word as it is used in the passage.

1. _____

_____

2. _____

_____

3. _____

_____

4. _____

_____

5. _____

_____

E. Ask another student to read your sentences. Then discuss these questions.

1. Do the sentences make sense?

2. Do the sentences show the meaning of the words?

EXERCISE 3

A. Write the words you chose in Exercises 1 and 2. Choose five or more of those words and make study cards for them.

B. Review your study cards alone and then with another student.

Inferring Meaning from Context

When you encounter an unfamiliar word, a good strategy is to infer (or guess) its meaning from the context. You may not always be able to infer an exact meaning, but you can often get the general meaning—enough to continue reading with understanding.

You can benefit from this strategy in three ways:

- It allows you to continue reading and stay focused on the ideas in the text.
- It helps you develop a more complete understanding of the word and the way it is used.
- It helps you remember the word in the future.

Guidelines for Inferring Meaning from the Immediate Context

- Analyze the way a word is used in a sentence. What part of speech is it (noun, verb, adjective, adverb, etc.)?

- Look at the words that are used with it. These often help determine meaning. For example, if it is an adjective, what is the noun? If it is a verb, what is the subject?

- Think about the topic and the meaning of the sentence. How does the word fit in?

Example:

Follow the guidelines above to infer the general meaning of the underlined word in each of the three sentences below. Then write the inferred meaning (in English or another language). Do not use a dictionary.

The president's spokesman said that it was too early to comment on the <u>outcome</u> of the meeting.

One unfortunate <u>outcome</u> of the elections was that both parties were weaker than before.

The <u>outcome</u> of hospital-based treatment was clearly better than home-based treatment.

Inferred meaning: *the result or effect of something*

Note: In Exercises 1–3, the underlined words are used with their most common definition, usually listed first in the dictionary.

A. Follow the guidelines to infer the general meaning of the underlined word in each set of three sentences below. Then write the inferred meaning (in English or another language). Do not use a dictionary.

1. Dark clouds appeared and ten minutes later everyone at the football match was completely <u>drenched</u>.

   When he pulled her out of the swimming pool, her dress was <u>drenched</u> and hung close to her body.

   Seymour screamed and sat up suddenly in bed, <u>drenched</u> in a cold sweat.

   Inferred meaning: _____

2. The stranger never said a word, but <u>thrust</u> a folded piece of paper into Pilar's hand.

   He <u>thrust</u> his hands into his pockets and walked slowly away.

   As she straightened up, she felt a sudden pain like a knife being <u>thrust</u> into her lower back.

   Inferred meaning: _____

B. Compare your answers with those of another student. Then look up drenched and thrust in the dictionary. Compare the dictionary definitions with your inferred meanings and write the dictionary definitions below:

drenched: _____

thrust: _____

EXERCISE 2

A. Follow the guidelines to infer the general meaning of the underlined word in each set of three sentences below. Then write the inferred meaning (in English or another language).

1. Never <u>tamper</u> with electrical fittings without first switching off the main power supply.

   It is illegal to add, take away, or otherwise <u>tamper</u> with the content of these videos.

   Several research assistants were accused of <u>tampering</u> with the results of the experiments.

   Inferred meaning: _____

2. When the train pulled out and the crowd had thinned, he could see a small, <u>forlorn</u> figure sitting on a suitcase.

   Drennan held on to a <u>forlorn</u> hope that somehow at the end of the war they would all be together again.

Two <u>forlorn</u> trees stood out, black and naked against the snow-covered fields.

Inferred meaning: _____

B. Compare your answers with those of another student. Then look up tamper *and* forlorn *in the dictionary. Compare the dictionary definitions with your inferred meanings and write the dictionary definitions below:*

tamper: _____

forlorn: _____

EXERCISE 3

A. Follow the guidelines to infer the general meaning of the underlined word in each set of three sentences below. Then write the inferred meaning (in English or another language).

1. The financial <u>woes</u> of Fiat and other big Italian companies could lead to some important changes in the Italian economy.

   Take a vacation in the South Pacific and leave behind all your winter worries and <u>woes</u>.

   It did not take long for him to discover the source of all his friend's <u>woes</u>, but there was little he could do to help.

   Inferred meaning: _____

2. Recent surveys show that many parents are very worried about the possibility of their child being <u>abducted</u>.

   In 1976, a school bus driver and twenty-six children were <u>abducted</u> at gunpoint in California.

   The young woman admitted in tears that she had made up the story of how she was <u>abducted</u> and held by the men for thirty-six hours.

   Inferred meaning: _____

B. Compare your answers with those of another student. Then look up woes *and* abducted *in the dictionary. Compare the dictionary definitions with your inferred meanings and write the dictionary definitions below:*

woes: _____

abducted: _____

Using Context to Choose a Dictionary Definition

If you are able to infer the general meaning of a word from the context, you can make better use of the dictionary. In fact, many words have more than one definition and you need to choose the most appropriate one. For example, the word *laugh* (as a verb) has eleven different definitions in the *Longman Advanced American Dictionary*. Definitions for the word *get* cover three pages!

Guidelines for Choosing a Definition in the Dictionary

- Determine the part of speech of the unknown word. This is necessary because there may be several dictionary entries for one word as different parts of speech.

- Look at the words that are used with it. If it is a part of a frequent combination of words, the definition may be listed separately. For example, you will find separately numbered definitions for *sign up* and *sign off*. The same is true of *on sight* and *sight unseen* (both listed in the dictionary under *sight*).

- Analyze the context for clues to the general meaning of the word.

- Think about the topic and the meaning of the sentence in which the word is found.

- Look at the definitions listed in the dictionary and choose the most appropriate one—the one that best fits the way the word is used in the sentence.

Example:

A. Read the sentence, write the part of speech of the underlined word, and choose the most appropriate definition. Follow the guidelines for choosing a dictionary definition.

Finally managing to <u>wrench</u> herself free, she turned and stared at him.

Part of speech: *verb*

Definitions: (1.) to use your strength to pull yourself away from someone who is holding you

2. to take someone away from somewhere without their permission

3. to twist a joint in your body suddenly and painfully

B. What basic meaning do all three definitions of wrench have in common?

They all include the idea of a movement that causes pain, either physical or psychological.

A. Read the sentences, write the part of speech of the underlined word, and choose the most appropriate definition. Follow the guidelines for choosing a dictionary definition.

a. No matter how thirsty it is, a horse that has been used to drinking out of a pond or stream will often refuse water from a <u>trough</u>.

Part of speech: _____

Definitions: 1. a short period when prices are low, when there is little economic activity

2. a long open container that holds water or food for animals

3. the hollow area between two waves in the ocean or between two hills

b. It was their job to buy horses for the army and to <u>scour</u> the countryside for food and supplies.

Part of speech: _____

Definitions: 1. to search an area very carefully and thoroughly

2. to clean something very thoroughly by rubbing it with a rough material

3. to form a hole by continuous movement over a long period

B. Compare your answers with those of another student. Work together and answer the following questions.

a. What basic meaning do the three definitions of *trough* have in common?

b. What basic meaning do the three definitions of *scour* have in common?

A. Read each sentence and choose the most appropriate definition of the underlined word.

a. To make the perfect crepe, put some butter in the pan and <u>tilt</u> it in every direction so the butter covers the bottom.   _____

b. She ran full <u>tilt</u> out the back door, never noticing the car parked at the side.   _____

c. With the new evidence, public opinion was <u>tilted</u> once again, this time in favor of the suspect.   _____

d. In Leonardo da Vinci's famous portrait *Mona Lisa*, the slightly upward <u>tilt</u> of her eyes adds to the mystery of her smile.   _____

Definitions:

1. v. to move or make something move into a position where one side is higher than the other

2. v. to move your head or chin up or to the side

3. v. to change (as in belief or situation), so that people prefer one person or belief over another

4. n. full tilt—as fast as possible

5. n. a situation in which someone prefers one person or belief, or in which one person or belief has an advantage

6. n. a movement or position in which one side of something is higher than the other

B. Compare your answers with those of another student. Then discuss the definitions of tilt. What basic meaning do they have in common?

EXERCISE 6

A. Read each sentence and choose the most appropriate definition of the underlined word.

a. It was an obvious attempt to <u>shift</u> the blame for the accident onto the other driver. _____

b. Working the night <u>shift</u> can create family problems for both men and women. _____

c. Politicians argued that there was a strong need to <u>shift</u> more resources into education and research. _____

d. The lawyer's sharp questions made the witness <u>shift</u> uncomfortably in his seat. _____

Definitions:

1. v. to move from one place or position to another, or make something do this

2. v. to change the way money is paid or spent

3. v. to make someone else responsible for something, especially for something bad that has happened

4. n. a change in the way people think about something or the way something is done

5. n. one of the periods during each day and night when a particular group of workers in a factory, hospital, etc., are at work

6. n. the key on a computer keyboard that you press to print a capital letter

B. Compare your answers with those of another student. Then discuss the definitions of shift. What basic meaning do they have in common?

Inferring the Meaning of a Word in a Paragraph

Beyond the immediate context of the sentence, you can also find clues to the meaning of an unknown word in the larger context of a whole paragraph.

In the following exercises you will practice inferring meaning from a whole paragraph, with a nonsense word in the place of a real word.

Example:

Read the following paragraph and answer the questions about the underlined nonsense word.

As the harmful effects of <u>mropping</u> on health have become widely known, many cities and some countries have passed laws that limit where it is allowed. In many places, <u>mropping</u> is no longer permitted in restaurants and bars. Owners of restaurants and bars were against the laws because they believed that their businesses would suffer, but that happened only in the first few months. After that, business returned to normal. The laws have also had another positive effect, apart from making the air cleaner for everyone: More people have given up <u>mropping</u> altogether.

a. What part of speech is it? *noun*

b. What words are found around it? *effects of mropping, mropping is no longer permitted, more people have given up mropping*

c. What word or phrase could replace it? *smoking*

EXERCISE 7

A. Working with another student, read the paragraphs and fill in the information about the nonsense words in each paragraph.

1. At the beginning of World War II, when the Germans moved into northern France, they searched the towns and countryside for escaping French soldiers, who were sent to prisoner-of-war camps in Germany. Next, they tried to <u>zep</u> all the guns or other arms they could find, though many people hid theirs on farms or underground. The Germans also took all the horses from farms and towns, because they were needed in the army. This loss really hurt the French, since the lack of gasoline made horses necessary to work the farms and for transport. Not long after this, the Germans <u>zepped</u> radios as well, so that people could not listen to foreign news reports.

   a. What part of speech is it? _____

   b. What words are found around it? _____

   c. What word or phrase could replace it? _____

2. In many countries, there are electronic signs along roads that <u>zop</u> drivers about dangers or problems ahead. These may be short-term dangers, such as an accident or bad weather, or longer-term problems, such as roadwork. Studies have shown, however, that drivers do not always notice these signs. To be sure that drivers are <u>zopped</u> about the condition of the road, the highway management service in Scotland has developed a new electronic system that sends messages directly to special

electronic systems built into the cars. Do these systems work better to <u>zop</u> drivers than the roadside signs? It is too soon to tell. The results of the first studies will be published next year.

a. What part of speech is it? _____

b. What words are found around it? _____

c. What word or phrase could replace it? _____

B. Compare your answers with those of another pair of students. If you disagree, look again at the paragraphs and explain your answers.

EXERCISE 8

A. Working with another student, read the paragraphs and fill in the information about the underlined nonsense words.

1. During my stay in the city, I often used to sit on a stone wall by the riverbank in the early evening, hoping for a cool breeze—though there never was one. On one side was the "white" city, on the other side were the African villages, and all day long there were large <u>dreels</u> that went back and forth, bringing people, bicycles, cars, and trucks to and from the city. At this time of day, city workers were eager to get back to their own world on the far side of the river. Brightly dressed and joking, the Africans pushed forward when the <u>dreel</u> arrived. Many were carrying loads on their heads or bicycles on their shoulders. Some were so anxious not to miss the chance to get home that they leaped down the steps and jumped into the <u>dreel</u> as it pulled out.

a. What part of speech is it? _____

b. What words are found around it? _____

c. What word or phrase could replace it? _____

2. The foreign news reporters had been warned not to dress in a way that marked them obviously as foreigners. They were also told not to walk down the middle of the street, where they could be a <u>zeem</u> for enemies on the roofs. They should always stay close to the buildings, ready to run into a doorway if they heard or saw anything suspicious. They should always wear a bulletproof vest. They all did as they had been told, but still did not feel safe. It was impossible not to think of the colleagues who had been wounded and killed in these streets. They walked quickly, looking up at the rooftops. There was no telling when and where a sharpshooter might decide it was time for <u>zeem</u> practice—and they rarely missed their <u>zeem</u>.

a. What part of speech is it? _____

b. What words are found around it? _____

c. What word or phrase could replace it? _____

B. Compare your answers with those of another pair of students. If you disagree, look again at the paragraphs and explain your answers.

Using the Larger Context to Infer Meaning

Sometimes you cannot infer the meaning of an unfamiliar word by using just the sentence or paragraph in which it appears. You need to read more of the surrounding text to look for clues to its meaning.

Guidelines for Using the Larger Context to Infer Meaning

- Determine the part of speech.

- Look at the words that are used with it.

- Think about the meaning of the sentence and the topic of the passage.

- Notice if the word is repeated elsewhere in the passage or if the writer has used any synonyms (words with the same meaning) or antonyms (opposites).

- Look for an explanation or definition of the word somewhere else in the passage (especially in a textbook).

- Infer an approximate meaning of the word.

- Read the sentence with your meaning instead of the original word. Does it make sense? If not, check steps 1–5 again (or look in a dictionary!).

Example:

A. Working with another student, read the passage below from Never Cry Wolf **by the biologist Farley Mowat. Then answer the questions and infer the meaning of the underlined word.**

Note: The book describes a summer that Mowat spent in the Canadian Arctic studying wolves. In this passage, he describes three wolves whom he has named George, Albert, and Angeline.

One day the wolves killed a caribou[1] close to home and this convenient food supply gave them an opportunity to take a holiday. They did not go hunting at all that night, but stayed near the den[2] and rested.

The next morning dawned fine and warm, and a general air of contented <u>lassitude</u> seemed to overcome all three. Angeline lay at her ease on the rocks overlooking the summer den, while George and Albert rested in sandy beds on the ridge.[3] The only signs of life from any of them through the long morning were occasional changes of position, and lazy looks about the countryside.

(Source: Farley Mowat, *Never Cry Wolf*, Boston: Bantam Books, 1963, p. 114)

---

[1] *caribou:* reindeer
[2] *den:* the home of some types of animals, for example, wolves
[3] *ridge:* a long area of high land

1. What part of speech is it? _noun_

2. What phrase is used with it? _general air of contented lassitude_

3. What words in the paragraph give clues to the meaning? (synonyms, antonyms, or other) _seemed to overcome, at her ease, rested, occasional changes of position, lazy_

B. Now infer an approximate meaning of the word and write it here.

laziness

C. Now look up lassitude in the dictionary and write the definition that best fits its use in the passage.

laziness or lack of energy

EXERCISE 9

A. Working with another student, read another passage from Never Cry Wolf. Then answer the questions and infer the meaning of the underlined word.

The realization that the wolves' summer diet consisted chiefly of mice did not conclude my work in the field of dietetics.[1] I knew that the mouse-wolf relationship was a revolutionary one to science and would be treated with suspicion, and possibly with ridicule, unless it could be so thoroughly substantiated that there would be no room to doubt its validity.

I had already established two major points:

1. That wolves caught and ate mice.
2. That the small rodents [mice] were sufficiently[2] numerous to support the wolf population.

There remained, however, a third point vital to the proof of my contention. This concerned the nutritional value of mice. It was imperative for me to prove that a diet of small rodents would suffice to maintain a large carnivore in good condition.

(Source: Farley Mowat, *Never Cry Wolf*. Boston: Bantam Books, 1963, p. 75)

---
[1] *dietetics:* science of diet and nutrition
[2] *sufficiently:* enough

1. What part of speech is it? _____

2. What phrase is used with it? _____

3. What words in the paragraph give clues to the meaning? (synonyms, antonyms, or other)

_____

B. Now infer an approximate meaning of the word and write it here.

_____

C. Compare your answers in A and B with those of another pair of students. Then look up substantiated in the dictionary. If what you wrote does not match any of the definitions in the dictionary, choose the most appropriate definition and write it here.

_____

A. Working with another student, read the passages from Bury Me Standing by the journalist Isabel Fonseca. Then infer the meaning of the underlined words.

(This book of anthropology describes the history of Gypsy, or Roma, families in Eastern Europe and their lives in the 1990s.)

1. Even at [the Gypsies'] home I was never allowed to be alone: not ever. The Dukas did not share gadjo [non-Gypsy] notions of or need for privacy. Or for quiet. The more and the noisier the better was their <u>creed</u>—one that I found to be universal among Roma. There was something wrong with you, some shame, if you had to be alone. The Gypsies have endured unimaginable hardships, but one could be sure that loneliness wasn't one of them.

   Inferred meaning of *creed*: _____

2. Every morning Bexhet stretched out his shaving ritual for as long as he could. One by one, he would produce the <u>implements</u> from his locked trunk: a shaving brush, a shaving bowl with the soap stuck in it, the folding razor. Wearing his morning suit—striped pajama bottoms and a khaki military shirt—he would make three trips in and out of the house for these tools, holding each with a ten-fingered delicacy you might reserve for the handling of a small but perfectly preserved Minoan [antique] pot. After all the <u>implements</u> had been arranged along the courtyard ledge, which became barber's corner for a good part of each morning, Bexhet would make a final trip for his special cracked shaving mirror.

   Inferred meaning of *implement*: _____

3. Jeta's father, Sherif (just for example), like most traditional Gypsy men, wore a suit all the time, the same suit, no matter what the occasion or the weather. And he would wear that suit until it fell to pieces and had to be replaced. This habit <u>flourished</u> alongside the foppish[1] tastes of many Gypsy men: they loved flash cuts and flapping lapels, in shiny, striped fabrics; they liked hats, wore watch fobs[2], mustaches, and lots of (gold) jewelry.

   (Source: Isabel Fonseca, *Bury Me Standing: The Gypsies and Their Journey*. New York: Vintage Books, 1995)

   ----
   [1] *foppish:* fashionable in an extreme way
   [2] *fob:* a short chain to which a watch is fastened

   Inferred meaning of *flourished*: _____

B. Compare your answers with those of another pair of students. Then look up the underlined words in the dictionary. If what you wrote does not match any of the definitions in the dictionary, choose the most appropriate definitions and write them here.

_____

UNIT 4   Word Parts

In this unit you will learn the important strategy of analyzing the parts of a word for information about its meaning. Many words in English can be broken down into several parts. When you know the meaning and function of some common word parts, you can

- guess the meaning of some new words;
- remember the meaning of new words better;
- increase the number of words you know.

Words in English can have three parts: a root, a prefix, and a suffix.

- The root of a word contains the basic meaning.

  Example: *happy*

- A prefix is a letter or group of letters that is added before the root to change its meaning.

  Example: *un* (not) + *happy* = *unhappy* (*not happy*)

- A suffix is a letter or group of letters that is added after the root to change its grammatical function. (Note that when suffixes are added, the spelling of the root may change.)

  Example: *happy* (adjective) + *ness* = *happiness* (noun)

Many words are combinations of these parts.

Examples:

create	+	*ive*		=	*creative*
un	+	*break*	+ *able*	=	*unbreakable*
il	+	*logic*	+ *al*	=	*illogical*

Roots of English Words

Knowing the meanings of some common roots can help you understand the words that are made from those roots. The words built around a single root are called related words.

There are two types of roots:

- Roots that can stand alone as words in English.

    Examples: *cheer, happy, usual, break*

- Roots that cannot stand alone in English. These include many of the roots that come from Latin, Greek, and other languages. Note that the spelling of the roots from other languages is often changed when they are part of an English word.

    Example: *philos* (from the Greek word for love) is contained in: *philosopher* (lover of knowledge) and *bibliophile* (lover of books).

EXERCISE 1

Latin roots			
annus	= year	manus	= hand
dictus	= say, speak	versum	= turn
locatum	= place	visus	= see

A. Working with another student, write the word, the root, and the definition if you know it or can guess it. Then look it up in the dictionary to check your definition.

Example: Because of problems with his <u>vision</u>, Sanjay can no longer drive a car.

Word: _vision_____   Root: _visus_____

Your definition: _being able to see_____

Dictionary definition: _ability to see_____

1. <u>Manual</u> workers with no special training are unlikely to find a job that pays well.

    Word: _____   Root: _____

    Your definition: _____

    Dictionary definition: _____

2. If you <u>reverse</u> the flow of water in the experiment, you will get the opposite results as well.

    Word: _____   Root: _____

    Your definition: _____

    Dictionary definition: _____

3. Historically, the earliest churches in this region were <u>located</u> outside the city walls.

Word: _____   Root: _____

Your definition: _____

Dictionary definition: _____

4. It was difficult to <u>predict</u> whether the injury would result in death.

Word: _____   Root: _____

Your definition: _____

Dictionary definition: _____

5. The bank's <u>annual</u> report gave details of the growth of its activities over the past twelve months.

Word: _____   Root: _____

Your definition: _____

Dictionary definition: _____

6. The <u>dictator</u> ruled his country with an iron hand.

Word: _____   Root: _____

Your definition: _____

Dictionary definition: _____

B. The related words in this table are based on the same Latin roots. Write the words from part A beside the words that have the same root. Then write the dictionary definitions of the related words.

Word from part A	Related word	Definition of related word
vision	visibility	the distance it is possible to see
	revert	
	visualize	
	manipulate	
	anniversary	
	dictation	
	local	

C. Compare your answers with those of another pair of students. If you disagree, use a dictionary to check your work.

	Greek roots		
bios	= life	logos	= word, speak, reason
chronos	= time	metron	= measure
genos	= race, kind	pathos	= suffering, feeling
geo	= earth		

A. Working with another student, write the word, the root, and the meaning if you know it or can guess it. Then look it up in the dictionary to check your work.

1. She spoke to him roughly because she didn't want to look lonely and <u>pathetic</u> in his eyes.

   Word: _____ Root: _____

   Your definition: _____

   Dictionary definition: _____

2. A new study that includes both men and women shows many <u>gender</u> differences.

   Word: _____ Root: _____

   Your definition: _____

   Dictionary definition: _____

3. According to marine <u>biologists</u>, the temperature of the world's oceans has risen in recent years.

   Word: _____ Root: _____

   Your definition: _____

   Dictionary definition: _____

4. After much study, we have concluded that there is only one <u>logical</u> solution to this problem.

   Word: _____ Root: _____

   Your definition: _____

   Dictionary definition: _____

5. Because schools do not emphasize <u>geography</u>, many children in the United States lack knowledge about other parts of the world.

Word: _____   Root: _____

Your definition: _____

Dictionary definition: _____

6. The documents in these files are arranged in <u>chronological</u> order from the earliest date to most recent.

Word: _____   Root: _____

Your definition: _____

Dictionary definition: _____

7. Someone has altered the <u>meter</u> for the building so that it no longer shows how much water is used.

Word: _____   Root: _____

Your definition: _____

Dictionary definition: _____

B. The related words in this table are based on the same Greek roots. Write the words from part A beside the words that have the same root. Then write the dictionary definitions of the related words.

Word from part A	Related word	Definition of related word
	sympathy	
	geocentric	
	chronicle	
	dialogue	
	gene	
	metric	
	biodegradable	

C. Compare your answers with those of another pair of students. If you disagree, use a dictionary to check your work.

Prefixes

Since each prefix has a meaning, adding a prefix creates a word with a new meaning. The following meanings are often added with prefixes:

- Negative or opposite

    Example: *un + happy = not happy*

- Number or quantity

    Example: *bi + cycle = two-wheeled vehicle*

- Time

    Example: *pre + view = to look at something before or earlier*

- Space

    Example: *inter + national = between two or more nations*

Sometimes a prefix can function like a root.

Examples: *uni* (one) + *ify* (make) = *unify*

du (two) + *et* = *a piece of music for two performers*

EXERCISE 3

A. Study the prefixes that give words a negative meaning. In the items below, all of the words except one have a prefix with a negative meaning. Working with another student, cross out the word that does not have a prefix. If necessary, you may use a dictionary.

Prefixes	Words with a negative meaning
dis- = not, opposite of	dissatisfied = not satisfied
in-, im- = not	incorrect = not correct
non- = not	nonalcoholic = not containing alcohol
un- = not, opposite of	unsympathetic = not sympathetic

Example:

im-	*impossible*	~~*imagine*~~	*imperfect*	*impersonal*	*impatient*
1. un-	unaware	uncle	unspoken	unable	unbearable
2. non-	nonsense	nonverbal	nonsmoking	nonfiction	normal
3. in-	inaccurate	inspire	inactive	incomplete	infinite
4. dis-	disapprove	diskette	discontent	displace	disfavor

B. Think of another word with each of the negative prefixes. If necessary, you may use a dictionary. Write the words and their definitions.

Prefix	Word	Definition
Example:		
un-	unattractive	not physically attractive or beautiful.
1. un-	_____	_____
2. non-	_____	_____
3. in-	_____	_____
4. dis-	_____	_____

C. Compare your answers with those of another pair of students. If you disagree, use a dictionary to check your work.

EXERCISE 4

A. Study the prefixes with a numerical meaning. In the items below, all of the words except one have a prefix with a numerical meaning. Working with another student, cross out the word that does not have a prefix. If necessary, you may use a dictionary.

Prefixes	Words with a numerical meaning
bi- = two	bicycle = a vehicle with two wheels
cent- = hundred	century = a hundred years
du- = two	duplex = a house that is divided to have two homes in it
mono- = one	monogamy = marriage with only one person
quad- = four	quadrangle = a shape that has four sides
tri- = three	triangle = a shape with three sides
uni- = one	unique = the only one of a type

1. uni-	united	union	universe	unimportant	uniform
2. bi-	biped	biannual	biology	binoculars	biceps
3. tri-	triplets	trial	tripod	triathlon	tricycle
4. quad-	quadrille	quadrant	quadruplets	quality	quadrant
5. cent-	central	centigrade	centenarian	centurion	centiliter
6. mono-	monotony	monocle	monograph	money	monolog
7. du-	duplicate	duet	duplicity	durable	dual

B. Think of another word with each prefix. If necessary, you may use a dictionary. Write the words and their definitions.

Prefix	Word	Definition
1. uni-	_____	_____
2. bi-	_____	_____
3. tri-	_____	_____
4. quad-	_____	_____
5. cent-	_____	_____
6. mono-	_____	_____
7. du-	_____	_____

C. Compare your answers with those of another pair of students. If you disagree, use a dictionary to check your work.

EXERCISE 5

A. Study the prefixes with meaning related to time. In the items below, all of the words except one have a prefix with a time meaning. Working with another student, cross out the word that does not have a prefix. If necessary, you may use a dictionary.

Prefixes	Words with a meaning related to time
post- = after, behind	posterity = generations of your family that come after you
pre- = before	predecease = to die before someone else
prime- = first	primitive = belonging to an early or very simple society
re- = again	reread = to read something again

1. pre-	preview	pretty	precaution	preliminary	prehistoric
2. re-	reason	rebuild	renew	rearm	relocate
3. post-	postpone	poster	posterior	posthumous	postnatal
4. prime-	primary	primer	primeval	primrose	primacy

B. Think of another word with each prefix. If necessary, you may use a dictionary. Write the words and their definitions.

Prefix	Word	Definition
1. pre-	_____	_____
2. re-	_____	_____
3. post-	_____	_____
4. prime-	_____	_____

C. Compare your answers with those of another pair of students. If you disagree, use a dictionary to check your work.

EXERCISE 6

A. Study the prefixes that show relationships. In the items below, all of the words except one have a prefix with a meaning that shows a relationship. Working with another student, cross out the word that does not have a prefix. If necessary, you may use a dictionary.

Prefixes	Words that show relationships
com-, con- = with, together	committee = a group of people who work together
contra- = against	contradict = to express the opposite of a statement
ex- = out, from	exhale = to breathe out
inter- = between	interpret = to translate one language to another
sub- = under	subterranean = underground
super- = above, over	superstructure = the part of a building above ground
sym-, syn- = same, together	synagogue = meeting place for Jewish religious services
tele- = distant	teleconference = a conference at which people are in different places and communicate by phone or video

1. com-	compatible	compatriot	company	comma	community
2. inter-	intermission	interact	interval	intercede	interest
3. sym-, syn-	symmetry	synchronize	symptom	syringe	symphony
4. ex-	exit	exercise	exile	exempt	except
5. sub-	subconscious	subordinate	subdivide	sublime	submit
6. tele-	telegram	telescope	telethon	telephoto	teller
7. super-	superficial	superb	supervisor	supersonic	superior
8. contra-	contraindication	contract	contrarian	contradiction	contraposition

B. Think of another word with each of the prefixes. If necessary, you may use a dictionary. Write the words and their definitions.

Prefix	Word	Definition
1. com-	_____	_____
2. inter-	_____	_____
3. sym-, syn-	_____	_____
4. ex-	_____	_____
5. sub-	_____	_____
6. tele-	_____	_____
7. super-	_____	_____
8. contra-	_____	_____

C. Compare your answers with those of another pair of students. If you disagree, use a dictionary to check your work.

Suffixes

Since most suffixes are related to grammar, adding a suffix to the end of a word usually changes the word's part of speech. Notice that when a suffix is added to the end of a root, the spelling of the root often changes.

- Some suffixes form nouns.

    Examples: *understand* (verb) + *ing* = *understanding*

    comprehend (verb) + *ion* = *comprehension*

    happy (adjective) + *ness* = *happiness*

- Some suffixes form adjectives.

    Examples: *understand* (verb) + *able* = *understandable*

    success (noun) + *ful* = *successful*

- Some suffixes form adverbs.

    Examples: *understand* (verb) + *ably* = *understandably*

    happy (adjective) + *ly* = *happily*

EXERCISE 7

A. Study the suffixes that change words into nouns. Working with another student, create nouns by adding an appropriate suffix to each word below. Write the noun and the meaning if you know it or can guess it. If necessary, you may use a dictionary.

Suffixes	Nouns
-ance, -ancy	insure + ance = insurance; truant + ancy = truancy
-ence	differ + ence = difference
-er, -or	teach + er = teacher; act + or = actor
-ion, -tion	confuse + ion = confusion; compete + tion = competition
-ism	real + ism = realism
-ment	refresh + ment = refreshment
-ness	ready + ness = readiness

Suffix	Word	Noun	Definition
Example:			
-ion	digest	*digestion*	*the process of digesting food*
1. -ance	endure		
2. -ence	competent		
3. -er	organize		
4. -or	conquer		
5. -ion	discuss		
6. -tion	delete		
7. -ism	mystic		
8. -ment	commit		
9. -ness	effective		
10. -ion	restrict		

B. Compare your answers with those of another pair of students. If you disagree, use a dictionary to check your work.

EXERCISE 8

A. Study the suffixes that change words into adjectives. Working with another student, create adjectives by adding an appropriate suffix to each word below. Write the adjective and the meaning if you know it or can guess it. If necessary, you may use a dictionary.

Suffixes	Adjectives
-able	adore + able = adorable
-al	spine + al = spinal
-ful	beauty + ful = beautiful
-ic	specify + ic = specific
-ious	space + ious = spacious
-ive	create + ive = creative
-less	care + less = careless
-ous	fame + ous = famous
-y	stick + y = sticky

Suffix	Word	Adjective	Definition
1. -able	conceive	_____	_____
2. -al	season	_____	_____
3. -ful	bounty	_____	_____
4. -ic	angel	_____	_____
5. -ous	monotony	_____	_____
6. -ious	deviate	_____	_____
7. -ive	suggest	_____	_____
8. -y	panic	_____	_____
9. -ic	strategy	_____	_____
10. -less	law	_____	_____

B. Compare your answers with those of another pair of students. If you disagree, use a dictionary to check your work.

EXERCISE 9

A. Study the suffixes that change words into verbs. Working with another student, create verbs by adding an appropriate suffix to each word below. Write the verb and the meaning if you know it or can guess it. If necessary, you may use a dictionary.

Suffixes	Verbs
-ate	liberty + ate = liberate
-ify	significant + ify = signify
-ize	final + ize = finalize

Suffix	Word	Verb	Definition
1. -ate	valid	_____	_____
2. -ify	justice	_____	_____
3. -ize	custom	_____	_____
4. -ate	equal	_____	_____
5. -ify	quantity	_____	_____
6. -ize	economy	_____	_____

B. Compare your answers with those of another student. If you disagree, use a dictionary to check your work.

A. Working with another student, read each word, underline the suffix, and write the part of speech (noun, adjective, or verb). Then try to guess the meaning of the word and write it down.

Word	Part of speech	Meaning
Example: meaningless	*adjective*	*having no purpose or importance*
1. harmonize		
2. environmental		
3. differentiate		
4. ethnic		
5. qualitative		
6. optional		
7. negate		
8. identical		
9. precedence		
10. investigative		

B. Compare your answers with those of another pair of students. If you disagree, use a dictionary to check your work.

A. In each sentence find a word with a prefix or suffix that you have worked with in this unit. Underline the word and write it again, divided into its parts. Then look for the definition in the dictionary.

Example: The <u>supervisor</u> of the factory expects all the employees to arrive on time every morning.

Word: *supervisor*   Parts: *super + vis + or*

Definition: *someone who oversees a person or activity*

1. It was necessary to revise the plan numerous times before everyone could agree.

Word: _____   Parts: _____

Definition: _____

2. The magic show included a woman who claimed she could perform mental telepathy.

Word: _____   Parts: _____

Definition: _____

3. In any language it is possible to generate an endless number of new sentences.

Word: _____ Parts: _____

Definition: _____

4. The young Swiss tennis player has demonstrated his total dominance of the game by winning ten major tournaments.

Word: _____ Parts: _____

Definition: _____

5. When James Joyce published his novel *Ulysses,* many critics did not appreciate the unconventional style of his writing.

Word: _____ Parts: _____

Definition: _____

6. The university president was insensitive to the women on the faculty and so he was fired from his job.

Word: _____ Parts: _____

Definition: _____

7. The firefighters acted heroically to save as many people as possible.

Word: _____ Parts: _____

Definition: _____

8. Some European clocks are synchronized by satellite with a clock in Frankfurt, Germany.

Word: _____ Parts: _____

Definition: _____

9. In his first lecture for the astronomy course, the professor gave a brilliant explanation of how the universe began.

Word: _____ Parts: _____

Definition: _____

B. Compare your answers with those of another student. If you disagree, use a dictionary to check your work.

UNIT 5 Collocations

Collocations are groups of words that frequently occur together. Every language develops different collocations. For example, in these three languages, different adjectives are used to describe tea:

English: *strong tea, weak tea*

Italian: *strong tea, long tea*

Japanese: *dark tea, thin tea*

When you are reading in English, it is very important to notice collocations and to learn them together with the individual words. You will gain fluency and improve comprehension if you are familiar with common collocations.

Noticing Collocations

Some Common Types of Collocations Found in Academic Texts*	
Collocations	**Examples**
Adjective + noun	key issues, persistent problems, wide range, further research, current theory, larger context, detailed references, essential information, prior knowledge, practical applications, straightforward approach
Verb + adverb (or adverb + verb)	develop further, demonstrate conclusively, present effectively, explore thoroughly, highly appreciate, successfully complete
Verb + noun	acquire vocabulary, gain awareness, reach a goal, address the issue, raise the question, develop a theory, provide a framework, set the scene, clarify the point
Phrasal verbs	depend on, relate to, focus on, bring together, deal with, consist of, respond to, lead to, serve as, point out
Prepositional phrases	in that case, in any case, on the whole, with regard to, in other words

*These examples of collocations were compiled by the authors from several academic texts.

Example:

A. Read the passage, find three collocations like those listed in the table, and underline them. Then write them below.

Millions of people now rent their movies the Netflix way. They <u>fill out</u> a wish list from the 50,009 titles on the company's Web site and receive the first few DVD's in the mail; when they mail each one back, the next one on the list is sent.

The Netflix model has been <u>exhaustively analyzed</u> for its disruptive, new-economy implications. What will it mean for video stores like Blockbuster, which has, in fact, started a similar service? What will it mean for movie studios and theaters? What does it show about "long tail" businesses—ones that amalgamate many niche markets, like those for Dutch movies or classic musicals, into a single <u>target audience</u>?

But one other major implication has <u>barely been mentioned</u>: what this and similar Internet-based businesses mean for that stalwart of the old economy, the United States Postal Service.

(Source: *The New York Times*, September 4, 2005)

fill out, exhaustively analyze, target audience, barely mention

B. Check the definitions of any words you are not sure about.

C. Compare your work with that of another student. If you disagree or are not sure about a collocation, check with your teacher.

▰EXERCISE 1

A. Read the passage, find at least three collocations like those listed in the table, and underline them. Then write them below.

The eclipse of "snail mail" in the age of instant electronic communication has been predicted at least as often as the coming of the paperless office. But the consumption of paper keeps rising. (It has roughly doubled since 1980, with less use of newsprint and much more of ordinary office paper.) And so, with some nuances and internal changes, does the flow of material carried by mail. On average, an American household receives twice as many pieces of mail a day as it did in the 1970s.

"Is the Internet hurting the mails, or helping?" asks Michael J. Critelli, a co-chairman of the public-private Mail Industry Task Force. "It's doing both." Mr. Critelli's day job is chief executive of Pitney Bowes—yes, that Pitney Bowes, once known for its postage meters and now a "mail and document management" company. In the last few years, it has also functioned as a research group for the mail industry, commissioning a series of studies, available free at PostInsight@PB.com, that contain startling findings about the economic, technological and cultural forces that affect use of mail.

(Source: *The New York Times*, September 4, 2005)

_____

B. Check the definitions of any words you are not sure about.

C. Compare your work with that of another student. If you disagree or are not sure about a collocation, check with your teacher.

A. Read the passage, find at least three collocations like those listed in the table on page 62, and underline them. Then write them below.

The harmful side of the Internet's impact is obvious but statistically less important than many would guess. People naturally write fewer letters when they can send e-mail messages. To leaf through a box of old paper correspondence is to know what has been lost in this shift: the pretty stamps, the varying look and feel of handwritten and typed correspondence, the tangible object that was once in the sender's hands. To stay in instant touch with parents, children and colleagues around the world is to know what's been gained.

But even before e-mail, personal letters had shrunk to a tiny share of the flow. As a consultant, Fouad H. Nader, wrote in a Pitney Bowes study, personal mail had "long ago been reduced to a minimum with the proliferation of telephone services in the last 50 years."

Personal letters of all sorts, called "household to household" correspondence, account for less than 1 percent of the 100 billion pieces of first-class mail that the Postal Service handles each year. Most of that personal mail consists of greeting cards, invitations, announcements, and other mail with "emotional content," a category that is generally holding its own.

The same higher-income households that rely the most on e-mail correspondence also send and receive the most letters. Whatever shrinkage e-mail has caused in personal correspondence, it is not likely to do much more.

(Source: *The New York Times*, September 4, 2005)

B. Check the definitions of any words you are not sure about.

C. Compare your work with that of another student. If you disagree or are not sure about a collocation, check with your teacher.

Using Concordance Sentences to Identify Collocations

A concordance is a computerized collection of sentences that all contain the same word or phrase. The sentences are taken from authentic texts, not texts written for language learning. From these sentences you can learn how a word or phrase is actually used and how it combines with other words.

The concordancing program used in Exercises 3–6 can be found at http://langbank.engl.polyu.edu.hk/corpus/microconcord.html.

Note: In the exercises that follow, the concordance "sentences" are often not complete sentences because of the way the computer selects a limited sample of text. Some of the words at the beginning or end may also be incomplete. You should not pay attention to the incomplete words or to any words you are not familiar with, but focus instead on the target word and the words around it.

A. Read the concordance sentences containing the word assumption **and answer the questions below. The first two have been started for you.**

1. to make the kind of general	assumption	made by Morgan and Engles. We can say
2. that a theory based on the	assumption	of a common mechanism must be
3. inside. It was a not unreasonable	assumption	that a man who developed a
4. different. Dubos started from the	assumption	that all organic matter added to
5. trality still rests on the further	assumption	that it was vital to us to keep
6. Fig. 5.6, as this depends on the	assumption	that stimulus A acquired
7. about these debates is the shared	assumption	that the area was a "good thing"
8. (p. 24) It dared to question the	assumption	that the creation of wealth, at
9. state. There was also the general	assumption	that the fact of a state populated
10. This entire case depends on the	assumption	that the trust to set up a building
11. growing tendency to question the	assumption	that, prior to the advent of
12. of justice. The fundamental	assumption	was that Time will always

1. List the words or phrases used before *assumption*.

   to make the kind of general assumption, based on the assumption

2. Find two patterns in the words or phrases in 1. above and write them here.

   1. Adjectives are often used before <u>assumption</u>: <u>general, unreasonable, further.</u>
   2. <u>Assumption</u> *often follows a phrasal verb.*

3. List the words or phrases used after *assumption*.

4. Find a pattern in the words or phrases in 3. above and write it here.

_____

B. Compare your answers with those of another student. Write three of the collocations for the word assumption **that you think would be useful to learn.**

A. Read the concordance sentences containing the word strategy and answer the questions below.

1.	countries adopt a development	strategy	away from dependence on fossil fuel
2.	maximum possible score that any	strategy	could achieve was 15,000
3.	Therefore the only rational	strategy	for either of us to play on the 100
4.	ed that his rats tended to adopt a	strategy	for sampling the stimuli in the fir
5.	can judge which is the truly best	strategy,	in a more general and less arbitra
6.	has really changed course. Its new	strategy	is called the Tropical Forestry Act
7.	ring. To a Darwinian, a successful	strategy	is one that has become numerous
8.	that do not fit in the long term	strategy	of the group. Money Page 24 Da
9.	short break and plan a date and a	strategy	for the return to your exercise rou
10.	than their authors. The winning	strategy,	remarkably, was the simplest and
11.	point of view this is a reasonable	strategy,	since it tends to cut down energy
12.	According to the regional	strategy,	the government aims to flood an

1. List the words or phrases used before *strategy*.

2. Find two patterns in the words or phrases in 1. above and write them here.

3. List the words or phrases used after *strategy*.

4. Find a pattern in the words or phrases in 3. above and write them here.

B. Compare your answers with those of another student. Write three of the collocations for the word strategy that you think would be useful to learn.

A. Read the concordance sentences containing the word process *and answer the questions below.*

1.	This is a relatively simple	process	and divides the egg up into a numbe
2.	certainly, the most ancient	process,	and one which continues to play a
3.	we are talking about the political	process,	and understand what this involves
4.	leep stages. Sleep is not a single	process,	as we know from our own experience
5.	But it had not been a smooth	process.	During the preceding fifty or sixt
6.	about what causes the historical	process	has been very widely discussed and
7.	in other ways, however. The main	process	is competition. Whenever one indivi
8.	lowly, go carefully and enjoy the	process	of change. Your lists of goals shou
9.	possible for doctors to extend the	process	of dying through the use, for examp
10.	between those involved in the	process	of production can be extremely vari
11.	piece of writing. Maybe it is this	process	of revision, and therefore of selec
12.	an autobiography is part of the	process	of understanding and interpreting
13.	appears to have been a gradual	process.	Various stories lend drama to the

1. List the words or phrases used before *process*.

2. Find two patterns in the words or phrases in 1. above and write them here.

3. List the words or phrases used after *process*.

4. Find a pattern in the words or phrases in 3. above and write them here.

B. Compare your answers with those of another student. Write three of the collocations for the word process *that you think would be useful to learn.*

A. Read the concordance sentences containing the word perception **and answer the questions below.**

1.	we do not understand what sense-	perception	actually is. In thinking about this
2.	This deals with motion and sense	perception,	and is laid out, after the manner
3.	He saw the problem of visual	perception	as a particular difficulty for it
4.	a world of objects beyond direct	perception.	But he is not, he claims, denying
5.	between ideas, and that where this	perception	is lacking we have only "belief"
6.	Malebranche, whose theories of	perception	involved both material things
7.	was not just a matter of my own	perception.	It was definitely an attitude on
8.	werful influence upon the popular	perception	of Islam. Christian polemicists
9.	of the relationship between their	perception	of the good of the state and public
10.	in society depends on the public's	perception	of what life imprisonment means:
11.	ways. First, there is a widespread	perception	recorded in the surveys of specific
12.	clusion was based on the general	perception	that pre-1939 aviation was overly

1. List the words or phrases used before *perception*.

2. Find two patterns in the words or phrases in 1. above and write them here.

3. List the words or phrases used after *perception*.

4. Find a pattern in the words or phrases in 3. above and write them here.

B. Compare your answers with those of another student. Write three of the collocations for the word perception **that you think would be useful to learn.**

A. Working with another student, choose five adjectives from the list to combine with each noun and write them on the lines. Try not to look back at the concordance sentences.

direct	gradual	lower	rational	successful
each	higher	main	regional	unreasonable
fundamental	historical	political	shared	visual
further	important	popular	single	widespread
general	long-term	public's	smooth	winning

1. _general_
   _____
   _____ assumption
   _____
   _____

2. _____
   _____
   _____ strategy
   _____
   _____

3. _____
   _____
   _____ process
   _____
   _____

4. _____
   _____
   _____ perception
   _____
   _____

B. Compare your answers with those of another pair of students. Then look back at the concordance sentences in Exercises 3–6 to check your answers. Check with your teacher or in a collocations dictionary about any new combinations that you have made.

A. Write an appropriate adjective in each sentence. Use each adjective only once.

1. The _____ assumption of the scientists was that their theory could be applied to both men and women.

2. The _____ perception of the president was that he had not told the whole truth about the war.

3. The company's vice president decided that it was important to adopt a _____ strategy for marketing the product.

4. It was not a _____ process but a sudden and dramatic change of government after 1989.

5. Birds have a very different _____ perception from humans. In fact, some birds can see colors that we do not perceive at all.

6. With so many people involved, making a decision about the new library was not a
   _____ process.

7. It was not easy for my grandmother to be accepted as a scientist because she
   questioned many _____ assumptions about women in science.

8. To reduce air pollution, the government has adopted a _____ strategy
   encouraging people to use public transportation.

B. Compare your answers with those of another student. Then look back at Exercise 6 to check your answers. Check with your teacher or in a collocations dictionary about any new combinations you have made.

EXERCISE 9

A. Working with another student choose three verbs (or phrasal verbs) to combine with each of the nouns and write them on the lines, adding articles as needed. Try not to look back at the concordance sentences. (You may use a verb more than once.)

adopt	belong to	extend	make	question
base on	cause	fall within	place in	rest on
be involved in	deal with	fit in	plan	start from
be part of	depend on	involve in		

1. _based on the_

   _____

   _____ assumption

2. _____

   _____

   _____ strategy

3. _____

   _____

   _____ process

4. _____

   _____

   _____ perception

B. Compare your answers with those of another student. Then look back at the concordance sentences in the Example and Exercises 3–6 to check your answers. Check with your teacher or in a collocations dictionary about any new combinations that you have made.

A. Write an appropriate verb (and preposition if necessary) in each sentence. Make sure it is in the correct tense for the context. Use each verb only once.

1. The public's perception of the war _____ the way it is shown on the news.

2. Taking the patient's complete medical history _____ the process of preparing for an operation.

3. When you are reading, you need to _____ a successful strategy for dealing with new words.

4. A lot of people _____ the assumption that all politicians are liars.

5. The decision _____ the widespread perception that air travel had become more costly and less safe.

6. General Howard _____ a strategy for attacking and entering the town, but it proved to be very unrealistic.

7. For democracy to function well, people must _____ the political process at the local level.

8. The doctor _____ the assumption that it was not a good idea to operate on a very elderly person.

B. Compare your answers with those of another student. Then look at Exercise 8 to check your answers. Check with your teacher or in a collocations dictionary about any new combinations that you have made.

Guidelines for Learning Collocations

- **Read extensively.** (See Part 1.)

  Research has shown that this is the best way to expand your knowledge of the collocations used in written English. By reading a lot—not just a few passages, or stories, but whole books—you will encounter many examples of how words are used and how they combine with each other. As a result, you will become a more effective and fluent reader (and writer).

- **Notice collocations as you read.**

  When you encounter an unfamiliar word, look at the words that are used with it.

- **Include collocations in your vocabulary study.**

  Focus on collocations that include words in word lists in Appendices 1 and 2 (pages 303–309).

PART 3

Comprehension Skills

Introduction to Comprehension

Comprehending what you read is more than just recognizing and understanding words. True comprehension means making sense of what you read and connecting the ideas in the text to what you already know. It also means remembering what you have read. In other words, comprehending means thinking while you read.

In Part 3, you will practice some important reading comprehension skills and you will learn to think in new ways about what you are reading.

At the end of each unit in Part 3, you will work on vocabulary-learning exercises. The words for the vocabulary exercises will be words that you encountered in the unit. The words are all found in either Appendix 1 or 2 (pages 303–309).

UNIT 1 Previewing

Previewing is a rapid kind of reading that allows you to get a general sense of what a passage, article, or book is about and how it is organized. Your eyes scan quickly over the page looking for answers to general questions about the material.

Previewing an Article or an Essay

In previewing an article or essay, you look at most of the first paragraph, the first sentence of each paragraph, and the concluding sentences. You should ask yourself questions like the ones below.

Previewing questions for an article or essay

- What is it about? What is the title? What do I already know about this?

- What kind of text is this? Is it a description? An explanation? An argument? A narrative (history)?

- Is the text divided into parts? How is it organized?

- Are there any maps, numbers, italicized words, or names in the text?

EXERCISE 1

A. Preview this essay by quickly, <u>reading only the underlined parts</u>. After previewing, answer the questions that follow. Your teacher will time you or you can time yourself for one minute.

How Dictionaries Are Made
by S. I. Hayakawa

I<u>t is widely believed that every word has a correct meaning, that we learn these meanings principally from teachers and grammarians</u> (except that most of the time we don't bother to, so that we ordinarily speak "sloppy English"), <u>and that dictionaries and grammars are the supreme authority in matters of meaning and usage</u>. [...] Few people ask by what authority the writers of dictionaries and grammars say what they say.

<u>Let us see how dictionaries are made and how the editors arrive at definitions</u>. What follows applies, incidentally, only to those dictionary offices where first-hand, original research goes on—not those in which editors simply copy existing dictionaries. The task of writing a dictionary begins with the reading of vast amounts of the literature of the period or subject that the dictionary is to cover. As the editors read, they copy on cards every interesting or rare word, every unusual or peculiar occurrence of a common word, a large number of common words in their ordinary uses, and also the sentences in which each of these words appears, thus:

pail
The dairy <u>pails</u> bring home increase of milk
Keats, Endymion 1, 44–45

That is to say, <u>the context of each word is collected, along with the word itself</u>. For a really big job of dictionary writing, such as the *Oxford English Dictionary* (usually bound in about twenty-five volumes) millions of such cards are collected, and the task of editing occupies decades. As the cards are collected, they are alphabetized and sorted. When the sorting is completed, there will be for each word anywhere from two to three to several hundred illustrative quotations, each on its card.

<u>To define a word, then, the dictionary editor places before him the stack of cards illustrating that word; each of the cards represents an actual use of the word</u> by a writer of some literary or historical importance. He reads the cards carefully, discards some, rereads the rest, and divides up the stack according to what he thinks are the several senses of the word. Finally, he writes his definitions, following the hard-and-fast rule that each definition *must* be based on what the quotations in front of him reveal about the meaning of the word. The editor cannot be influenced by what *he* thinks a given word *ought* to mean. He must work according to the cards or not at all.

<u>The writing of a dictionary, therefore, is not a task of setting up authoritative statements about the "true meanings" of words</u>, but a task of *recording*, to the best of one's ability, what various words have meant to authors in the distant or immediate past. *<u>The writer of a dictionary is a historian, not a lawgiver.</u>* [...] To regard the dictionary as an "authority," therefore, is to credit the dictionary writer with gifts of prophecy which neither he nor anyone else possesses. <u>In choosing our words when we speak or write, we can be *guided* by the historical record afforded us by the dictionary, but we cannot be *bound* by it, because new situations, new experiences, new inventions, new feelings, are always compelling us to give new uses to old words. Looking under a "hood," we should ordinarily have found, five hundred years ago, a monk; today, we find a motorcar engine.</u>

(Source: S. I. Hayakawa, *Language in Thought and Action*, 2nd Edition. New York: Harcourt, Brace & World, Inc., 1939)

B. Answer the following questions without looking back at the essay. Notice how much you are able to remember from just one minute of previewing!

1. What is this essay about?

2. What kind of text is this (i.e., description, explanation, argument, narrative)?

3. Where do dictionary meanings come from? *use of the world*

4. What is the role of a dictionary writer? *historians*

5. Do words keep the same meaning forever? *no because are change any.*

6. Write any words, phrases, or numbers you noticed.

C. Compare your answers with those of another student. If you disagree about your answers, read the article to check your work.

Previewing a Textbook

Previewing is especially important in textbooks. You should always read the table of contents and the outline of a chapter to find out what they contain. You should also preview the text in a chapter or a section of a chapter before reading it.

EXERCISE 2

A. Read the table of contents from a sociology textbook. Then answer the questions that follow.

Society: The Basics

Brief Contents

(Source: J. J. Macionis, *Society: The Basics*, 4th Edition. Upper Saddle River, NJ: Prentice Hall, 1998)

1. How many chapters does this book contain?

2. Which topics are not familiar to you?

3. Which chapters do you think would be most interesting to read?

4. Besides chapters, what other sections are listed?

B. Compare your answers with those of another student. If you disagree, look back at the table of contents to check your work.

A. *Read the outline for Chapter 3 of* Society: The Basics *and answer the questions that follow.*

CHAPTER 3: SOCIALIZATION

The Importance of Social Experience
Human Development: Nature and Nurture
Social Isolation

Understanding Socialization
Sigmund Freud: The Elements of Personality
Jean Piaget: Cognitive Development
Lawrence Kohlberg: Moral Development
Carol Gilligan: The Gender Factor
George Herbert Mead: The Social Self

Agents of Socialization
The Family
The School
The Peer Group
The Mass Media

Socialization and the Life Course
Childhood
Adolescence
Adulthood
Old Age
Death and Dying
The Life Course: An Overview

Resocialization: Total Institutions

Summary

Key Concepts

Critical-Thinking Questions

(Source: J. J. Macionis, *Society: The Basics*, 4th Edition. Upper Saddle River, NJ: Prentice Hall, 1998)

1. What is the title of Chapter 3?

2. Which topics are familiar to you?

3. Which topics do you think would be most interesting to read about?

4. Are there many unfamiliar words or names in this outline? List some of them.

5. Would this chapter be difficult for you to read? If so, why?

6. What study aids are included at the end of Chapter 3?

B. *Compare your answers with those of another student. If you disagree, look back at the outline to check your work.*

Guidelines for previewing a textbook passage

- Read the main heading.

- Check to see if the passage is divided into parts.

- Read the first few sentences.

- Read the first sentence of each paragraph after that.

- Read the final sentences of the passage.

EXERCISE 4

A. Preview the following passage from Chapter 3 of Society: The Basics *for <u>one minute</u>. Then answer the questions that follow.*

Introduction: The Importance of Social Experience

On a cold winter day in 1938, a concerned social worker walked anxiously to the door of a rural[1] Pennsylvania farmhouse. Investigating[2] a case of possible child abuse,[3] the social worker soon discovered a five-year-old girl hidden in a second-floor storage room. The child, whose name was Anna, was wedged into an old chair with her arms tied above her head so she could not move. She was wearing filthy garments, and her arms and legs were as thin as matchsticks.

Anna's situation can only be described as tragic. She was born in 1932 to an unmarried mentally impaired woman of twenty-six who lived with her father. Enraged by his daughter's "illegitimate" motherhood, the grandfather did not even want the child in his home. Anna, therefore, spent the early months of her life in the custody of various welfare agencies. But her mother was unable to pay for this care, so Anna returned to the home where she was not wanted. Because of her grandfather's hostility and her mother's indifference, Anna lived alone in a room where she received little attention and just enough milk to keep her alive. There she stayed—day after day, month after month, with virtually no human contact—for five years.

Upon learning of the discovery of Anna, sociologist Kingsley Davis traveled immediately to see the child. He found her in a county home, where local authorities had taken her. Davis was appalled by the sight of the emaciated child, who could not laugh, speak, or even smile. Anna was completely apathetic, as if alone in an empty world.

(Source: J. J. Macionis, *Society: The Basics*, 4th Edition. Upper Saddle River, NJ: Prentice Hall, 1998)

---

[1] *rural:* relating to the country, not the city
[2] *investigate:* to try to find out the truth about something
[3] *child abuse:* cruel treatment of a child

1. What is the section about?

2. Have you ever heard or read about other children like Anna?

3. Is this part of the chapter divided into parts?

4. Do you think this chapter would be difficult to read and understand?

5. What words, phrases, or numbers do you remember from previewing the passage?

C. Compare your answers with those of another student. If you disagree, read the passage to check your work.

EXERCISE 5

A. Preview another passage from Chapter 3 of Society: The Basics *for two minutes. Then answer the questions that follow.*

Social Isolation

For obvious ethical reasons, researchers cannot subject human beings to experimental isolation. But research on the effects of social isolation has been conducted on nonhuman primates.

Research with monkeys. Psychologists Harry and Margaret Harlow (1962) observed rhesus monkeys whose behavior is in some ways surprisingly similar to that of human beings in various conditions of social isolation. They found that complete isolation (with adequate nutrition) for a period of even six months was sufficient to cause developmental disturbances. When reintroduced to others of their kind, these monkeys were anxious, fearful, and defenseless against aggression.

The Harlows also placed infant rhesus monkeys in cages with an artificial 'mother' constructed of wire mesh and a wooden head and the nipple of a feeding tube where the breast would be. These monkeys, too, were subsequently unable to interact with others. But when they covered the artificial 'mother' with soft terry cloth, the infant monkeys clung to it, thereby deriving some emotional benefit, which reduced developmental harm. The experiment revealed the profound importance of the simple act of cradling as part of parent-infant interaction.

Finally, the Harlows discovered that, when socially isolated for shorter periods of time (about three months), infant monkeys eventually regained normal emotional patterns after rejoining others. But they concluded that longer-term isolation causes irreversible emotional and behavioral damage.

Isolated children. The later development of Anna roughly squares with the Harlows' findings. After her discovery, Anna benefited from extensive social contact and soon showed some improvement. When Kingsley Davis (1940) revisited her after ten days, he noted that she was more alert and displayed some human expression, and even smiled with obvious pleasure. Over the next year, as she experienced the humanizing effects of socialization, Anna showed more interest in other people and gradually gained the ability to walk. After a year and a half, she was able to feed herself, walk alone for short distances, and play with toys.

Consistent with the observations of the Harlows, however, it was apparent that Anna's five years of social isolation had left her permanently damaged. At age eight her mental and social development was still below that of a normal two-year-old. Only as she approached ten did she begin to use language. Of course, since Anna's mother was mentally retarded,

perhaps Anna was similarly disadvantaged. The riddle was never solved, however, because Anna died at age ten of a blood disorder, possibly related to her years of abuse (Davis, 1940).

In a more recent case of childhood isolation, a thirteen-year-old California girl was victimized in a host of ways by her parents from the age of two (Curtiss, 1977; Pines, 1981; Rymer, 1994). Genie's ordeal included being locked alone in a garage for extended periods. Upon discovery, her condition was similar to that of Anna. Genie was emaciated (weighing only fifty-nine pounds) and had the mental development of a one-year-old. She received intensive treatment by specialists and thrived physically. Yet even after years of care, her ability to use language remains that of a young child, and she lives today in a home for developmentally disabled adults.

All the evidence points to the crucial role of social experience in personality development. Human beings are resilient creatures, sometimes able to recover from even the crushing experience of prolonged isolation. But there may well be a point—precisely when is unclear from the small number of cases studied—at which isolation in infancy results in damage, including a reduced capacity for language, that cannot be fully repaired.

(Source: J. J. Macionis, *Society: The Basics*, 4th Edition. Upper Saddle River, NJ: Prentice Hall, 1998)

B. Answer the following questions without looking back at the passage.

1. What is the title of this section?

2. What is it about?

3. How is it divided into parts?

4. How do the parts relate to the topic of the section?

5. What words, phrases, or numbers do you remember from your preview?

C. Compare your answers with those of another student. If you disagree, read the passage to check your work.

Focus on Vocabulary

In the exercises that follow, you will build your knowledge of some of the words you encountered in this unit. These words are all found on the Academic Word List in Appendix 2 (page 308).

EXERCISE 6

A. Check your understanding of the following target words (the words that you will study). Read each word aloud and then write S, M, or N beside it.

S = you are sure of the meaning of the word
M = you think you might know the meaning of the word
N = you don't know the meaning of the word at all

____ principally	____ original	____ context	____ reveal
____ authority	____ task	____ bound by	____ incidentally
____ apply	____ period	____ decade	____ credit
____ influence	____ occurrence	____ illustrative	____ thus

B. Read the passage from Exercise 1. As you read, look for the target words and circle them. Note that the words in part A are listed in the same order as they appear in the passage but the form may be different. For example, in the passage, you will find applies **instead of** apply.

How Dictionaries Are Made
by S. I. Hayakawa

It is widely believed that every word has a correct meaning, that we learn these meanings principally from teachers and grammarians (except that most of the time we don't bother to, so that we ordinarily speak "sloppy English"), and that dictionaries and grammars are the supreme[1] authority in matters of meaning and usage. [...] Few people ask by what authority the writers of dictionaries and grammars say what they say.

Let us see how dictionaries are made and how the editors arrive at definitions. What follows applies, incidentally, only to those dictionary offices where first-hand, original research goes on—not those in which editors simply copy existing dictionaries. The task of writing a dictionary begins with the reading of vast[2] amounts of the literature of the period or subject that the dictionary is to cover. As the editors read, they copy on cards every interesting or rare word, every unusual or peculiar occurrence of a common word, a large number of common words in their ordinary uses, and also the sentences in which each of these words appears, thus:

> pail
> The dairy _pails_ bring home increase of milk
> Keats, _Endymion_ 1, 44–45

---

[1] _supreme:_ having the highest position of importance
[2] _vast:_ extremely large

That is to say, the context of each word is collected, along with the word itself. For a really big job of dictionary writing, such as the *Oxford English Dictionary* (usually bound in about twenty-five volumes) millions of such cards are collected, and the task of editing occupies decades. As the cards are collected, they are alphabetized and sorted. When the sorting is completed, there will be for each word anywhere from two to three to several hundred illustrative quotations, each on its card.

To define a word, then, the dictionary editor places before him the stack[3] of cards illustrating that word; each of the cards represents an actual use of the word by a writer of some literary or historical importance. He reads the cards carefully, discards[4] some, rereads the rest, and divides up the stack according to what he thinks are the several senses of the word. Finally, he writes his definitions, following the hard-and-fast[5] rule that each definition *must* be based on what the quotations in front of him reveal about the meaning of the word. The editor cannot be influenced by what *he* thinks a given word *ought* to mean. He must work according to the cards or not at all.

The writing of a dictionary, therefore, is not a task of setting up authoritative statements about the "true meanings" of words, but a task of *recording*, to the best of one's ability, what various words have meant to authors in the distant or immediate past. *The writer of a dictionary is a historian, not a lawgiver.* [...] To regard the dictionary as an "authority," therefore, is to credit the dictionary writer with gifts of prophecy[6] which neither he nor anyone else possesses. In choosing our words when we speak or write, we can be *guided* by the historical record afforded[7] us by the dictionary, but we cannot be *bound* by it, because new situations, new experiences, new inventions, new feelings, are always compelling[8] us to give new uses to old words. Looking under a "hood," we should ordinarily have found, five hundred years ago, a monk[9]; today, we find a motorcar engine.

(Source: S. I. Hayakawa, *Language in Thought and Action,* 2nd Edition. New York: Harcourt, Brace & World, Inc., 1939)

---

[3] *stack:* a neat pile
[4] *discard:* to get rid of something
[5] *hard-and-fast:* not able to be changed
[6] *prophecy:* a statement that tells what will happen in the future
[7] *afforded:* given
[8] *compelling:* forcing
[9] *monk:* a man who is a member of a religious group

C. Working with another student, check to be sure that you have located all of the target words. Then check your comprehension of this passage. Mark each statement T (true) or F (false).

1. The government decides the true meanings of the words in a dictionary.

2. Writing a dictionary is a very big job that takes a long time.

3. The meanings of words always stay the same.

4. Often, hundreds of examples are collected for a single word.

5. The definitions written in the dictionary must show how the words are actually used.

D. Compare your answers with those of another pair of students. If you disagree about the answers, look back at the passage to check your work.

A. *These sentences are taken from the passage in Exercise 6. Working with another student, read each sentence aloud. Then circle the best meaning or synonym for the underlined word as it is used in the sentence.*

1. It is widely believed that every word has a correct meaning, that we learn these meanings <u>principally</u> from teachers and grammarians. . . .

   a. easily   b. mainly   c. only

2. Few people ask by what <u>authority</u> the writers of dictionaries and grammars say what they say. . . .

   a. unusual ability   b. power   c. opinion

3. What follows <u>applies</u>, incidentally, only to those dictionary offices where first-hand, original research goes on. . . .

   a. points to   b. belongs to   c. relates to

4. What follows applies, <u>incidentally</u>, only to those dictionary offices where first-hand, original research goes on. . . .

   a. in that case   b. in particular   c. by the way

5. What follows applies, incidentally, only to those dictionary offices where first-hand, <u>original</u> research goes on. . . .

   a. new   b. language   c. informal

6. As the editors read, they copy on cards every interesting or rare word, every unusual or peculiar occurrence of a common word, a large number of common words in their ordinary uses, and also the sentences in which each of these words appears, <u>thus</u>: . . .

   a. at the same time   b. in some cases   c. in this way

7. The <u>task</u> of writing a dictionary begins with the reading of vast amounts of the literature of the period or subject that the dictionary is to cover.

   a. idea   b. job   c. organization

8. The task of writing a dictionary begins with the reading of vast amounts of the literature of the <u>period</u> or subject that the dictionary is to cover.

   a. time   b. language   c. type

9. As the editors read, they copy on cards every interesting or rare word, every unusual or peculiar <u>occurrence</u> of a common word, a large number of common words in their ordinary uses. . . .

   a. spelling   b. example   c. lesson

10. That is to say, the <u>context</u> of each word is collected, along with the word itself.

    a. sentence   b. grammar   c. meaning

11. For a really big job of dictionary writing, such as the *Oxford English Dictionary* (usually bound in about twenty-five volumes) millions of such cards are collected, and the task of editing occupies <u>decades</u>.

    a. many years   b. many editors   c. many desks

12. When the sorting is completed, there will be for each word anywhere from two to three to several hundred <u>illustrative</u> quotations, each on its card.

    a. colorful   b. explanatory   c. unusual

13. The editor cannot be <u>influenced by</u> what he thinks a given word ought to mean. He must work according to the cards or not at all.

    a. measured by   b. interested in   c. affected by

14. To regard the dictionary as an "authority," therefore, is to <u>credit</u> the dictionary writer with gifts of prophecy which neither he nor anyone else possesses.

    a. believe   b. hope   c. understand

15. In choosing our words when we speak or write, we can be guided by the historical record afforded us by the dictionary, but we cannot be <u>bound by</u> it. . . .

    a. led to   b. free from   c. tied to

16. Finally, he writes his definitions, following the hard-and-fast rule that each definition must be based on what the quotations in front of him <u>reveal</u> about the meaning of the word.

    a. prove   b. show   c. decide

B. Compare your answers with those of another pair of students. If you disagree, explain your answers and look back at the passage to check your work.

A. In this table, write as many different forms of the words as you can think of without looking in the dictionary. The first one is done for you.

Noun	Verb	Adjective	Adverb
application	apply	*applicable, applied*	———
authority			
		bound	———
context			
	credit		
		illustrative	———
	———		incidentally
	influence		———
occurrence		———	———
		original	
period	———		
	———		principally
	reveal		

B. Compare your work with that of another student. Then look in the dictionary for the forms you did not know and write them in the table.

A. Working with another student, read each sentence aloud. Then write a form of one of the target words in each of the sentences below. Each word may be used only once.

apply	credit	influence	principally
authority	decade	occurrence	reveal
bound	illustrative	original	task
context	incidentally	period	thus

1. The _____ immediately after World War II was one of great hardship in many European countries.

2. At the committee meeting, the members listened carefully as the man spoke with great _____ on the topic.

3. The university system has grown, _____ allowing many more young people to get a higher education.

4. Computer programs, called concordancing programs, can count the number of _____ of any given word in thousands of texts.

5. To give the students a better understanding of the theory, the textbook included an _____ example.

6. One of a schoolteacher's many _____ is to teach children how to work together in the classroom.

7. Only _____ documents will be accepted by the visa and immigration office.

8. The new president was _____ her pre-election promises to give certain jobs to certain people.

9. The doctors learned of the problem only _____, when they were examining the patient for a different condition.

10. The rules about minimum grades do not _____ to all students, but only to those who have a scholarship.

11. In making his films he was undoubtedly _____ by the great masters of Italian neo-realism.

12. Studying vocabulary words out of _____ can lead to misunderstandings about their meaning.

13. The elephant is generally _____ with exceptional intelligence and memory.

14. After the success of his first novel, he lived for several _____ and never wrote another book.

15. No new schools have been built for many years, _____ because of the lack of children.

16. The author of the book did not _____ the truth about the murderer until the final page.

B. Compare your work with that of another pair of students. If you disagree, explain your answers and then use a dictionary to check your work.

EXERCISE 10

A. Make word study cards for the target words that you are still unsure about. Use the cards to study the words, first on your own and then with another student. (See Part 2, Unit 1, page 29).

B. 1. Write a sentence for each of the words, leaving a blank instead of the target word. Ask another student to read your sentences and write the target word that should go in each blank.

2. Look at your sentences again. If your classmate wrote a different word, discuss the sentences to find out why. Was your sentence unclear, or did your classmate not know the target word?

UNIT 2 Making Inferences

Good readers make inferences as they read. That is, in addition to reading the words, they use their imagination and their knowledge about the world to fill in facts and ideas that are not stated in the text. This is sometimes called "reading between the lines."

It is often necessary to read between the lines because a writer cannot include all the possible information about a topic or situation. Writers leave out information that they think readers will know already or will be able to guess.

Separating Fact from Inference

In many kinds of writing, the author presents facts about a situation or topic and also makes inferences from those facts.

Facts are statements of information that can be verified.

For example:

> Chile is considered one of the most conservative Catholic countries in South America.

> On January 15, 2006, Chileans elected their first woman president, the Socialist Michelle Bachelet, with 53.5 percent of their votes.

> She is a former defense minister, a doctor, a single mother and a non-Catholic.

> Her father, a general in the army, was killed in 1973 under the military dictatorship of Pinochet.

> Her election campaign was based on promises of social and economic reform aimed at more equality.

Inferences are educated guesses that are based on facts.

For example:

> People in Chile are not as conservative as generally thought.

> People in Chile want changes in their society and economy.

> President Bachelet's background and experience should help her understand the problems in Chile.

> The fact that she served as defense minister may have reassured conservatives afraid of radical change.

> The fact that her father was killed under Pinochet probably raised her standing among leftists.

A. Preview the passage. Then read it and underline the facts. Working with another student, answer the questions that follow. The first two have been done for you.

Olive Oil Works as a Natural Painkiller

It is not just price that makes extra virgin olive oil different from other oils. Now scientists have discovered that it contains a chemical compound[1] that acts similarly to the painkiller ibuprofen.

Paul Breslin from the Monell Chemical Senses Center in Philadelphia and colleagues describe in *Nature* how they isolated a compound called oleocanthal from extra virgin olive oil. Pouring 50 gm of the best olive oil on your food each day is equivalent to about 10 percent of the average ibuprofen dose.[2]

---

[1] *chemical compound:* containing atoms from two or more chemical elements
[2] *dose:* a measured amount of a medicine

1. What facts are included in the first paragraph?

   Extra virgin olive oil contains a chemical compound that acts like a painkiller.

2. What can you infer about the price of extra virgin olive oil?

   It costs more than other olive oils.

3. What can you infer about other kinds of oil?

4. What facts are included in the second paragraph?

5. What inferences can you make about Paul Breslin?

6. What can you infer about *Nature*?

B. Compare your answers with those of another pair of students. If you disagree, explain your answers and look back at the passage to check your work.

A. Preview the passage. Then read it and underline the facts. Working with another student, answer the questions that follow.

A New Pesticide in India

In two states in India, Andhra Pradesh and Chattisgarh, farmers have discovered a new kind of pesticide.[1] Instead of paying large sums of money to international chemical companies for chemical pesticides, they are spraying their cotton and chili pepper fields with Coca-Cola.

In the past month there have been reports of hundreds of farmers spraying cola on their fields. Thousands of others are expected to make the switch[2] to cola from the usual pesticides as word spreads about the new spray. A farmer in Andhra Pradesh interviewed by a local newspaper said he was very satisfied with his new cola spray, which he applied this year to several acres of cotton. He observed that the insects on his cotton plants began to die soon after he sprayed his fields with cola.

Local agriculture officials would not comment on this new development, except to note that the cola spray cost considerably less than the pesticides produced by Montsanto, Shell and Dow Chemical. The Coca-Cola Company already is in legal difficulties in Andhra Pradesh state, where it has been accused of taking water away from farmers for its bottling plants. So far, representatives of the Coca-Cola Company have refused to comment on the new use of their product. It is not known if or how sales of the soft drinks have been affected, though it is likely that the company may try to profit from this new market.

(Source: Adapted from "Things grow better with Coke." *The Guardian Weekly*, November 5–11, 2004)

---

[1] *pesticide:* a chemical used to kill insects that destroy plants
[2] *switch:* the replacement of an object with a similar object

1. What facts are included in the first paragraph?

2. What can you infer about the cost of pesticides in India?

3. What facts are included in the second paragraph?

4. What can you infer about the cola spray?

5. What facts are included in the third paragraph?

6. What can you infer about the economic situation of the farmers in Andhra Pradesh?

7. What can you infer about the Coca-Cola Company in India?

B. Compare your answers with those of another pair of students. If you disagree, explain your answers and look back at the passage to check your work.

A. Preview the passage. Then read it and underline the facts. Working with another student, answer the questions that follow.

Mysterious "Piano Man" Puzzles British Doctors

The photograph shows a tall, blond young man holding what looks like a musical score.[1] His eyes scared, his shoulders rounded and slightly turned away, he appeared to avoid contact with the camera.

Found several weeks ago on a windy road beside the sea on the Isle of Sheppey in Kent, England, he was dripping wet and apparently very disturbed. He would not answer questions or speak with anyone. He was wearing a black suit and a white shirt, but since all the labels had been mysteriously cut out from his clothes, authorities had no way of even identifying his nationality. Since then he has continued to remain silent, refusing or unable to give information about who he is or where he comes from. He was taken to the accident and emergency department at the Medway Maritime Hospital in Gillingham, but later was moved to the psychiatric clinic in Dartford, where he continues to baffle[2] doctors.

A spokesman for the hospital says that the first clue to his identity came when someone in the hospital had the idea of leaving him with a piece of paper and pencils and he drew a detailed sketch of a grand piano. Hospital staff then took him to the hospital's chapel, which contains a piano. He sat down immediately at the piano and began to play, appearing calm and relaxed for the first time since he had been found. According to reports from the hospital, he is also a good musician and a pleasure to listen to, even if he tends to play rather melancholy[3] music. One staff member identified a piece from Tchaikovsky's *Swan Lake*, but acknowledged that she was not an expert in classical music.

According to a social worker assigned to the case, the young man is shy in the extreme and avoids any kind of social interaction. Though interpreters in various northern and central European languages have been called to the hospital to visit him, he has failed to respond to any of them. His photograph has been circulated in newspapers around the world, prompting hundreds of phone calls to the Missing Persons Bureau. However, none of these has provided useful information about his identity.

There is, of course, the delicate question of whether the man is really in need of psychiatric care or just pretending to be ill. Doctors at the hospital say that they have no reason not to take him seriously and they have a duty to care for him as long as he needs it.

---

[1] *score:* a printed copy of a piece of music
[2] *baffle:* If something baffles someone, they cannot understand or explain it.
[3] *melancholy:* sad

1. What has the writer inferred from the photograph of the "Piano Man"?

2. What can you infer from the fact that he was wearing a black suit and a white shirt?

3. What can you infer about the fact that the labels had been cut out of his clothes?

4. What can you infer from the fact that the police brought him to the hospital?

5. What did the hospital staff infer from his drawing of a piano?

6. What can you infer from the description of the way he played the piano?

7. What have people at the hospital inferred about his nationality?

8. What can you infer from the doctors' reported statements in the last sentence?

B. Compare your answers with those of another pair of students. If you disagree, explain your answers and look back at the passage to check your work.

EXERCISE 4

A. This exercise has four parts. For each part, preview and then read the passage and underline the facts. Working with another student, answer the questions that follow each part.

Part A

Our Not So Distant Relative

When archaeologists started to excavate[1] a limestone cave on the Indonesian island of Flores, they weren't prepared for what they found: the tiny skeleton[2] of an entirely new species of human, *Homo floresiensis*, that lived as recently as 18,000 years ago.

"I would have been less surprised if someone had uncovered an alien,"[3] says Peter Brown, an anthropologist from the University of New England in Armidale, New South Wales.

Among the stone tools and bones of seven individuals found by the Indonesian and Australian team in the Liang Bua cave were the skull[4] and incomplete skeleton of an adult whose shape suggests that it was female. It had long arms and its legs were light and apparently chimpanzee-like, but it walked upright. Its brain capacity was far smaller than any other known human species. Since the bones are not fossilised,[5] they may contain DNA and answer questions about their genetic links with *Homo sapiens*.

"When we first unearthed the skeleton, I was [...] puzzled and amused," says Australian scientist Bert Roberts of the University of Wollongong. "We had been looking for the remains of the earliest modern humans in Indonesia, so when we found the skeleton of a completely new species of human, with so many primitive traits,[6] and that survived until so recently, it really opened up a whole series of new questions [...]."

_____
[1] *excavate:* to dig carefully to find ancient objects, bones, etc.
[2] *skeleton:* the bones of a human body
[3] *alien:* a creature that comes from another world
[4] *skull:* the bones of a person's or animal's head
[5] *fossilized:* to be kept the same because it became hard as a rock
[6] *traits:* particular qualities

1. What can you infer about seven other "individuals" found in the cave by the scientists?

2. What have the scientists inferred about the skeleton?

Part B

Roberts says the island's population seems to have disappeared at about the same time as the pygmy[1] elephants they hunted, both apparently wiped out by a volcanic explosion.

The discovery, described in the journal *Nature* last week, could alter our outlook[2] on our own place in nature. It raises obvious questions about the diversity of the human family, such as whether undiscovered human-like species might survive today. Are we really the sole human caretakers of our planet? Could the existence of *Homo floresiensis* bring back persistent rumors[3] of undiscovered human-like species elsewhere, notably the orang pendek, or "jungle yeti" of Malay folklore?

---

[1] *pygmy:* a very small type of animal
[2] *outlook:* view
[3] *rumor:* information that is passed from one person to another and which may not be true

3. What has Roberts inferred about the disappearance of *Homo floresiensis*? Explain.

4. What does the writer of this article infer about the discovery? Explain.

Part C

Unlike parts of Indonesia closer to the Asian mainland, Flores has been an island for at least a million years. As is the case with islands elsewhere, its fauna[1] evolved in its own way, producing creatures larger or smaller than their mainland relatives: a [...] lost world of tiny elephants, giant rats, Komodo dragons and even larger extinct[2] lizards.

This isolation had its effects on the human inhabitants[3]. One of the most surprising things about the Liang Bua skeleton is its size: in life, no more than a meter (about 3 ft) tall, about the same size as one of the giant rats. Living in a hole in the ground and chased by lizards of giant proportions, the creature has been nicknamed "hobbit" by some researchers—a reference to the small, hole-dwelling heroes of *The Lord of the Rings*.

For Brown, it was the smallness of the skull which showed that *Homo floresiensis* was truly different. When he measured the skull volume and found it a chimp-sized 380 cc, he says his jaw "dropped to my knees. Small stature[4] is easy to explain but small brain capacity is a bigger problem—it still is." Yet these tiny-brained creatures were skilled enough to make finely crafted[5] stone tools.

---

[1] *fauna:* animals living in a particular area
[2] *extinct:* an animal that does not exist anymore
[3] *inhabitants:* people who live in a particular place
[4] *stature:* someone's height or size
[5] *crafted:* made with skill

5. From the facts here, what can you infer about the process of evolution on islands?

6. "This isolation had its effects on the human inhabitants." Is this a fact or an inference?

7. What do scientists usually infer about small brain size?

8. Why was Brown so surprised about the small brain size?

Part D

The clue to the origin of *Homo floresiensis* comes from previous work suggestive of the presence on Flores of earlier, full-sized prehumans. Michael Morwood, of the University of New England, codirector of the excavation, is working closely with his Indonesian colleague, R. P. Soejono, of the Indonesian Centre for Archaeology in Jakarta, whose team discovered the skeleton. In the mid-1990s Morwood and his colleagues unearthed stone tools on the island dating back 800,000 years. The implication was that the toolmakers, presumably *Homo erectus*, were capable of navigating the open sea. It is possible that once marooned[1] on Flores, a population of *Homo erectus* set its own evolutionary course, changing into *Homo floresiensis*.

When a small population of animals is cut off from the parent population for an extended[2] period, it follows its own evolutionary course. Size change is a typical response. Small size is an advantage on isolated islands, where resources are scarce, so this might have been what predisposed[3] the inhabitants of Flores toward smallness.

It is hard to comprehend the significance of the survival of such a strange species of human until what is, in geological terms, a very recent date. To put this in context, by 18,000 years ago, modern *Homo sapiens* had been in Indonesia for at least 20,000 years.

(Source: Henry Gee, *The Guardian Weekly*, November 5–11, 2004)

———
[1] *marooned:* to be left in a place from which you cannot escape
[2] *extended:* long
[3] *predisposed:* tending to behave or develop in a particular way

9. When Morwood found stone tools on Flores that were 800,000 years old, what inferences did he make?

10. What inference does the writer of this article make about why *Homo floresiensis* was small?

11. What can you infer from the last paragraph about *Homo sapiens* and *Homo floresiensis*?

B. Compare your answers with those of another pair of students. If you disagree, explain your answers and look back at the passage to check your work.

Making Inferences in Fiction

Writers of fiction often choose not to tell "the whole story" to the reader. They may have stylistic reasons for this, or they may keep back some information from the reader in order to increase the mystery or the suspense. When you are reading fiction, you should look for words and phrases that will help you fill in the information that the writer has left out.

EXERCISE 5

A. In this exercise you will read Chapter One of Tell Me That You Love Me, Junie Moon, *a novel by American writer Marjorie Kellogg that was published in 1968. The exercise is divided into four parts. Read each part and working with another student, write the answers to the inference questions that follow each part.*

Part A

Chapter One

Once there were three patients who met in the hospital and decided to live together. They arrived at this decision because they had no place to go when they were discharged.[1]

Despite the fact that these patients often quarreled and nagged each other, and had, so far as they knew, nothing in common, they formed an odd balance—like three pawnshop[2] balls.[3]

The first patient was called Warren. When he was seventeen, he and a friend were out hunting rabbits when the friend's gun went off and the bullet struck Warren in the middle of his spine.[4] From then on he was a paraplegic and spent the rest of his days in a wheelchair.

---

[1] *discharge:* to allow to leave the hospital
[2] *pawnshop:* a business where money is lent in exchange for objects
[3] *pawnshop balls:* a symbol outside a pawnshop
[4] *spine:* the long row of bones down the center of your back

The second patient was Arthur. He had a progressive neurological disease which no one had been able to diagnose. He estimated that he had been asked to touch his finger to his nose 6,012 times, and he could recite the laboratory findings on himself for the past five years, in case the doctors wanted them reviewed. Arthur walked with a careening gait[5] and his hands fluttered about his face like butterflies.

The third patient was a woman named Junie Moon. That was her real name. An irate[6] man had beaten her half to death in an alley one night and had topped off his violence by throwing acid over her. She had a number of pitiful and pesky[7] deformities.[8]

---

[5] *careening gait:* a way of walking that is very unsteady
[6] *irate:* extremely angry
[7] *pesky:* annoying
[8] *deformities:* parts of the body that are not the average shape

1. What kind of hospital do you think this is?
   It probably is a hospital or part of a hospital that specializes in helping people recover after illness or injury.
2. What can you infer about each of these patients?

3. What can you infer about the families of these patients?

Part B

The idea of their living together originated with Warren. He was fat and lazy and did not relish[1] the thought of being alone or looking after himself. He was also a cheerful organizer of other people's time and affairs and could paint lovely pictures of how things would be later on.

"My dear friends," he said to Arthur and Junie Moon one night after the evening medications had been given out, "I have a solution to our collective dilemma." Junie Moon, who was playing checkers with Arthur in the far end of the corridor, scowled[2] at Warren from her torn, disfigured face.

"With the various pittances[3] we could collect from this and that source," Warren went on, as Arthur inadvertently knocked two checkers on the floor, "we could live fairly comfortably." Warren retrieved[4] the checkers and patted Arthur on the shoulder. "What do you think?"

"Nobody wants to live with me," Junie Moon said, "so shut up about it."

"I think the idea stinks,"[5] Arthur said, as his hand flew into the air.

Then he and Junie Moon bent closer to the board as if to dismiss Warren's preposterous[6] scheme.

---

[1] *relish:* to enjoy the thought of something that is going to happen
[2] *scowl:* to look at someone in an angry or disapproving way
[3] *pittances:* a very small amount of money
[4] *retrieve:* to find something and bring it back
[5] *stinks:* an expression that means that something is bad or that you do not like it
[6] *preposterous:* completely unreasonable or silly

"Don't pretend that either of you have a place to go," Warren said, leaning forward in his wheelchair so that his face was on a level with theirs, "because you haven't!" He gave Junie Moon a lascivious wink: "You'll end up at the old-ladies home and you know what goes on *there*!"

"At least it's better than nothing," she said. Her scarred mouth shifted painfully to permit a laugh. Warren was still not used to her face, but he loved her quick humor.

"But I'm better than a dozen old ladies," he said, "and more responsible."

"Baloney!"[7] shouted Arthur, which set off a terrible spasm[8] of his body and almost lifted him from his chair. Automatically, Warren and Junie Moon laid a hand on his shoulders to quiet him.

---

[7] *baloney:* nonsense
[8] *spasm:* sudden uncontrolled tightening of muscles

4. What can you infer about the three patients' financial situation?

5. What can you infer about the relationship between Warren and the other two patients?

6. What can you infer from the fact that Junie Moon and Warren automatically laid a hand on Arthur's shoulder?

Part C

"You are many things," Arthur said when he had regained control of himself, "but responsible is not one of them."

"But he may be better than the poorhouse at that," Junie Moon said. "What do you have in mind?"

"Well now!" Warren reared[1] back in his wheelchair and stroked his bright blond beard. He said: "We will each have our own room. Junie Moon will do the cooking. Arthur will go to the store. I can see it all now."

"And I can see you have planned nothing for yourself in the way of expended effort," Arthur said.

"Who in their right minds would rent us an apartment?" Junie Moon said. "Three freaks,[2] one a female."

"We'll do it by phone," Warren said. "We'll say we're much too busy to come in person."

"When the landlord takes one look at us, he will throw us out," Junie Moon said.

"He couldn't," Arthur said. "We represent at least three different minority[3] groups." By making this last remark, Arthur had cast his vote[4] in favor of the plan. Junie Moon held out a little longer.

---

[1] *reared:* to rise upright
[2] *freak:* someone who looks very strange or behaves in an unusual way
[3] *minority:* belonging to a group of people who do not have the same opinion, religion, race, or physical condition as most of the larger group they are in
[4] *cast a vote:* to vote

7. What can you infer from what Arthur says about "three different minority groups"?

8. What can you infer about the relationship between Warren and Arthur?

Part D

"It's bad enough seeing the two of you in this hospital every day," she said, "let alone living with you."

At this, the two men banded together and attacked her.

"You're no prize yourself," Warren said.

"And you probably have a lot of disgusting personal habits of which we are not aware and to which you will expose us once we agree to a common arrangement," Arthur said.

"Let's not talk about prizes," Junie Moon said to Warren. "If we did, you might take the cake."

Arthur, who was the more sensitive of the men, realized by something in Junie Moon's voice that they had hurt her feelings. Because her face was so disfigured, it was difficult to read her emotions.

"I suppose none of us would take a prize," Arthur said. "On the other hand, we have a few things in our favor, I believe." He turned his head abruptly[1] so the other two could not see him blush over this self-compliment.

"What are you three up to?" Miss Oxford, the chief nurse, asked, looking thin and suspicious.

"We are plotting your demise,"[2] Warren said, cheerfully. Miss Oxford scurried[3] away, glancing over her shoulder.

Junie Moon then decided to join the two men in their plan. "I've thought of a number of ways to get that nurse," she said. "We must try a few of them before we leave here to set up housekeeping."

That was the way they decided.

(Source: Marjorie Kellogg, *Tell Me That You Love Me, Junie Moon*, New York: Farrar, Strauss & Giroux. 1968.)

---

[1] *abruptly:* suddenly and unexpectedly
[2] *demise:* death
[3] *scurry:* to move quickly with short steps

9. What can you now infer about Junie Moon?

10. What can you infer about Warren?

11. What can you infer about the nurse, Miss Oxford, and her relationship with patients?

12. From the title of the novel, what can you infer about what will happen later?

13. Now that you have read this part of the novel, would you like to read the rest of it? Explain.

B. Compare your answers with those of another pair of students. If you disagree, explain your answers and look back at the passage to check your work.

Focus on Vocabulary

EXERCISE 6

A. Check your understanding of the following target words. Read each word aloud and then write S, M, or N beside it.

S = you are sure of the meaning of the word
M = you think you might know the meaning of the word
N = you don't know the meaning of the word at all

___ apparently	___ alter	___ elsewhere	___ presumably
___ capacity	___ diversity	___ proportion	___ evolutionary
___ survive	___ sole	___ previous	___ resource
___ wipe out	___ persistent	___ implication	___ significance

B. Read the passage from Exercise 4. As you read, look for the target words and circle them. Note that the words in Part A are listed in the same order as they appear in the passage but the form may be different.

Our Not So Distant Relative

When archaeologists started to excavate a limestone cave on the Indonesian island of Flores, they weren't prepared for what they found: the tiny skeleton of an entirely new species of human, *Homo floresiensis*, that lived as recently as 18,000 years ago.

"I would have been less surprised if someone had uncovered an alien," says Peter Brown, an anthropologist from the University of New England in Armidale, New South Wales.

Among the stone tools and bones of seven individuals found by the Indonesian and Australian team in the Liang Bua cave were the skull and incomplete skeleton of an adult whose shape suggests that it was female. It had long arms and its legs were light and apparently chimpanzee-like, but it walked upright. Its brain capacity was far smaller than any other known human species. Since the bones are not fossilized, they may contain DNA and answer questions about their genetic links with *Homo sapiens*.

"When we first unearthed the skeleton, I was [...] puzzled and amused," says Australian scientist Bert Roberts of the University of Wollongong. "We had been looking for the remains of the earliest modern humans in Indonesia, so when we found the skeleton of a completely new species of human, with so many primitive traits, and that survived until so recently, it really opened up a whole series of new questions [...]" Roberts says the island's population seems to have disappeared at about the same time as the pygmy elephants they hunted, both apparently wiped out by a volcanic explosion.

The discovery, described in the journal *Nature* last week, could alter our outlook on our own place in nature. It raises obvious questions about the diversity of the human family, such as whether undiscovered humanlike species might survive today. Are we really the sole human caretakers of our planet? Could the existence of *Homo floresiensis* bring back persistent rumors of undiscovered human-like species elsewhere, notably the orang pendek, or "jungle yeti" of Malay folklore? [...]

Unlike parts of Indonesia closer to the Asian mainland, Flores has been an island for at least a million years. As is the case with islands elsewhere, its fauna evolved in its own way, producing creatures larger or smaller than their mainland relatives: a [...] lost world of tiny elephants, giant rats, Komodo dragons and even larger extinct lizards.

This isolation had its effects on the human inhabitants. One of the most surprising things about the Liang Bua skeleton is its size: in life, no more than a meter (about 3 ft) tall, about the same size as one of the giant rats. Living in a hole in the ground and chased by lizards of giant proportions, the creature has been nicknamed "hobbit" by some researchers—a reference to the small, hole-dwelling heroes of *The Lord of the Rings*.

For Brown, it was the smallness of the skull which showed that *Homo floresiensis* was truly different. When he measured the skull volume and found it a chimp-sized 380 cc, he says his jaw "dropped to my knees. Small stature is easy to explain but small brain size is a bigger problem—it still is." Yet these tiny-brained creatures were skilled enough to make finely crafted stone tools.

The clue to the origin of *Homo floresiensis* comes from previous work suggestive of the presence on Flores of earlier, full-sized prehumans. Michael Morwood, of the University of New England, codirector of the excavation, is working closely with his Indonesian colleague, R. P. Soejono, of the Indonesian Centre for Archaeology in Jakarta, whose team discovered the skeleton. In the mid-1990s Morwood and his colleagues unearthed stone tools on the island dating back 800,000 years. The implication was that the toolmakers, presumably *Homo erectus*, were capable of navigating the open sea. It is possible that once marooned on Flores, a population of *Homo erectus* set its own evolutionary course, changing into *Homo floresiensis*.

When a small population of animals is cut off from the parent population for an extended period, it follows its own evolutionary course. Size change is a typical response. Small size is an advantage on isolated islands, where resources are scarce, so this might have been what predisposed the inhabitants of Flores toward smallness.

It is hard to comprehend the significance of the survival of such a strange species of human until what is, in geological terms, a very recent date. To put this in context, by 18,000 years ago, modern *Homo sapiens* had been in Indonesia for at least 20,000 years.

(Source: Henry Gee, *The Guardian Weekly*, November 5–11, 2004)

C. Working with another student, check to be sure that you have located all of the target words.

EXERCISE 7

A. *These sentences are taken from the passage in Exercise 6. Working with another student, read each sentence aloud. Then circle the best meaning or synonym for the underlined word as it is used in the sentence.*

1. It had long arms and its legs were light and <u>apparently</u> chimpanzeelike, but it walked upright.

   a. extremely   b. seemingly   c. undoubtedly

2. Its brain <u>capacity</u> was far smaller than any other known human species.

   a. damage   b. power   c. size

3. ". . . so when we found the skeleton of a completely new species of human, with so many primitive traits, and that <u>survived</u> until so recently, it really opened up a whole series of new questions."

   a. continued to live   b. became alive   c. appeared to be dead

4. Roberts says the island's population seems to have disappeared at about the same time as the pygmy elephants they hunted, both apparently <u>wiped out</u> by a volcanic explosion.

   a. eaten up   b. found out   c. killed off

5. It raises obvious questions about the <u>diversity</u> of the human family, such as whether undiscovered humanlike species might survive today.

   a. variety   b. strangeness   c. similarity

6. The discovery, described in the journal *Nature* last week, could <u>alter</u> our outlook on our own place in nature.

   a. change   b. prove   c. limit

7. Are we really the <u>sole</u> human caretakers of our planet?

   a. highest   b. only   c. best

8. Could the existence of *Homo floresiensis* bring back <u>persistent</u> rumors of undiscovered humanlike species elsewhere, notably the orang pendek, or "jungle yeti" of Malay folklore?

   a. sudden   b. scientific   c. continuing

9. As is the case with islands <u>elsewhere</u>, its fauna evolved in its own way, producing creatures larger or smaller than their mainland relatives: . . .

   a. in this place   b. in other places   c. a long time ago

10. Living in a hole in the ground and chased by lizards of giant <u>proportions</u>, the creature has been nicknamed "hobbit" by some researchers—a reference to the small, hole-dwelling heroes of *The Lord of the Rings*.

    a. hunger   b. size   c. age

11. The clue to the origin of *Homo floresiensis* comes from <u>previous</u> work suggestive of the presence on Flores of earlier, full-sized prehumans.

    a. later   b. unknown   c. earlier

12. The <u>implication</u> was that the toolmakers, presumably *Homo erectus*, were capable of navigating the open sea.

    a. suggestion   b. discovery   c. history

13. The implication was that the toolmakers, <u>presumably</u> *Homo erectus*, were capable of navigating the open sea.

    a. certainly   b. unlikely   c. probably

14. When a small population of animals is cut off from the parent population for an extended period, it follows its own <u>evolutionary</u> course.

    a. gradually changing   b. definitely fixed   c. strangely mysterious

15. Small size is an advantage on isolated islands, where <u>resources</u> are scarce, so this might have been what predisposed the inhabitants of Flores towards smallness.

    a. animals   b. large families   c. food supplies

16. It is hard to comprehend the <u>significance</u> of the survival of such a strange species of human until what is, in geological terms, a very recent date.

    a. difficulty   b. importance   c. secret

B. Compare your answers with those of another pair of students. If you disagree, explain your answers and then use a dictionary to check your work.

A. *In this table, write as many different forms of the words as you can think of without looking in the dictionary.*

Noun	Verb	Adjective	Adverb
	alter		—
			apparently
capacity	—		—
diversity			
		evolutionary	—
implication			
		persistent	
			presumably
—	—	previous	
proportion			
resource	—		
significance			
—	—	sole	
	survive		—

B. *Compare your work with that of another student. Then look in the dictionary for the forms you did not know and write them in the table.*

A. *Working with another student, write a form of one of the target words in each of the sentences below. Each word may be used only once.*

alter	elsewhere	presumably	significance
apparently	evolutionary	previous	sole
capacity	implication	proportion	survive
diversity	persistent	resource	wipe out

1. The _____ work of this writer leads us to expect more from this novel, which has proved a major disappointment.

2. Despite _____ efforts to convince the committee to follow his plan, it was rejected.

3. When the storm hit the ferryboat in the North Sea, it was carrying fifty more passengers than its legal _____.

4. The _____ of her silence was clear to the police: she knew, but would not tell.

5. After ten years in prison, the man's appearance had _____ so much his old friends did not recognize him.

6. The _____ of scientists' findings about global warming has not been fully understood by ordinary people and politicians.

7. Of the 145 passengers and crew members on the plane, only twelve _____ the crash.

8. After Mr. Jetson died, his wife became _____ owner of the company.

9. Though there were once millions of passenger pigeons (a species of bird) in North America, they were _____ by hunters by the end of the nineteenth century.

10. Anne Frank lived for three years with her family and another family in a few rooms of tiny _____ .

11. Scientists rarely have the opportunity to see _____ change in action.

12. We can _____ accept the reports of witnesses, who blamed the accident on the wet road and the poor visibility.

13. In Europe, the economic situation was not favorable, but _____ there were signs of improvement.

14. The company does not have the _____ to update its computer systems and software.

15. The bridge was _____ not built with strong enough material, as it fell during the earthquake.

16. Many American colleges and universities tried to create more _____ among the students by searching for young people from minority groups.

B. Compare your work with that of another pair of students. If you disagree, explain your answers and then use a dictionary to check your work.

EXERCISE 10

A. Make word study cards for the target words that you are still unsure about. Use the cards to study the words, first on your own and then with another student. (See Part 2, Unit 1, page 29).

B. 1. Write a sentence for each of the words, leaving a blank instead of the target word. Ask another student to read your sentences and write the target word that should go in each blank.

2. Look at your sentences again. If your classmate wrote a different word, discuss the sentences to find out why. Was your sentence unclear, or did your classmate not know the target word?

Understanding Paragraphs

English is a topic-centered language: a paragraph, or longer text, has a single main topic, and all the details relate to that topic. Writers in English almost always mention the topic at or near the beginning of a passage. Good readers look for the topic when they read.

Identifying the Topic of a Paragraph

The topic is the word or phrase that best describes what all of the sentences in the paragraph are about. Words relating to the topic are usually repeated several times in a paragraph. Looking for these words can help you focus on the topic.

Example:

Read the paragraph and underline the words that are repeated. Then write a topic that is not too specific or too general.

In developing countries, poor people have suffered the most from shortages of clean <u>water</u>. There are several reasons for this. First, in many developing countries, the majority of houses in <u>poor</u> villages and urban slums are not yet served by a piped <u>water</u> system. People living in these places often have to walk many miles to find <u>water</u> and carry it home in jugs and plastic containers. Second, these people usually have few alternatives to the piped <u>water</u> supply. There may be water closer by in rivers or lakes, but this is often dangerously polluted. In <u>poor</u> areas, street vendors often sell water by the liter, but they often charge extremely high prices for <u>water</u> that is not always safe to drink.

Topic: <u>*shortage of clean water in poor areas*</u>

A. Read each paragraph and underline words that are repeated. Then write a topic that is not too specific or too general.

Mexico City: Water Shortages and a Sinking City

1. Like many other fast-growing cities around the world, Mexico City is facing severe water shortages. Many of its 20 million inhabitants receive only one hour of piped water per week. Others receive none at all for weeks on end. Those who can afford the expense build their own home water system to catch and keep rainwater to supplement the city water. The situation, according to international experts, is the result of a combination of factors. First, the system of pipes is old and poorly managed, with the result that the pipes lose almost 40 percent of the water that they distribute around the city. Second, the demand for water, which has grown with the rapid population growth, far exceeds the supply. Furthermore, the water is consumed not only by residents for household use, but also by thirsty industries such as beer-brewers and soft-drink bottlers, and there is little incentive[1] for them to conserve[2] or recycle water.

---

[1] *incentive:* something that encourages you to do something
[2] *conserve:* to use less

Topic: _____

2. The current water shortages in Mexico City contrast remarkably with the city's situation in the past. When the Spanish arrived at the Aztec capital in 1519, they found stone buildings and gardens set on an island in the middle of a vast series of interconnected lakes—an "enchanted vision," according to one Spanish soldier. The Spanish destroyed the buildings, and began draining[1] the water from the lakes to build what became Mexico City. For the next four centuries, the city was able to meet its water needs from springs, shallow wells, and the remaining lake water. In the mid-nineteenth century, the residents of the city began taking water from the underlying aquifer.[2] In the twentieth century, as water needs grew and supplies from the aquifer became inadequate, city authorities brought water up from two nearby river systems. Twenty-five years ago, they began piping in water from 80 miles (130 km) away. Because Mexico City is located on a highland, the water must all be pumped uphill at considerable expense.

---

[1] *drain:* to make the water flow away
[2] *aquifer:* a layer of stone or earth under the surface of the ground that contains water

Topic: _____

3.   Related to the shortages is another problem: the city is sinking. Other cities around the world (such as Venice, Italy) are also experiencing this phenomenon, but the situation is most dramatic in Mexico City. Some neighborhoods are going down by as much as 15 inches (40 cm) a year, or a total of about 30 feet (9.1 m) over the last century. The cause is simply the fact that water is being removed from the aquifers faster than it can be replaced by rainwater. As water is removed, the spongy soil dries up and becomes more compact,[1] and the city slowly settles down. The effects are evident. At the Monument to Independence, which was built at ground level in 1910, twenty-three more steps were recently added to reach the base from the current ground level. Buildings and streets have been damaged by the uneven settling of the city, and so have the water and sewage systems. Since the city is now 6 feet below the level of nearby Lake Texcoco, flooding has become a frequent problem and because of the poor state of the sewage system, the flood waters are often full of untreated waste.

---

[1] *compact:* packed or put together firmly

Topic: _____

B. Compare your answers with those of another student. If you disagree, explain your answers and look back at the paragraphs to check your work.

Topic Sentences

Paragraphs in English usually contain a topic sentence that lets the reader know what the paragraph is about. Although this sentence is usually near the beginning of the paragraph, it can also be found in the middle or at the end.

EXERCISE 2

A. Each of the paragraphs is missing a topic sentence. The missing sentences are listed at the end of the exercise (with one extra sentence). Working with another student, read the paragraphs and write the letter of the sentence that fits each paragraph best.

The Pollution of the Oceans

1. _____ No one can calculate the quantity of solid waste that has been dumped[1] in the world's oceans, but the total certainly exceeds many millions of tons. For example, from 1880 to 1895, 75 percent of the solid waste from New York City was dumped untreated into the Atlantic Ocean. Although it is now prohibited by law, the dumping of solid waste, including wastewater sludge,[2] industrial waste, and high-level radioactive waste were common in the United States until 1970. Cruise

---

[1] *dump:* to get rid of something you do not want
[2] *sludge:* mud, waste, and oil mixed together

ships and huge floating fishing factories still regularly dispose of their solid waste products directly into the ocean.

2.   The earth naturally recycles water and refreshes the land in what is called the hydrological cycle. The hydrological cycle not only renews the supply of water, but cleans it as well. The process begins as heat from the sun causes sea water, 97 percent of the earth's total water reserve, to evaporate[3] and form clouds. Because water evaporates at lower temperatures than most pollutants, the water vapor that rises from the seas is relatively pure and free of the contaminants, which are left behind. Next, water returns to earth as rain, which drains into streams and rivers and rushes toward the sea. _____

3.   Chemicals, petroleum products, and other dangerous substances such as radioactive materials remain in the ocean, polluting it permanently. The polluted ocean water kills fish or makes them dangerous to eat, posing health problems for those who consume them. It kills the tiny sea creatures that are the source of food for larger fish, sharks, and whales. It also spoils a source of great beauty and pleasure when some solid waste is thrown onto beaches during storms. Discharged[4] petroleum products are frequently found on beaches and they not only ruin the beach, the petroleum residue[5] kills hundreds of shore birds. _____

4.   _____ Nonpoint pollutants are dumped into lakes, rivers, and streams that may be far away from any ocean. However, these pollutants flow, eventually, into the oceans. They can come from a variety of sources, from road salt to agricultural pesticides. One source of nonpoint pollution is runoff from farming, including fertilizers, manure, and pesticides. Another source is industrial runoff, including heavy metals, phosphorous, and many other chemicals. Urban runoff (oils, salts, various chemicals) and atmospheric fallout of airborne pollution are other sources of nonpoint pollutants that reach the oceans.

5.   _____ This includes water and waste from sinks, toilets, washing machines, and bathtubs. The problem with this type of waste is that it provides massive amounts of nutrients for water plants, such as algae, so that they grow rapidly. This sudden growth causes concentrations or algae blooms, which use up the oxygen in the water. As the oxygen levels of the water decline, many organisms suffer and die, and the ocean ecosystem is radically altered. This can be prevented by the installation of waste treatment plants that prevent waste from entering the sea, but such facilities do not exist in many poorer countries.

---

[3] *evaporate:* when a liquid changes into a gas
[4] *discharged:* to send out from someplace
[5] *residue:* something left after most of the material is gone

Missing topic sentences:

a. Although the hydrological cycle produces clean water in the form of rain, it does not remove the pollutants that steadily build up in the oceans.

b. New laws and regulations make it difficult for people to dump their trash into the oceans.

c. The oceans have long served as a vast dumping ground for all kinds of waste.

d. These are just a few of the problems caused by using the oceans as dumping grounds.

e. Wastewater dumping is yet another major form of ocean pollution.

f. Some pollutants in the ocean are not dumped there directly.

B. Compare your answers with those of another pair of students. If you disagree, explain your answers and look back at the paragraphs to check your work.

Main Ideas of Paragraphs

Topic sentences and main ideas

In addition to stating the topic, most topic sentences also tell the writer's main idea, or in other words, the idea that the writer wants to express about the topic. To explain the idea, the writer includes several supporting details in the paragraph and these details are more specific than the main idea.

Example

Working with another student, read the paragraph and underline the topic sentence. Choose the best main idea statement below.

The global demand for water (estimated at about 5 billion cubic feet per year) has tripled since 1950. One reason for the increased demand for water is the rapid growth in population. Each person on earth consumes, on average, 10 million gallons of water in a lifetime! More people means a need for more water for agricultural and household use. A second reason for the increased consumption of water is the rapid development of complex technology. Factories and food production facilities cannot function without water. Power-generating facilities also use vast amounts of water to make the steam that is needed to run the turbines and cool the system.

Main idea:

a. More people means a need for more water for agricultural and household use.

b. Factories and food production facilities cannot function without water.

c. The global demand for water has tripled since 1950.

The main idea is choice *c*. It states the topic and the general idea that the writer explains about the topic. Choices *a* and *b* are details about the topic.

Inferring the Main Idea

In some paragraphs, the topic sentence may not state the complete main idea. The topic may be stated in one sentence, and the writer's idea about the topic may be expressed in another sentence or in several sentences in the paragraph. In this case, the reader must combine ideas from several sentences to infer the complete main idea.

Note: To make sure that it is really expressing a complete idea, the main idea statement should always be stated in a complete sentence with a subject and verb.

EXERCISE 3

A. *Working with another student, read the paragraph, write the topic, and underline the supporting facts and ideas. Then choose the best main idea statement.*

Floodplains are the flat land near a river that is covered with water when the river rises following a storm. They provide several benefits. They can control flooding when the waters of a narrow river rise rapidly. As soon as the river's water has exceeded its banks and enters a floodplain, the water spreads out over a wide area and slows down. There, the floodplain holds the water, allowing it to be slowly released into the river system and into underground bodies of water. Floodplains also help clean rivers and streams. They keep the water long enough for sediment (small particles of dust, rock, and organic matter) to settle into the earth under the floodplain. This keeps the sediment out of the river or stream.

Topic: _____

Main idea:

  a. Floodplains are the flat land near a river that is covered with water when the river rises following a storm.

  b. Floodplains can control flooding when the waters of a narrow river rise rapidly.

  c. Floodplains near a river provide several benefits.

B. *Compare your answers with those of another pair of students. If you disagree, explain your answers. Discuss the other main idea choices and explain why they were too general or too specific.*

A. Working with another student, read each paragraph, write the topic, and underline the supporting facts and ideas. Then choose the best main idea statement.

Controlling Water in the Netherlands

1.   The Netherlands, in Europe, is more than 60 percent near or below sea level. Flooding has always been a major worry because its major cities, factories, and greenhouse farms are built on floodplains. The greatest risk of flooding comes from the North Sea itself with its severe winter storms and massive tides. However, flooding can also occur along the Rhine, Maas, and Scheldt Rivers, which are swollen every spring with snowmelt from the Alps. And when these major rivers meet the North Sea, they form a delta region that consists of additional floodplains.

Topic: _____

Main idea:

 a. The Netherlands, in Europe, is more than 60 percent near or below sea level.

 b. Floods in the Netherlands are caused by severe winter storms.

 c. The Netherlands is at a high risk of flooding because much of it is on floodplains.

2.   As the Dutch built their cities, farms, and factories on the floodplains, they also built a system of barriers[1] to keep the floodwaters back. The Dutch barriers are the strongest in the world, designed to protect the country from the usual high tides and heavy rainfall, as well as possible "monster" storms that occur only rarely. The first line of defense is the dikes,[2] dams,[3] and storm barriers, which over the centuries have become ever longer and higher. Today they stretch for about 2,200 miles (3,500 km) along the sea and the major rivers. They are aided by secondary defenses, such as canal dikes and holding ponds, as well as by thousands of water pumps and pumping stations.

---

[1] *barrier:* a fence or gate that keeps two things apart
[2] *dike:* wall along a river or seacoast built to prevent flooding
[3] *dam:* special wall built across a river

Topic: _____

Main idea:

 a. The Dutch built cities, farms, and factories on the floodplains.

 b. The Dutch built a system of barriers to keep water out of the floodplains.

 c. The Dutch system of barriers is the strongest in the world.

3.   A recent government study on the effects of climate change has led the Dutch government to change its traditional water protection strategies. The study concluded that the combination of higher rainfall in Northern Europe and rising sea levels would lead to an increased risk of flooding. At the same time, hotter summers could lead to cracking and weakening in the traditional earthen dikes. Thus, in the future, it might no longer be possible to hold back the water. Though it will continue to maintain the barriers, the government is shifting to a "softer," more environmentally friendly approach. The aim is to rely more on the natural protection of flood plains, sand dunes, salt marshes, and mud flats. The government has begun buying land along major waterways, where water could be directed when floods threaten.

(Source: Adapted from "Netherlands relinquishes some of itself to the waters," by Cole Nickerson, *Boston Globe*, June 12, 2005)

Topic: _____

Main idea:

   a. The Dutch government has been studying the effects of climate change.

   b. As a result of climate change, the Dutch will change their water protection strategies.

   c. More rainfall in Northern Europe and rising sea levels may increase the risk of flooding.

   B. Compare your answers with those of another pair of students. If you disagree, explain your answers. Discuss the other main idea choices for each paragraph and explain why they were too general or too specific.

EXERCISE 5

A. Working with another student, read each paragraph and write the topic. Then choose the best main idea statement below and underline the supporting facts and ideas.

Lake Baikal

1. Lake Baikal, the world's largest lake, is located in southern Siberia, in Russia. It measures 395 miles (636 km) long by 50 miles (80 km) wide and it has 1,245 miles (2,100 km) of coastline. The lake's rocky basin consists of three depressions, which hold a total volume of 14,656 cubic miles (23,600 cubic km) of water, 20 percent of the freshwater in the world. The lake is also very deep, with its deepest point at over 1 mile (1,637 meters) and an average depth of 2,066 feet (630 meters). Furthermore, scientists have determined that Lake Baikal is the oldest lake in the world. From sediment obtained by drilling deep down below the lake, researchers estimate it to be at least 25 million years old.

Topic: _____

Main idea:

  a. Lake Baikal is the world's largest and oldest lake.

  b. Lake Baikal is over 1 mile deep at its deepest point.

  c. Lake Baikal is located in southern Siberia, in Russia.

Supporting facts and ideas: _____

_____

_____

2.   To scientists, Lake Baikal is of particular interest because of its unique and isolated ecosystem. More than 1,000 species of plants and animals found at Lake Baikal exist nowhere else on earth and some can be dated to prehistoric times. Among its unique fauna is the Baikal freshwater seal. This creature, which local people call *nerpa*, is the only mammal which inhabits the lake. Researchers speculate that these seals, which have been breeding at Lake Baikal for 22 million years, are the descendents of ocean-dwelling seals which migrated inland in search of food, when the lake was still connected to the sea. Another creature that is unique to this Siberian Lake is the *omul*, a fish, which is caught by local fisherman and is considered a great delicacy.

Topic: _____

Main idea:

  a. Scientists can study many unique species that exist only at Lake Baikal.

  b. The fauna at Lake Baikal includes a freshwater seal called nerpa and a fish called omul.

  c. Many unique species can be found in the isolated ecosystem of Lake Baikal.

Supporting facts and ideas: _____

_____

_____

3.   For centuries, the water in Lake Baikal was so clear that it was possible to see down to depths of 40 to 60 feet. Several factors contributed to keeping the water crystal clear. First, the lake contained certain small zooplankton and small crustaceans that consumed waterweeds, bacteria, and other material that would otherwise cloud the water. Furthermore, the water in the lake consisted of rainwater and melted snow that flowed down from a mountain range in about 300 streams and through uninhabited forest. Finally, most of the watershed has a rocky surface, so the water flowing into the lake did not accumulate mud or organic matter and had little mineral or chemical content.

Topic: _____

Main idea:

    a. The water in Lake Baikal was very clean for several reasons.

    b. Lake Baikal's water is famous for being clean and pure.

    c. Small crustaceans keep the waters of Lake Baikal clear.

Supporting facts and ideas: _____

_____

_____

B. Compare your answers with those of another pair of students. If you disagree, explain your answers and look back at the paragraph to check your work. Then discuss the other main idea choices and explain why they are too general or too specific.

Connecting Ideas in Paragraphs

Understanding a paragraph—or a longer passage—often involves more than just identifying the topic and main idea. It is also necessary to understand the way writers in English guide the reader through the logic of their ideas or show the connections between ideas.

Pronouns as Connectors

Pronouns often function as connecting words within a sentence or among different sentences. Some of the pronouns that can be used this way are:

- Personal pronouns—*he, it, they, him, us*, etc.

- Possessive pronouns—*his, her, our, their*, etc.

- Demonstrative pronouns—*this, that, these, those*

- Relative pronouns—*which, who, where, whose*, etc.

    Pronouns are used to refer to a noun or noun phrase that has already been mentioned. (A noun phrase is a group of words that functions as a noun in the sentence.) This noun or noun phrase is called the *referent*. In order to understand what you read, you need to be able to identify the referent for each pronoun. A good reader does this automatically.

Read the following paragraph, the main idea statement, and the list of pronouns and referents below. Working with another student, circle the pronouns, underline the referents, and draw an arrow from each pronoun to its referent. The first one is done for you.

Working Women

One of the most significant economic trends in the United States in the last half century has been the sharp increase in the number of women in paid employment. This trend is commonly seen as the result of various sociological developments. First, women are no longer bound to their traditional role of homemaker, thanks to smaller families and labor-saving household devices. There has also been a strong demand for women in the job market, where the range of opportunities for them is continually expanding. Furthermore, women are generally earning more than in the past, which means they can afford to pay for child care and help with household chores.

Main idea: _The number of women in paid employment has increased in the last half century._

Pronouns	Referents
This	increase in number of women in paid employment
their	women
where	the job market
them	women
which	women are generally earning more

A. Working with another student, read the paragraph and write the main idea. Then circle the pronouns, underline the referents, and draw an arrow from each pronoun to its referent. Write the pronouns and referents below.

The increase in paid employment for women may have contributed to various changes in social attitudes, but it has not completely changed the role of women in the home. Women who work outside the home still usually end up playing the leading role in managing the care of the house and family. Husbands may contribute by taking out the trash or mowing the lawn, but on average they spend a lot less time doing these and other household tasks than women do. This is true even for women who are working full-time and for those who can afford to pay for help in the home. In fact, if a woman can afford to pay for help, she is usually the one who has to manage this help, hiring and overseeing the baby-sitters, cleaners, repairmen, and so on. She is also more likely to attend school meetings, make appointments with teachers, and in general, attend to the needs of the children.

Main idea: _____

Pronouns	Referents
_____	_____
_____	_____
_____	_____
_____	_____
_____	_____
_____	_____
_____	_____
_____	_____

B. Compare your answers with those of another pair of students. If you disagree, look back at the paragraph to check your work.

Transition Words and Phrases as Connectors

Writers also show connections between ideas by using transition (connecting) words or phrases. These words help the reader to follow the logic of the writer's thinking.

Some common transition words and phrases			
also	especially	in fact	soon
as a result	finally	in other words	such as
as well as	first	in particular	that is
at the same time	for example	instead	then
at this point	for instance	in the same way	thus
at times	for this reason	likewise	whereas
before long	furthermore	now	
but	however	similarly	

Example:

A. *Working with another student, read the paragraph and write the main idea. Then underline the transitions listed below.*

The Transnational Corporation

The transnational corporation, or TNC, is not just a company that engages in business abroad. It is generally defined as a firm that has a direct investment in two or more countries. In other words, a TNC may have its headquarters in one country, its factories in another, and it may sell its products in yet another country. For instance, Nike, makers of sportswear, is based in the United States, but most of its shoes and clothes are manufactured in Southeast Asia or South America. They are then shipped back to the United States to be sold, or to Europe, Japan, or other emerging markets such as India. Thus, the TNC can potentially influence the economies of many different countries, especially the weaker economies of the developing world.

Main idea: _____

Transitions	*Pronouns and referents*
In other words	It—the transnational corporation
For instance	its—the transnational corporation
Thus	it—the transnational corporation
especially	its—Nike, They—Nike shoes and clothes

B. *Compare your work with that of another pair of students. If you disagree, look back at the paragraph to check your work.*

A. *Working with another student, read the paragraphs and underline the transitions. Circle the pronouns and draw an arrow from each pronoun to its referent. Then write the main idea.*

Henry Ford and Fordlandia

1. In the 1920s, the Ford Motor Company bought large quantities of rubber from Asian rubber growers for the tires of its Model A cars. However, the supply of rubber was not always reliable and at times, while waiting for shipments, the factory had to stop production. Henry Ford, who owned the company, could have ensured more reliable rubber supplies by making a long-term agreement with the rubber growers. In fact, carmakers often make such agreements now. But Henry Ford had another idea. He decided that the best solution would be to own a rubber supply of his own. Thus, in 1927, the company bought land in Brazil and started a rubber plantation.

    Main idea: _____

2. The new plantation, named Fordlandia, was situated in the jungle and covered about 3,600 square miles (5,800 square km). A vast area of tropical forest was cut down and replaced by rubber trees. Beside the plantation, a factory was built for processing the rubber, and a whole town was constructed for the workers, complete with schools, stores, churches, and even a golf course. Once the trees were producing rubber and the factory was operating, Ford thought his rubber supply was guaranteed. However, there were various factors in the situation that he had not taken into account. One was the suitability of the Amazon jungle for rubber production. In fact, the rubber trees were soon attacked by disease. Another factor was the political climate in South America, which was not favorable for

Americans. Before long, there were problems with the local workers at the plantation and in the factory. Finally, in 1945, Ford was forced to abandon Fordlandia, at great loss to the Ford Motor Company.

Main idea: _____

3.   Fordlandia is now viewed as a historical lesson for companies about the mistake of trying to control all phases of production. In fact, the Ford Motor Company has the opposite problem today. Whereas Henry Ford was afraid of running short of supplies, contemporary carmakers and other companies are afraid of having too many supplies and parts on hand. For this reason, they buy only what they need when they need it and try to have as little inventory as possible. This so called "just on time" system works fine as long as the parts are available when needed. However, in recent years a number of carmakers, as well as computer and electronics companies, have been faced with shortages. For example, soon after the Apple Computer Company introduced its iPod music player, there was so much demand that Apple ran out of parts and it had to suspend production, losing sales as a result.

Main idea: _____

B. Compare your work with that of another pair of students. If you disagree, look back at the paragraphs to check your work.

Thinking in English

In these exercises you will practice what you have learned so far about paragraphs. The last sentence in each paragraph is incomplete. In order to choose the best completion, you need to understand the main idea and how all the ideas in the paragraph are connected.

Example:

Read the incomplete paragraph and write the main idea. Then decide which ending best fits the logic of the paragraph.

The wine industry in the Burgundy region of France has proved to be an unexpected source of data about the history of climate change. From the Middle Ages until the twentieth century, churches in Burgundy were central to social, cultural, and even economic activity. They also often functioned as a bureaucratic center, holding records of all aspects of town life, including winemaking. Thus, every year careful note was made of a key date in the local agricultural calendar, the first day of the grape harvest. And since grape harvest time is closely related to temperature, scientists have been able to reconstruct

a. the medieval churches in northeastern Burgundy.

b. medieval winemaking methods in Burgundy.

c. climate data for Burgundy for the years after 2003.

d. summer temperatures in Burgundy from 1370 to 2003.

Main idea: *The wine industry in the Burgundy region of France has proved to be an unexpected source of data about the history of climate change.*

Which ending is best and why?

Ending *d* is the best ending because it refers to the main idea and the dates fit in with the information in the paragraph. All other endings are not relevant to the main idea or are not logical.

A. *Read each incomplete paragraph and write the main idea. Then decide which ending best fits the logic of the paragraph.*

The Price of Gold

1.   The attraction of gold is as old as history. Since ancient times, gold has been the object of dreams and obsessions.[1] Western literature is full of characters who kill for gold or hoard[2] it, from King Midas in the ancient Greek myths, to Fagin in Dickens' *Oliver Twist*. These characters go to evil extremes to get or keep their gold and they get the punishment they deserve. Most people would not be willing to go to such extremes, of course, but they would not question the assumption that gold has lasting value above and beyond any local currency. Societies change over time, customs and currencies evolve, but gold remains. A wedding ring, for example, must be gold, and so should any serious gift of jewelery. In fact, giving and wearing gold is still a mark of prestige in our postindustrial society,

   a. though gold is no longer valued as it used to be.
   b. even if most people prefer to wear silver.
   c. whereas in the past, gold was not so valuable.
   d. just as it has been for thousands of years.

Main idea: _____

_____

[1] *obsession:* unhealthy interest in something
[2] *hoard:* to collect and hide large amounts of food, money, etc.

2.   Why is gold so valuable? True, it is shiny, durable,[1] and rare, but it is far less useful than many other minerals or metals. It is also not like stock in a company, where the value of the stock depends on the performance of the company. Gold, on the contrary, like any currency, is valuable precisely because people believe it is valuable. That is, if people were willing to accept seashells for their labor and could use them to pay for food, fuel, and other commodities, then seashells would become a valuable currency. Thus, the value of gold depends on the collective belief that gold will continue to be valuable. As long as demand for gold remains steady, the price will hold steady; if demand is high, it will continue to increase in value. But if people should someday lose faith in gold,

   a. the demand for gold would increase.
   b. the price of gold could fall sharply.
   c. people would need more gold for industry.
   d. the dollar would be worth less than before.

Main idea: _____

_____

[1] *durable:* long lasting

3.   Another factor that has affected the price of gold has been the increasing difficulty in acquiring[1] it. Today, most of the gold left in the ground is in microscopic pieces mixed with rock. To get it, miners must dig up tons and tons of rock, and then spray it with diluted[2] cyanide (a poison) to separate out the gold. For one ounce of gold—a wedding ring, for example—the mine processes about 30 tons of rock. This is already a costly operation. But there are also hidden social and environmental costs. The mining and processing of gold is ruinous to the environment and to the health of people living nearby. Most of these mines are in poor regions where the people have had little voice in whether there should be mines and how the mines should be run. The large multinational mining companies simply bought the land and opened the mines. However, as people and governments begin to realize the extent[3] of the damage caused by the mines, the situation might change. Indeed, if the mining companies ever have to pay the full environmental and social costs of mining gold,

   a. the price of gold is likely to climb yet higher.
   b. people will probably stop buying gold.
   c. they will charge less for an ounce of gold.
   d. gold will be easier and cheaper to acquire.

Main idea: _____

---

[1] *acquire:* to get
[2] *dilute:* to mix with water
[3] *extent:* amount

B. Compare your answers with those of another student. If you disagree, look back at the paragraphs to check your work.

A. Read each incomplete paragraph and write the main idea. Then decide which ending best fits the logic of the paragraph.

Crisis Management

1.   In 1986, the drug company Johnson & Johnson was faced with a crisis. Several people had died after taking Tylenol, a Johnson & Johnson product. The deaths were not the fault of the company, but the work of a criminal who had put poison in some of the Tylenol capsules.[1] The criminal was later caught and punished, but in reaction to the deaths, people stopped buying Tylenol. The management of Johnson & Johnson realized that they had to act decisively and quickly to prevent serious consequences for the company. Within days, in fact, they recalled every Tylenol capsule in the United States to check for poisoning. Soon afterward they also introduced "tamperproof"[2] bottles to prevent future problems. Sales of Tylenol picked up again, and in the end,

   a. Johnson & Johnson had to discontinue the product.
   b. other companies avoided the same mistakes.
   c. people felt that Johnson & Johnson had acted well.
   d. customers felt that Johnson & Johnson had not done enough.

Main idea: _____

_____

[1] *capsules:* pills
[2] *tamperproof:* made in a way that prevents someone from opening it before it is sold

2.   Not all companies respond to crisis as well as Johnson & Johnson. The Firestone Company had a very different kind of reaction in 2000 when it became known that over a hundred people had died in accidents involving defective Firestone tires. The company's initial response was to blame others for the accidents. This way they hoped they might avoid having to recall their tires. First they said that the car owners were at fault because they had not inflated the tires enough. This naturally made the owners—and consumer groups—very angry, so Firestone tried next to place the blame on the carmakers, since the accidents had almost all involved Ford Explorer SUVs. This made the Ford Motor Company angry, and it threatened to take legal action. At this point, Firestone realized that it

had to recall all the tires—6.5 million of them. But by then it was too late. Not only did Firestone have to pay out millions of dollars in damage claims, but it suffered a dramatic drop in sales. Consumers

   a. no longer trusted the tire maker.
   b. stopped buying cars from Ford.
   c. realized they should inflate their tires more.
   d. still preferred to buy Firestone tires.

Main idea: _____

3.   The key to managing a crisis lies in the company's initial reaction. If they recognize a problem immediately and take measures to deal with it, they are less likely to suffer long-term consequences. One example of a quick reaction was that of the Pepsi Company in 1992, when hypodermic syringes were found in several soda cans. In a short time, the company was able to prove that the syringes had nothing to do with the production process, and they also found the criminals who had put the syringes in the cans. As a result, they lost few customers. On the other hand, Wendy's fast-food company lost millions of dollars in 2004 because it tried to deny bad news and did not act quickly enough. The bad news was very dramatic: A customer claimed to have found a human finger in a bowl of Wendy's chili. It took the company almost a month to prove that the finger belonged to the woman who claimed to have found it. During that month,

   a. all fast-food places changed their menu.
   b. Wendy's had more customers than ever before.
   c. families stopped drinking Pepsi sodas in cans.
   d. families took their children to other fast-food places.

Main idea: _____

B. *Compare your answers with those of another student. If you disagree, look back at the paragraphs to check your work.*

A. Read each incomplete paragraph and write the main idea. Then decide which ending best fits the logic of the paragraph.

A Market for Matisse

1.   In the early twentieth century, a Parisian financier named André Level started a new kind of investment fund. He persuaded twelve other people to contribute to a fund that he called *La Peau de l'Ours* ("the skin of the bear"). With a moderate sum of money, Level then began to invest in an unusual market for his day: modern art. In the course of the next ten years, this investment group bought over 100 paintings and drawings, including works by Picasso and Matisse. By the end of this period, modern art was attracting more buyers, the prices had risen, and Level decided it was time to sell. In 1914, he organized an enormous auction[1] in Paris and sold off all the paintings. The results were better than his wildest hopes. Some of the paintings sold for ten times the original price, and taken as a whole, the collection

    a. did not attract much interest or many investors.
    b. was a great disappointment to the investors.
    c. made a substantial profit for the investors.
    d. remained in Level's possession for many years.

Main idea: _____

_____
[1] *auction:* an event at which things are sold to the person who offers the most money

2.   One hundred years after Level's art fund, people are again enthusiastically investing their money in art. However, the new art investment funds show many changes in the way art is bought and sold today. In the past, art collectors were usually wealthy individuals who were more interested in showing off their wealth or enjoying the art than in making money from it. However, today's investors are mainly interested in making a profit. Some of the funds focus on contemporary painters. They often advertise expert consultants who can predict which works of art are sure to increase in value. Others focus on known artists and invite investors to pool their contributions and become part owners (a few square inches) of a painting, with an already established value, under the assumption that its value will continue to increase. In both cases, the fund managers promise that before long, they will sell the art, like Level, and investors will

    a. have a beautiful home.
    b. lose a lot of money.
    c. own beautiful paintings.
    d. make a lot of money.

Main idea: _____

3.   Buying artwork is appealing for many reasons. We all like to have nice pictures in our homes and to show them to others. But art as an investment may not be a good idea. Whether you are interested in contemporary or established artists, there is a good chance that you will not make a profit and you could even lose your money. With contemporary art, regardless of what "experts" say, it is very unlikely that any painting you buy will increase in value. In fact, only a very small percentage of all new paintings are worth more thirty years later. The situation is no better for the work of older, known painters. Prices for these paintings have soared in recent years, not only for the best paintings of the most famous painters like Picasso or Monet, but also for minor painters or minor media, like drawings or prints. Even if you could afford to buy them now, it would hardly make sense. It seems unlikely that prices will continue to climb at the same rate and they may soon begin to decline. All in all, you might be better off

   a. buying paintings by Picasso or Monet.
   b. investing in paintings by new artists.
   c. investing in something else.
   d. painting some pictures yourself.

   Main idea: _____

B. Compare your answers with those of another student. If you disagree, look back at the paragraphs to check your work.

EXERCISE 11

A. Read each incomplete paragraph and write the main idea. Then decide which ending best fits the logic of the paragraph.

A New Sales Method: The Home Party

1.   In 1948, Earl Tupper had invented a new type of airtight plastic food containers, but they were not selling well in the stores. He was convinced that housewives would love these containers if they had a chance to try them. The problem was how to get the containers out of the stores and into their homes. So he invented the Tupperware Party. At these parties, women invited their friends and neighbors to their home for a cup of coffee. Then they showed the containers

and offered them for sale. Since women usually liked the containers and they did not cost much, sales were usually brisk. This happy combination of a good product with the "home party" led to the enormous success of the Tupperware brand and

a. the end of the home party.
b. an interesting new marketing strategy.
c. the opening of Tupperware stores.
d. the invention of a new kind of container.

Main idea: _____

2.   More than a half-century after the first Tupperware parties, all sorts of products are being sold at home parties in America, including baskets, detergents, cosmetics, and health products. Sales of this type now total around $8 billion every year. The marketing methods of these parties are similar to the original Tupperware home parties. A salesperson (typically a middle-aged woman working part-time) convinces another woman to host a party and invite her friends, relatives, and neighbors to see the products, cosmetics, for instance. At the party, the women are served coffee and are encouraged to talk about cosmetics in general and to try some of the products that are for sale. News and enthusiasm about the parties—and the cosmetics—are passed from one woman to another and from one town to the next. This is what economists call "viral marketing," where new customers come to a product

a. almost entirely through existing customers.
b. mostly through their own research on the Internet.
c. through the company's sales and marketing team.
d. through effective television advertising.

Main idea: _____

3.   One business that has made good use of the home party method is the Longaberger Company in Ohio, which manufactures handwoven baskets. It produces baskets of all kinds—picnic baskets, laundry baskets, flower baskets, etc.—each one signed by an individual basket maker. The baskets are then marketed at home "shows," as they are called by the company. These home shows are so effective that many thousands of baskets are sold every day in the United States. There is also a strong market for old, used Longaberger baskets, which have become collectors' items and sell for large sums on eBay. For example, a "Two Pie Basket" that originally sold for $10 in 1986 recently sold for $450. When

Longaberger published his autobiography in 2001, he used the same marketing methods to promote it. As a result, although the book had not been advertised much outside of the Longaberger network, it nevertheless

a. sold only a few thousand copies.
b. was soon forgotten.
c. was very poorly written.
d. became a national best-seller.

Main idea: _____

B. *Compare your answers with those of another student. If you disagree, look back at the paragraphs to check your work.*

Focus on Vocabulary

=== EXERCISE 12 ===

A. *Check your understanding of the following target words. Read each word aloud and then write S, M, or N beside it.*

S = *you are sure of the meaning of the word*
M = *you think you might know the meaning of the word*
N = *you don't know the meaning of the word at all*

____ supplement	____ consume	____ inadequate
____ factor	____ recycle	____ locate
____ distribute	____ current	____ considerable
____ exceed	____ contrast	____ phenomenon
____ furthermore	____ underlying	____ evident

B. *Read the passage from Exercise 1. As you read, look for the target words and circle them. Note that the words in Part A are listed in the same order as they appear in the passage but the form may be different.*

Mexico City: Water Shortages and a Sinking City

Like many other fast-growing cities around the world, Mexico City is facing severe water shortages. Many of its 20 million inhabitants receive only one hour of piped water per week. Others receive none at all for weeks on end. Those who can afford the expense build their own home water system to catch and keep rainwater to supplement the city water. The situation, according to international experts, is the result of a combination of factors. First, the system of pipes is old and poorly managed, with the result that the pipes lose almost 40 percent of the water that they distribute around the city. Second, the demand for water, which has grown with the rapid population growth, far exceeds the supply. Furthermore, the water is consumed not only by residents for household use, but also by thirsty industries such as beer brewers and soft-drink bottlers, and there is little incentive for them to conserve or recycle water.

The current water shortages in Mexico City contrast remarkably with the city's situation in the past. When the Spanish arrived at the Aztec capital in 1519, they found stone buildings and gardens set on an island in the middle of a vast series of interconnected lakes—an "enchanted vision," according to one Spanish soldier. The Spanish destroyed the buildings and began draining the water from the lakes to build what became Mexico City. For the next four centuries, the city was able to meet its water needs from springs, shallow wells, and the remaining lake water. In the mid-nineteenth century, the residents of the city began taking water from the underlying aquifer. In the twentieth century, as water needs grew and supplies from the aquifer became inadequate, city authorities brought water up from two nearby river systems. Twenty-five years ago, they began piping in water from 80 miles (130 km) away. Because Mexico City is located on a highland, the water must all be pumped uphill at considerable expense.

Related to the shortages is another problem: The city is sinking. Other cities around the world (such as Venice, Italy) are also experiencing this phenomenon, but the situation is most dramatic in Mexico City. Some neighborhoods are going down by as much as 15 inches (40 cm) a year, or a total of about 30 feet (9.1 m) over the last century. The cause is simply the fact that water is being removed from the aquifers faster than it can be replaced by rainwater. As water is removed, the spongy soil dries up and becomes more compact, and the city slowly settles down. The effects are evident. At the Monument to Independence, which was built at ground level in 1910, twenty-three more steps were recently added to reach the base from the current ground level. Buildings and streets have been damaged by the uneven settling of the city, and so have the water and sewage systems. Since the city is now 6 feet below the level of nearby Lake Texcoco, flooding has become a frequent problem and because of the poor state of the sewage system, the flood waters are often full of untreated waste.

C. Working with another student, check to be sure that you have located all of the target words.

EXERCISE 13

A. These sentences are taken from the passage in Exercise 12. Working with another student, read each sentence aloud. Then circle the best meaning or synonym for the underlined word as it is used in the sentence.

1. Those who can afford the expense build their own home water system to catch and keep rainwater to <u>supplement</u> the city water.

   a. pay for   b. remove   c. add to

2. The situation, according to international experts, is the result of a combination of <u>factors</u>.

   a. causes   b. effects   c. people

3. First, the system of pipes is old and poorly managed, with the result that the pipes lose almost 40 percent of the water that they <u>distribute</u> around the city.

   a. drink   b. send   c. use

4. Second, the demand for water, which has grown with the rapid population growth, far <u>exceeds</u> the supply.

   a. goes beyond   b. uses up   c. adds to

5. <u>Furthermore</u>, the water is consumed not only by residents for household use, but also by thirsty industries such as beer-brewers and soft-drink bottlers, . . .

   a. however   b. in addition   c. for example

6. Furthermore, the water is <u>consumed</u> not only by residents for household use, but also by thirsty industries such as beer-brewers and soft-drink bottlers, . . .

   a. paid for   b. wasted   c. used

7. Furthermore, the water is consumed not only by residents for household use, but also by thirsty industries such as beer brewers and soft-drink bottlers, and there is little incentive for them to conserve or <u>recycle</u> water.

   a. use again   b. catch up   c. pipe in

8. The <u>current</u> water shortages in Mexico City contrast remarkably with the city's situation in the past.

   a. today's   b. past   c. future

9. The current water shortages in Mexico City <u>contrast</u> remarkably with the city's situation in the past.

   a. are different from   b. are similar to   c. are an example of

10. In the mid-nineteenth century, the residents of the city began taking water from the <u>underlying</u> aquifer.

   a. beneath   b. beside   c. above

11. In the twentieth century, as water needs grew and supplies from the aquifer became <u>inadequate</u>, city authorities brought water up from two nearby river systems.

   a. not enough   b. too much   c. undrinkable

12. Because Mexico City is <u>located</u> on a highland, the water must all be pumped uphill at considerable expense.

   a. not far from   b. positioned   c. far from

13. Because Mexico City is located on a highland, the water must all be pumped uphill at <u>considerable</u> expense.

   a. moderate   b. small   c. great

14. Other cities around the world (such as Venice, Italy) are also experiencing this <u>phenomenon</u>, but it is most dramatic in Mexico City.

    a. fact   b. news   c. substance

15. The effects are <u>evident</u>.

    a. surprising   b. serious   c. obvious

B. Compare your answers with those of another pair of students. If you disagree, explain your answers and then use a dictionary to check your work.

EXERCISE 14

A. In this table, write as many different forms of the words as you can think of without looking in the dictionary.

Noun	Verb	Adjective	Adverb
		considerable	
	consume		——
	contrast		——
	——	current	
	distribute		——
		evident	
	exceed		
factor		——	——
	——	inadequate	
	locate	——	——
phenomenon	——		
	recycle		——
	supplement		——
——		underlying	——

B. Compare your work with that of another student. Then look in the dictionary for the forms you did not know and write them in the table.

A. Working with another student, write a form of one of the target words in each of the sentences below. Each word may be used only once.

considerable	evident	locate
consume	exceed	phenomenon
contrast	factor	recycle
current	furthermore	supplement
distribute	inadequate	underlying

1. This new book _____ the social theories of two major thinkers of the twentieth centuries.

2. Some local pharmacies _____ free information about disease prevention.

3. The growing interest in American art is _____ from the number of people who visit museums of American art.

4. The food and clothing supplies that arrived after the earthquake were _____ to meet the needs of the people who lost their homes.

5. Many young dancers or singers have to _____ their professional income with other work.

6. Americans get much less vacation time than workers in other industrialized countries; _____, many Americans do not take all the vacation time they are given.

7. Today, because of air conditioning and their many household machines, the average family _____ far more electricity than it did thirty years ago.

8. The project, which was a total failure, wasted a _____ amount of time and money.

9. The company has not yet decided how much money it can spend on public relations for the _____ year.

10. Foreign competition was one of the _____ that influenced the company's decision to close the factory.

11. Some European countries are highly organized and manage to _____ a high percentage of the paper they use—85 percent in Denmark, for example.

12. In nineteenth-century America, an important factor in deciding where to _____ a new town was the presence of water.

13. One natural _____ that scientists are still not able to explain fully is the ability of birds to find their way over great distances.

14. The price he paid for the house _____ its market value.

15. When scientists started digging in the _____ rocks, they found the remains of an ancient forest.

B. Compare your work with that of another pair of students. If you disagree, explain your answers and then use a dictionary to check your work.

Exercise 16

A. Make word study cards for the target words that you are still unsure about. Use the cards to study the words, first on your own and then with another student. (See Part 2, Unit 1, page 29).

B. 1. Write a sentence for each of the words, leaving a blank instead of the target word. Ask another student to read your sentences and write the target word that should go in each blank.

2. Look at your sentences again. If your classmate wrote a different word, discuss the sentences to find out why. Was your sentence unclear, or did your classmate not know the target word?

For thousands of years, people have looked at groups of stars in the night sky and found patterns. They have given names to these constellations and have used them as guides for travel on land and sea.

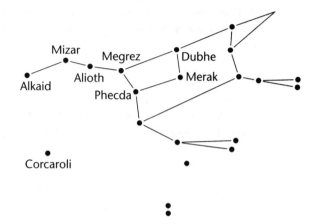

Ursa Major, The Great Bear

One of the most recognizable groups of stars in the northern sky is called Ursa Major, the "Great Bear." Can you see how this constellation might look like a bear? Within the constellation is another famous group of stars called the Big Dipper. This group resembles a long-handled drinking cup. Can you find it?

In fact, our brain helps us make sense of the world by sorting information into mental networks. These networks are organized in patterns, and we use those patterns to understand and remember what we see and experience.

Recognizing the pattern of organization is an important part of reading comprehension, since writers, too, use patterns to present their ideas in a way that makes sense. Once you recognize the pattern, you will understand and follow their ideas more efficiently. In this unit, you will learn to identify six common patterns that are often found in paragraphs in English:

- Listing
- Sequence
- Comparison/Contrast
- Cause/Effect
- Problem/Solution
- Extended Definition

Examples of the six patterns of organization

1. Listing

> In the listing pattern, the writer states the main idea in the form of a generalization and gives a list of details or examples to support that general statement.
>
> - Key words/phrases in the main idea: *many, several, a number of, a variety of, a few, kinds of.*
> - Signal words/phrases: *for example, for instance, first, second, another, also, besides, in addition, final, last, most important.*

Read the paragraph and the information below. Then underline the signal words in the paragraph.

There are several different theories about the origin of the Moon. One theory, called the fission[1] theory, states that early in the life of Earth, a piece broke off, and that piece became the Moon. A second, closely related theory is that the Moon is composed of several pieces of Earth that broke away from our planet. Yet another theory is that the Moon formed elsewhere in the solar system and was captured by Earth's gravity.[2] The final theory states that a huge piece of planetary rock struck Earth and broke up into pieces. One of the pieces became the Moon.

---

[1] *fission:* the act of splitting into parts
[2] *gravity:* the force that causes objects to fall to the ground

Topic: *Theories about the origin of the Moon*

Main idea: *There are several different theories about the origin of the Moon.*

Key word in the main idea: *several*

Supporting facts and ideas:

Signal words/phrases	Details
One theory	*A piece of Earth broke off (fission theory).*
A second	*Several pieces of Earth became the Moon.*
Yet another	*The Moon formed elsewhere in the solar system.*
The final	*A piece of a huge planetary rock struck Earth and became the Moon.*

2. Sequence

In the sequence pattern, the writer explains the main idea with *a series of events or steps in a process* that follow one after the other in time order.

- Key word/phrases in the main idea: *began, account, story, process, history, sequence.*
- Signal words/phrases: *first, second, then, next, after, while, since, then, soon, finally, at last, in 1965, last June, later, over time, the next step, the following week.*

A. Series of Events

Read the paragraph and the information below. Then underline the signal words in the paragraph.

Close-up study of the planet Mars began when rockets were developed that could send scientific instruments into space. In 1965, the first observations of Mars were done by the American spacecraft *Mariner 4*, which flew near the planet to collect data and take photographs. Four years later, more data and photographs were collected by *Mariners 6* and *7* as they flew past the planet. Then, in 1971, *Mariner 9* actually went into orbit[1] around Mars, and during the following eleven months, sent back more than 7,000 images before contact with the spacecraft was lost. The next major step, in 1976, was the landing of two Viking crafts on two different areas of Mars' surface. These landers were able to send back important data about the atmosphere[2] of the planet.

---

[1] *orbit:* the path that is traveled by an object that is moving around a larger object
[2] *atmosphere:* the mixture of gases that surround a planet

Topic: *Close-up study of Mars*

Main idea: *Close-up study of Mars began when rockets were developed that could send probes into space.*

Key word in the main idea: *began*

Supporting facts and ideas:

Signal words/phrases	Details
In 1965	*The first spacecraft flew near the planet*
Four years later	*More photographs were collected of the planet*
Then, in 1971	*Mariner 9 orbited Mars*
during the following eleven months	*It sent back more than 7,000 images.*
The next major step, in 1976	*The landing of two Viking crafts on Mars' surface*

B. Steps in a Process

Read the paragraph and the information below. Then underline the signal words in the paragraph.

Not all stars are the same age, so it is possible to see stars at every stage of their life cycle. From their observations, astrophysicists can explain the process of the formation of a star. A star begins life inside a *nebula,* a huge cloud of gas and dust in outer space. Over time, the force of gravity pulls some of the gas and dust together to form into clumps.[1] Then the temperature inside the nebula begins to rise. Next, several clumps come together and become denser and hotter, and they form a *protostar* (an early form of a star). After that, the protostar continues to grow until it has become about as large as our Sun. At that point, nuclear reactions begin to occur in its core (center), and these reactions send energy to the surface of the protostar. Finally, the energy escapes as heat and light and a new star begins to shine.

―――――――
[1] *clump:* a clustered mass; a lump

Topic: *The process of the formation of a star*

Main idea: *A star is formed in a process during which clumps of gas and dust form a protostar that becomes large and hot.*

Key word in the main idea: *process*

Supporting facts and ideas:

Signal words/phrases	Details
begins	*In a cloud of dust and gas in outer space*
Over time	*Gravity makes clumps of dust and gas*
Then	*The temperature begins to rise.*
Next	*Several clumps form a protostar*
After that	*The protostar grows larger.*
At that point	*Nuclear reactions send energy to the surface.*
Finally	*A new star begins to shine.*

3. Comparison/Contrast

In the comparison/contrast pattern, the writer's main idea is a general statement about two things and how they are similar and/or different. A comparison can include both similarities and differences, or only the similarities. A contrast states only differences.

- Key words/phrases in the main idea: *similarities, differences, both, in common, same, different, compare, comparison.*

- Signal words/phrases for similarities: *similarly, also, in the same way, as, like, both, in common.*

- Signal words/phrases for differences: *however, but, on the other hand, although, while, in contrast, than, conversely, yet, unlike.*

A. Similarities and Differences

Read the paragraph and the information below. Then underline the signal words in the paragraph.

Astronomy and astrology are similar in some ways, but they differ in a very important way. In both fields, the experts study planetary motion and constellations (groups of stars), and they use telescopes, tables, and charts to do their work. However, astronomers study the heavenly bodies as a science, and over the years people have used astronomy to discover more about the universe. Astrologers, on the other hand, use their knowledge of the heavenly bodies to advise people about their life situations. This is not science, but a belief that what happens in our lives is affected by the positions of the moon, sun, and planets.

Topic: _Astronomy and astrology_

Main idea: _Astronomy and astrology are similar in some ways, but they differ in an important way._

Key words in the main idea: _similar, differ_

Supporting facts and ideas:

Signal words/phrases	Details
both	_Experts study planetary motion and constellations._
However	_Astronomers study heavenly bodies as a science._
on the other hand	_Astrologers advise people about their lives._

B. Differences Only

Read the paragraph and the information below. Then underline the signal words in the paragraph.

Earth differs greatly from its two closest neighboring planets, Venus and Mars. The Venusian and Martian atmospheres are composed almost entirely of carbon dioxide, while Earth's atmosphere contains very little. The dominant material in our atmosphere is nitrogen (77 percent). The other major component of Earth's atmosphere is oxygen (21 percent), a gas that is almost nonexistent on Venus and Mars. Our planet has an abundance[1] of water, which covers about 70 percent of Earth's surface and supports life on our planet. In contrast, Venus and Mars are extremely dry planets and incapable of supporting life.

---

[1] *abundance:* a large quantity of something

Topic: _How Earth is different from Venus and Mars_

Main idea: _The Earth differs greatly from that of its two closest neighboring planets, Venus and Mars._

Key word in the main idea: _differs_

Supporting facts and ideas:

Signal words/phrases	Details
while	*The Venusian and Martian atmospheres are mostly carbon dioxide; Earth's contains little.*
however	*Our atmosphere has a lot of oxygen, there's almost none on Venus and Mars.*
in contrast	*Earth has lots of water; Venus and Mars are very dry.*

4. Cause/Effect

In this pattern, the writer's main idea is that one event or action caused another event or action.

- Key words/phrases in the main idea and the signal words for details are the same and often include: *causes, leads to, is the cause of, results in, creates, brings about, makes, provokes, produces, gives rise to, contributes to, is due to, is the result of, comes from, results from, is produced by, is a consequence of, follows, is caused by.*

Read the paragraph and the information below. Then underline the signal words in the paragraph.

In 2003, two robotic rovers landed on Mars and began sending back data about the possible existence of water on the red planet. This close examination of Mars was the result of new and improved technology. Because of advances in telecommunication systems, scientists on Earth can send commands faster and receive data in greater amounts. New software in the rovers led to their increased ability to make independent decisions and avoid dangers and hazards on their own. As a result of new technologies for severe environments, the rovers and their interior computers were able to survive the extreme cold and hot conditions in space and on Mars. And due to their new improved wheels the twin rovers could move around the rocky Martian landscape with ease.

Topic: *Close examination of Mars*

Main idea: *This close examination of Mars is the result of new and improved technology.*

Key word in the main idea: *the result of*

Cause: *New and improved technology*

Effect: *Close examination of Mars*

Supporting facts and ideas:

Signal words/phrases	Details
because of	Advances in telecommunication–send commands and receive data faster
led to	New software–increased abilities of the rovers
as a result of	New technology–rovers and computers can survive extreme conditions
due to	Improved wheels–the rovers can move around with ease

5. Problem/Solution

In this pattern, the main idea names a problem and indicates that one or more solutions. The paragraph always consists of two parts: 1) a statement and 2) a description and explanation of how it was solved. There are often no signal words for the details.

- Key words/phrases in the main idea: _situation, trouble, crisis, dilemma_ or _issue_.
- In the body of the paragraph, key words include: _solve, solution, resolved_.

Read the paragraph and the information below. Then underline the signal words in the paragraph.

Beginning in the 1600s, astronomers had realized that their telescopes had serious limits. They had managed to build stronger and better telescopes, but no matter how strong the new telescopes were, they were less than satisfactory. The astronomers were able to view objects only when the objects were in view of Earth. At the same time, however, Earth's light and atmosphere made it difficult to see many heavenly objects. Thanks to the Hubble Telescope, this has been solved, because the Hubble is not just a telescope. It is a digital camera on a satellite that travels about 370 miles (600 km) above Earth, making a complete orbit every ninty-seven minutes. Since 1990, Hubble has been able to take digital pictures of planets, galaxies, comets, and more, and these are sent back to Hubble headquarters for scientists to study.

Topic: _Telescopes_

Main idea: _Telescopes were limited, but the new Hubble telescope has solved the problem._

Key words in the main idea: _problem, solved_

Supporting facts and ideas:

Problem: _Telescopes could view objects only when they were in view of Earth._

Solution: _A new kind of telescope_

6. Extended Definition

In this pattern, the writer names a concept or complicated process that the paragraph will define and explain. Usually, the main idea or first sentence of the paragraph states a dictionary definition of the concept or process, followed by a description and/or an explanation. There are usually no signal words for the details.

- Key words/phrases in the main idea: *consists of, is, seems to be, are.*

Read the paragraph and the information below. Then underline the signal words in the paragraph.

A solar eclipse is an astronomical event during which the Moon seems to cover the Sun. When the Moon passes between the Earth and the Sun, all or part of the Sun's light is blotted out. The Moon, in fact, is much smaller than the Sun, but it is also a great deal closer to the Earth. As a result, both the Sun and the Moon seem to be about the same size to us. During a total eclipse, the Sun, the Moon, and the Earth are all in a straight line and the Moon completely hides the Sun from view. A partial eclipse occurs when the three bodies are not exactly in a straight line. In an annular solar eclipse, the Sun is visible as a bright ring around the Moon because the Moon is farthest from the Earth.

Topic: *Solar eclipse*

Main idea: *A solar eclipse is an astronomical event during which the Moon seems to cover the Sun.*

Supporting facts and ideas:

Explanation or description: *How and why a solar eclipse occurs. Three different types of solar eclipses.*

Identifying patterns

In the exercises that follow, you will practice using key words and signal words to identify the patterns. Remember that when the Extended Definition and Problem/Solution patterns are used, there are usually no signal words for the details.

EXERCISE 1

A. Each paragraph has a different pattern. Working with another student, read the paragraphs and write the topic, the main idea, the key words in the main idea, and the pattern. Then add the supporting facts and ideas as shown in the examples.

- *Listing, Sequence, Comparison/Contrast or Cause/Effect patterns: Signal words and details*

- *Problem/Solution pattern: The problem and the solution*

- *Extended Definition pattern: Explanation and/or description*

Moon Landings

1.   Only three and a half years passed between the first moon landing in 1969 and the sixth and last moon landing in 1972. But while the first landing was an enormous achievement in itself, the last landing contributed far more to the advancement of scientific knowledge. On the first mission, the two astronauts were on the Moon for only a few hours and remained close to the landing site. Their time on the Moon was just sufficient to conduct several experiments and collect a small sample of lunar rocks. On the last mission, however, the three men (one of whom was a geologist) spent much more time on the lunar surface—three periods of about seven hours. With their special moon vehicle, they could travel much further from the landing site to investigate more of the lunar environment and collect a wider range of soil and rock samples.

Topic: _____

Main idea: _____

_____

Key words in the main idea: _____

Pattern: _____

Supporting facts and ideas:

2.   The Apollo moon landings, may not have led to any great discovery—such as evidence[1] of life on the Moon—but it did have a significant impact on scientific and technological development in the twentieth century. One field that was undoubtedly affected by the moon landings was computer research. NASA, the U.S. space agency, did not invent the integrated circuit[2] (the basis of the computer), but it was the largest single consumer[3] of integrated circuits in the early 1960s. Working for the space program undoubtedly motivated computer engineers, pushing them toward the development of today's personal computer. Another, related technological development that could be attributed at least in part to the Apollo program was the invention of the Internet. In this case, too, the moon landings served as an indirect motivation for scientists and engineers in their search for ways to communicate from computers in spacecraft to computers on Earth.

---

[1] *evidencer: use:* facts, objects, or signs that make you believe that something exists or is true
[2] *integrated circuit:* very small electronic parts working together as a single unit in a computer
[3] *consumer*

Topic: _____

Main idea: _____

_____

Key words in the main idea: _____

Pattern: _____

Supporting facts and ideas:

3.   In planning for future lunar missions, scientists are faced with one serious
limitation to human exploration on the Moon, and that is the lack of water. The
availability of water would make an enormous difference for humans working on the
Moon for any length of time. The search for water, then, remains a high priority for
space scientists. One technique that they have used is to send rockets crashing into
the lunar surface. The crash creates a cloud of vapor[1] and dust that scientists can
collect and analyze for evidence of water. Several rockets have already been sent to
the Moon, but so far the results have not been conclusive. Another larger and heavier
rocket, which will be sent to the moon in 2009, will have a greater impact and may
produce different results. With the data from this larger rocket blast, scientists hope
to establish conclusively the presence or absence of water on the Moon.

_____
[1] *vapor:* a mass of very small drops of a liquid that floats in the air

Topic: _____

Main idea: _____

_____

Key words in the main idea: _____

Pattern: _____

Supporting facts and ideas:

4.   Lunar craters make travel on the Moon's surface a challenge for astronauts or robotic rovers. The surface of the Moon is marked by millions of the deep depressions or holes which are visible from the earth with just the naked eye. The craters are generally circular, range in size from a few feet to many hundreds of kilometers across, and can be surrounded by sharp mountainous peaks. They have been created by the impact of various objects—asteroids, comets, or meteorites. Since the Moon has no atmosphere to protect it from potentially dangerous objects in space, it is exposed to anything that may be in its path. The fact that there is no atmosphere on the Moon, and so no wind or rain, also means that the craters remain unchanged unless another object lands in the same spot.

Topic: _____

Main idea: _____

_____

Key words in the main idea: _____

Pattern: _____

Supporting facts and ideas:

B. Compare your answers with those of another pair of students. If you disagree, read the paragraphs again and check the examples on pages 135–141 to decide on the best answers.

EXERCISE 2

A. Each paragraph has a different pattern. Working with another student, read the paragraphs and write the topic, the main idea, the key words in the main idea, and the pattern. Then add further information for each pattern.

- **Listing, Sequence, Comparison/Contrast or Cause/Effect patterns: Signal words and details**

- **Problem/Solution pattern: The problem and the solution**

- **Extended Definition pattern: Explanation and/or description**

Telescopes: Tools for Examining the Heavens

1.   According to some accounts, the first optical telescope was accidentally invented in the 1600s by children who put two glass lenses together while playing with them in a Dutch optical shop. The owner of the shop, Hans Lippershey, looked through the lenses and was amazed by the way they made the nearby church look so much larger. Soon after that, he invented a device that he called a "looker," a long thin tube where light passed in a straight line from the front lens to the viewing lens at the other end of the tube. In 1608 he tried to sell his invention unsuccessfully. In the same year, someone described the "looker" to the Italian scientist Galileo, who made his own version of the device. In 1610 Galileo used his version to make observations of the Moon, the planet Jupiter, and the Milky Way. In April of 1611, Galileo showed his device to guests at a banquet in his honor. One of the guests suggested a name for the device: telescope.

Topic: _____

Main idea: _____

_____

Key words in the main idea: _____

Pattern: _____

Supporting facts and ideas:

2.   When Isaac Newton began using Galileo's telescope more than a century later, he noticed a problem. The type of telescope that Galileo designed is called a refractor because the front lens bends, or refracts, the light. However, the curved front lens also caused the light to be separated into colors. This meant that when Newton looked through the refracting telescope, the images of bright objects appeared with a ring of colors around them. This sometimes interfered with viewing. He solved this problem by designing a new type of telescope that used a curved mirror. This mirror concentrated the light and reflected a beam of light to the eyepiece at the other end of the telescope. Because Newton used a mirror, his telescope was called a reflector.

Topic: _____

Main idea: _____

_____

Key words in the main idea: _____

Pattern: _____

Supporting facts and ideas:

3.   Very much larger optical telescopes can now be found in many parts of the
world, built on hills and mountains far from city lights. For example, the world's
largest refracting telescope has lenses that are 40 inches (101 cm) across. It is
located at the Yerkes Observatory in Williams Bay, Wisconsin. Another telescope
stands on Mount Palomar in California. This huge reflecting telescope, with a 200-
inch (508 cm) lens, was for many years the largest reflecting telescope in the world
until an even larger reflecting telescope was built in the Caucasus Mountains. It
has a 237-inch (6 m) mirror. A fourth famous reflector telescope, the Keck
Telescope situated on a mountain in Hawaii, does not use a single large mirror to
collect the light. Instead, the Keck uses the combined light that falls on thirty-six
mirrors, each of which is 5.9 feet (1.8 m) in diameter.

Topic: _____

Main idea: _____

_____

Key words in the main idea: _____

Pattern: _____

Supporting facts and ideas:

4.   Radio telescopes, like optical telescopes, allow astronomers to collect data from outer space, but they are different in important ways. First of all, they look very different because instead of light waves, they collect radio waves. Thus, in the place of lenses or mirrors, radio telescopes employ bowl-shaped disks that resemble huge TV satellite dishes. Also, apart from their distinctive appearance, radio telescopes and optical telescopes use different methods to record the information they collect. Optical telescopes use cameras to take photographs of visible objects, while radio telescopes use radio receivers to record radio waves from distant objects in space. With both kids of telescopes, however, larger is better. In optical telescopes, images are clearer with larger lenses, and in radio telescopes, only really large dishes can capture radio waves.

Topic: _____

Main idea: _____

_____

Key words in the main idea: _____

Pattern: _____

Supporting facts and ideas:

B. Compare your answers with those of another pair of students. If you disagree, read the paragraphs again and check the Examples on pages 135–141 to decide on the best answers.

EXERCISE 3

A. In this exercise, each paragraph is missing a sentence. Working with another student, read each paragraph, identify its pattern of organization, and then choose the sentence that fits best. (There is one extra sentence.)

Use these abbreviations: Listing (L)   Cause/Effect (C/E)
                             Sequence (S)   Problem/Solution (P/S)
                             Comparison/Contrast (C/C)   Extended Definition (ED)

Modern Astronomy: From Optical to Infrared

1.   Infrared light was discovered in 1800 by an astronomer, Sir William Herschel, who was curious about sunlight as a source of heat. He knew that sunlight produced heat, and he knew that it was made up of all the colors of the spectrum (as in a rainbow), but he wanted to find out which color or colors were responsible for the heat. He did this in an experiment using a special piece of glass called a prism, which separates light rays into all the different colors. First, he allowed sunlight to pass through the prism. Then he passed a thermometer over each color to measure the temperature. He observed that the temperature increased as he moved the thermometer from the color violet to the color red. _____. To his surprise, this area gave off the most heat. Herschel called this invisible radiation "calorific rays." Today, we know it as infrared light rays.

Pattern: _____ Missing sentence: _____

2.   Herschel and other astronomers developed infrared telescopes in the hope that these new telescopes would allow them to see distant objects more clearly than optical telescopes. However, infrared telescopes presented a different problem: The Earth's atmosphere blocked out most infrared light. In 1946, astronomer Lyman Spitzer first came up with the idea of space telescopes that would operate from outside the Earth's atmosphere. It took more than four decades to develop the technology for a space telescope, but finally, NASA (National Aeronautics and Space Agency) launched the Hubble Space Telescope into orbit high above the Earth. _____. The problem was solved, and the photographs from the Hubble have revolutionized our view of the heavens.

Pattern: _____ Missing sentence: _____

3.   When astronomers try to view an object with the Hubble telescope, they must follow certain procedures very precisely. Operating the telescope by remote computer, they need to keep their target object in view. This is not easy because the Hubble telescope revolves around Earth at 17,500 mph and the Earth is moving around the Sun at 67,000 mph. First they must pinpoint their tiny target's exact location in the vast sky. Then they select a pair of "guide stars" from the Space Telescope Science Institute's Guide Star Catalog, which lists the brightness and positions of 15 million stars. They choose guide stars whose apparent positions are near their desired viewing target. These guide stars will help center the target in the telescope's field of view. _____. Next, the telescope's guidance sensors search for the guide stars and "lock on" to them. From then on, the telescope can maintain the precise direction needed for a Hubble observation.

Pattern: _____ Missing sentence: _____

4.   The Hubble Space Telescope and the new Spitzer Space Telescope were both launched from Earth and sent out beyond the Earth's atmosphere so that they could make full use of infrared detectors and cameras. _____ . The two telescopes are operated in a similar way by connecting to the computers of ground-based technicians. However, there is one big difference between them. The Hubble orbits the Earth and so has a limited view of the dark reaches of outer space. The Spitzer, on the other hand, was not launched to orbit the Earth. It was sent much further out, about 26 million miles from Earth. Thus, the Spitzer has been able to collect information about the outer reaches of space, including clues about how planets form and evidence of young galaxies that were present at the beginning of time.

Pattern: _____   Missing sentence: _____

Missing Sentences:

a. There, far away from the Earth's atmosphere, the telescope could easily detect infrared light.

b. Then he moved the thermometer farther to an area next to the red light, where he could see no light or color.

c. Both have been highly successful in their missions, sending back thousands of exciting images of the heavens.

d. Some radio telescopes are set up in a group called an "array" to increase their capacity for collecting data from space.

e. Then the guide star information is transmitted to Hubble's onboard computers via satellite.

B. Compare your answers with those of another pair of students. If you disagree, read the paragraphs again and check the examples on pages 135–141 to decide on the best answers.

Focus on Vocabulary

A. Check your understanding of the following target words. Read each word aloud and then write S, M, or N beside it.

S = *you are sure of the meaning of the word*
M = *you think you might know the meaning of the word*
N = *you don't know the meaning of the word at all*

____ achievement	____ affect	____ analyze
____ conduct	____ impact on	____ conclusive
____ vehicle	____ motivate	____ potential
____ investigate	____ attribute to	____ expose
____ environment	____ availability	

B. Read the paragraphs from Exercise 1 again. As you read, look for the target words and circle them. Note that the words in Part A are listed in the same order as they appear in the passage but the form may be different.

Moon Landings

Only three and a half years passed between the first moon landing in 1969, and the sixth and last moon landing in 1972. But while the first landing was an enormous achievement in itself, the last landing contributed far more to the advancement of scientific knowledge. On the first mission, the two astronauts were on the moon for only a few hours and remained close to the landing site. Their time on the moon was just sufficient to conduct several experiments and collect a small sample of lunar rocks. On the last mission, however, the three men (one of whom was a geologist) spent much more time on the lunar surface—three periods of about seven hours. With their special moon vehicle, they could travel farther from the landing site to investigate more of the lunar environment and collect a wider range of soil and rock samples.

The Apollo moon landings may not have led to any great new discovery—such as evidence of life on the moon—but they did have a significant impact on science and technology in the twentieth century. One field that was undoubtedly affected by the moon landings was computer research. NASA, the U.S. space agency, did not invent the integrated circuit (the basis of the computer), but it was the largest single consumer of integrated circuits in the early 1960s. Working for the space program motivated computer engineers, pushing them toward the development of today's personal computer. Another, related development that could be attributed at least in part to the Apollo program was the invention of the Internet. In this case, too, the moon landings served as indirect motivation for scientists and engineers in their research for ways to communicate from computers in spacecraft to computers on Earth.

In planning for future lunar missions, scientists are faced with one serious limitation to human exploration on the moon, and that is the lack of water. The availability of water would make an enormous difference for humans working on the moon for any length of time. The search for water, then, remains a high priority for space scientists. One technique that they have used is to send rockets crashing into the lunar surface. The crash creates a cloud of vapor and dust that scientists can collect and analyze for evidence of water. Several rockets have already been sent to the moon, but so far the results have not been conclusive. Another larger and heavier rocket, which will be sent to the moon in 2009, will have a greater impact and may produce different results. With the data from this larger rocket blast, scientists hope to establish conclusively the presence or absence of water on the moon.

Lunar craters make travel on the moon's surface a challenge for astronauts or robotic rovers. The surface of the moon is marked by millions of deep depressions or holes which are visible from the earth with just the naked eye. The craters are generally circular, range in size from a few feet to many hundreds of kilometers across, and can be surrounded by sharp mountainous peaks. They have been created by the impact of various objects—asteroids, comets, or meteorites. Since the moon has no atmosphere to protect it from potentially dangerous objects in space, it is exposed to anything that might be in its path. The fact that there is no atmosphere on the moon, and so no wind or rain, also means that the craters remain unchanged unless another object lands in the same spot.

C. Working with another student, check to be sure that you have located all of the target words.

Exercise 5

A. These sentences are taken from the passage in Exercise 4. Working with another student, read each sentence aloud. Then circle the best meaning or synonym for the underlined word as it is used in the sentence.

1. But while the first landing was an enormous <u>achievement</u> in itself, the last landing contributed far more to the advancement of scientific knowledge.

   a. success   b. ability   c. job

2. Their time on the moon was just sufficient to <u>conduct</u> several experiments and collect a small sample of lunar rocks.

   a. take off   b. look at   c. carry out

3. With their special moon <u>vehicle</u>, they could travel farther from the landing site to investigate more of the lunar environment and collect a wider range of soil and rock samples.

   a. light   b. car   c. tool

4. With their special moon vehicle, they could travel farther from the landing site to <u>investigate</u> more of the lunar environment and collect a wider range of soil and rock samples.

   a. find out about   b. take away   c. look around

5. With their special moon vehicle, they could travel farther from the landing site to investigate more of the lunar <u>environment</u> and collect a wider range of soil and rock samples.

   a. weather   b. tests   c. conditions

6. The Apollo moon landings may not have led to any great new discovery—such as evidence of life on the moon—but they did have a significant <u>impact</u> on science and technology in the twentieth century.

    a. effect   b. explosion   c. invention

7. One field that was undoubtedly <u>affected</u> by the moon landings was computer research.

    a. interested   b. influenced   c. limited

8. Working for the space program <u>motivated</u> computer engineers, pushing them toward the development of today's personal computer.

    a. disappointed   b. encouraged   c. produced

9. Another, related development that could be <u>attributed</u> at least in part <u>to</u> the Apollo program, was the invention of the Internet.

    a. controlled by   b. prevented by   c. caused by

10. The <u>availability</u> of water would make an enormous difference for humans working on the moon.

    a. presence   b. lack   c. production

11. The crash creates a cloud of vapor and dust that scientists can collect and <u>analyze</u> for evidence of water.

    a. examine   b. experiment   c. develop

12. Several rockets have already been sent to the moon, but so far the results have not been <u>conclusive</u>.

    a. direct   b. certain   c. simple

13. Since the moon has no atmosphere to protect it from <u>potentially</u> dangerous objects in space, it is exposed to anything that might be in its path.

    a. possibly   b. partly   c. plainly

14. Since the moon has no atmosphere to protect it from potentially dangerous objects in space, it is <u>exposed</u> to anything that might be in its path.

    a. covered by   b. harmful   c. without protection

B. Compare your answers with those of another pair of students. If you disagree, explain your answers and look back at the passage to check your work.

A. In this table, write as many as possible of the missing forms below, without looking in a dictionary.

Noun	Verb	Adjective	Adverb
achievement			———
	affect		———
	analyze		
	attribute		
availability			———
		conclusive	
	conduct	———	———
environment	———		
		exposed	———
impact		———	———
	investigate		———
	motivate		———
	———	potential	
vehicle	———		———

B. Compare your work with that of another student. Look in the dictionary for the forms you did not know and write them in the table.

A. Working with another student, write a form of one of the target words in each of the sentences below. Each word may be used only once.

achievement	conclusive	impact
affect	conduct	motivate
analyze	environment	potential
attribute	expose	vehicle
availability	investigate	

1. Patients who need to have X-rays should be _____ to as little radiation as possible.

2. The company designed a plan to _____ employees to work more efficiently.

3. In American supermarkets the _____ of certain fruits and vegetables no longer depends on the weather or the season.

4. After the remarkable _____ of his first novel that won several prizes, this writer never managed to write anything else as interesting or original.

5. Scientists are _____ the relationship between air quality and cancer.

6. The police _____ the cause of the accident to the bad weather and wet roads.

7. Both young and middle-aged women were considered _____ customers of the new clothing store.

8. The study was _____ by a well-known company with long experience in political matters.

9. The areas most severely _____ by the storm were those along the coast.

10. Living in an unhealthy _____ can influence a child's behavior and development.

11. The police are waiting for _____ evidence before they can arrest the man they think is responsible for the crime.

12. Motor _____ are not allowed on the roads in many national parks.

13. When the bones found on the mountain top were _____, scientists were surprised to discover they were five centuries old.

14. The stores in the downtown area are beginning to feel the _____ of the huge new shopping center on the edge of town.

B. Compare your work with that of another pair of students. If you disagree, explain your answers and then use a dictionary to check your work.

EXERCISE 8

A. Make word study cards for the target words that you are still unsure about. Use the cards to study the words, first on your own and then with another student. (See Part 2, Unit 1, page 29).

B. 1. Write a sentence for each of the words, leaving a blank instead of the target word. Ask another student to read your sentences and write the target word that should go in each blank.

   2. Look at your sentences again. If your classmate wrote a different word, discuss the sentences to find out why. Was your sentence unclear, or did your classmate not know the target word?

Reading Longer Passages Effectively

Like a paragraph, a longer passage focuses on a single topic, expresses a general idea about that topic, follows a pattern of organization, and uses signal words and phrases to indicate supporting ideas.

The Topic

The topic of a longer passage is usually repeated many times to focus the reader's attention and to reinforce connections between the topic and the supporting ideas. It is generally mentioned in:

- the title;

- the topic sentence of each paragraph;

- at least one other sentence in each paragraph.

Example:

A. Read the following passage. What is the topic?

Topic: _____

_____ are everywhere these days—on buses, in restaurants, at school, and at the workplace. You see people of all ages, from young children to the elderly, conversing on their _____ as they walk down the street. Clearly, _____ have become an important part of our lives and represent a major technological shift. However, it could also be argued that they have had a significant impact on how we communicate and on social relations in general.

The fact that _____ allow us to stay in touch at all times has clearly had an impact on the way we work. In many professions _____ have in fact been enormously helpful, and probably on many occasions they have made it possible for doctors or firefighters to save lives through quick intervention[1]. However, in many other professions, _____ have basically meant more work. The fact that it is possible to stay in touch constantly makes people feel they ought to stay in touch constantly. For these people—especially business managers and others in positions of responsibility—the work day is never over and they end up answering calls from the office while dining with their family or vacationing on the beach.

In daily life, _____ have also brought about some changes in our habits. They can, of course, help solve some of the problems of our busy lives. Motorists stuck in traffic, for example, can use _____ to let people know they will be late. However, this ease of daily communication seems to have fostered[2] a certain inability to make a decision or stick to a plan. This is especially true of young people who have grown up with _____ and who have become extremely impatient. For instance, if a bus does not arrive exactly on time, they are incapable of waiting a few minutes. Instead, they pull out their _____ and immediately start calling friends or family to arrange other transportation.

Furthermore, apart from the users, _____ can also have an impact on others who happen to be nearby. At concerts or movies, people often forget to turn off their _____, which inevitably start ringing at the worst possible moment. On trains or buses, there is nothing more annoying that someone nearby conversing on a _____, especially since they tend to speak more loudly than normal.

To conclude, though there are certainly many good reasons for having and using _____, we should be aware of how they affect our lives and condition us in many ways. Sometimes it might be useful to remember that until just a few years ago, _____ did not exist, and life went along just fine without them.

_____

[1] *intervention:* action to help
[2] *foster:* to help to develop a skill, feeling, idea etc.

B. Write the topic at the top of the passage and then compare it with that of another student. (You can find the answer at the bottom of this page.)

C. Write the same topic on all of the blank lines in the passage. Then read the passage again. Why is it easier to understand and follow the ideas with the topic included?

(Topic of the Example Exercise passage: cell phones)

The Thesis Statement

In a longer passage, the writer's idea about the topic is stated in a sentence called the thesis statement. Like the main idea in a paragraph, the thesis statement tells the writer's overall idea about the topic. Recognizing and understanding the writer's thesis statement is the key to understanding the ideas in a passage.

Look again at the passage above. The topic is *cell phones*. The thesis statement is: *It could also be argued that they (cell phones) have had a significant impact on how we communicate and on social relations in general.*

Read the passage again. Notice that each paragraph explains a way cell phones influence our lives.

Identifying the Thesis Statement

The thesis statement in English

- includes the topic;

- is usually found in the first paragraph (or paragraphs);

- is always a complete sentence;

- often indicates how the ideas will be developed in the passage;

- is supported by the ideas and information found in all of the paragraphs of the passage.

In English, the thesis statement is near the beginning of a passage because readers expect to learn right away what the passage is about. In other languages and cultures, this is not necessarily true.

Think about how writers express their ideas in your language. Where can you usually find the thesis in a longer passage in your language? Is it the same as in English or different?

A. Read the passage and ask yourself, "What is the topic? What is the writer's idea about that topic?" Then decide what the topic and the thesis statement are and write them below.

Human Responses to Disaster

Catastrophic events, such as natural disasters and major terrorist attacks, are extremely traumatic[1] for the people involved. In these situations, where one's own and others' physical safety is threatened, feelings may range from fear, to horror or helplessness. Studies of catastrophe survivors have taught psychologists how individuals who have undergone such traumas and losses respond to these circumstances. Such research is difficult: Ethics prevent psychologists from creating disastrous events in order to study their effects on volunteer subjects. The only way to study these events is to be on the scene after the catastrophe, getting the story from the survivors while it is fresh on their minds. From these stories, psychologists have theorized that responses to extreme natural and human-caused disasters occur in five stages.

The first stage begins immediately after the event and may last for a few moments or several days. During this period, victims experience psychological numbness—a certain inability to think or feel. They may be in a state of shock and confusion, and they have difficulty comprehending what has happened. This reaction occurs whether or not they have been physically injured themselves during the event.

During the next stage, victims continue to lack awareness of what is going on around them. They appear to function automatically, without conscious[2] control of their thinking or reacting. Later, they may not remember these moments or their actions. When there has been no warning at all of the disaster—as in an earthquake or the September 11, 2001 attacks in New York—this

stage lasts longer. While people are in this phase, they are also unable to focus their attention on their surroundings or coordinate their actions with other people. This can result in delays in rescue efforts and the loss of lives.

In the third stage after a disaster, victims turn to each other. They pool[3] resources and collaborate in trying to deal with the consequences. At this point, they may experience some pride at having managed to survive, they may be hopeful about the future, and they express their willingness to "roll up their sleeves" and try to rebuild. At the same time, they are physically worn out by the impact of the experience and they may not have much reserve energy.

The fourth stage is when victims are most likely to become depressed or even attempt suicide. They experience a letdown[4] and finally comprehend the full extent of the tragedy. By this time, the public and the media may have lost interest in the disaster and the victims are no longer given special consideration. Though the state of emergency may continue, the survivors feel abandoned and forgotten.

The final period of recovery is the most extended stage, as the survivors struggle to adapt to the changes in their lives. These changes may be personal or they may involve the whole community. In some cases, the victims may have to move elsewhere and start a completely new life. During this phase, survivors feel a basic need to find a meaning in their loss. "Why?" they ask themselves, and they demand answers from those in authority.

(Source: From Zimbardo, Philip G., Robert L. Johnson & Ann L. Weber, *Psychology: Core Concepts* 5/e. Published by Allyn & Bacon, Boston, MA. © by Pearson Education. By permission of the publisher.)

---

[1] *traumatic:* shocking and upsetting
[2] *conscious:* intended, awake and thinking
[3] *pool:* to combine and share
[4] *letdown:* a feeling of disappointment

Topic: _____

Thesis statement: _____

_____

B. Compare your work with that of another student. Explain how all the paragraphs support the thesis statement you have written. If you disagree, look back at the passage to check your work.

EXERCISE 2

A. Read the passage and ask yourself, "What is the topic? What is the writer's idea about that topic?" Then decide what the topic and the thesis statement are and write them below the passage.

Cultural Universals in Emotional Expression

You can usually tell when your friends are happy or angry by the looks on their faces or by their actions. This is useful because reading their emotional expressions helps you to know how to respond to them. [...] Emotions have evolved to help us respond to important situations and to convey[1] our intentions to others. But does raising the eyebrows and rounding the mouth say the same thing in Minneapolis as it does in Madagascar? Much research on emotional expression has centered on such questions.

According to Paul Ekman, the leading researcher in this area, people speak and understand substantially[2] the same "facial language" the world around (Ekman, 1984,1992, 2003; Ekman & Rosenberg, 1997). Studies by Ekman's group have demonstrated that humans share a set of universal emotional expressions that testify to the common biological heritage[3] of the human species. Smiles, for example, signal happiness and frowns indicate sadness on the faces of people in such far-flung places as Argentina, Japan, Spain, Hungary, Poland, Sumatra, the United States, Vietnam, the jungles of New Guinea, and the Eskimo villages north of the Artic Circle (Biehl et al., 1997; Ekman et al., 1987; Izard, 1994).

Ekman and his colleagues claim that people everywhere can recognize at least seven basic emotions: sadness, fear, anger, disgust, contempt,[4] happiness, and surprise (Ekman & Friesen, 1971, 1986; Ekman et al., 1969, 1987; Keating, 1994). There are, however, huge differences across cultures in both the context and intensity of emotional displays—the so-called display rules. In many Asian cultures, for example, children are taught to control emotional responses—especially negative ones—while many American children are encouraged to express their feelings more openly (Matsumoto, 1994, 1996).

Regardless of culture, however, emotions usually show themselves, to some degree, in people's behavior. From their first days of life, babies produce facial expressions that communicate their feelings (Ganchrow et al., 1983). And the ability to read facial expressions develops early, too. Very young children pay close attention to facial expressions, and by age five they nearly equal adults in their skill at reading emotions on people's faces (Nelson, 1987). [...]

This evidence all points to a biological underpinning[5] for our abilities to express and interpret a basic set of human emotions. Moreover, as Charles Darwin pointed out over a century ago, some emotional expressions seem to appear across species boundaries. Darwin especially noted the similarity of our own facial expressions of fear and rage to those of chimpanzees and wolves (Darwin, 1998/1862; Ejnabm, 1984).

But are *all* emotional expressions universal? No. Cross-cultural psychologists tell us that certain emotional responses carry different meanings in different cultures (Ekman, 1992, 1994; Ellsworth, 1994). These, therefore, must be learned rather than innate.[6]

[1] *convey:* to communicate a message with or without words
[2] *substantially:* to a great degree
[3] *heritage:* something that is passed down from the past
[4] *contempt:* a feeling that someone or something does not deserve any respect
[5] *underpinning:* basis or inheritance
[6] *innate:* something you are born with

For example, what emotion do you suppose might be conveyed by sticking out your tongue? For Americans, this might indicate disgust, while in China it can signify surprise.

Likewise, a grin[7] on an American face may indicate joy, while on a Japanese face it may just as easily mean embarrassment. Clearly, culture influences emotional expression.

---

[7] *grin:* a wide smile

Topic: _____

Thesis statement: _____

_____

B. Compare your work with that of another student. Explain how all the paragraphs support the thesis statement you have written. If you disagree, look back at the passage to check your work.

The Thesis Statement, Pattern of Organization, and Supporting Points

The thesis statement will help you determine the overall pattern of organization of the whole passage and what kind of supporting points to look for. In each of the paragraphs after the thesis statement, the main idea supports the thesis statement and often includes a signal word for the overall pattern of the passage.

Example:

Read the information about the example passage on pages 155–156. Then turn back to the passage and underline the supporting points.

Thesis statement: *It could also be argued that they (cell phones) have had a significant impact on how we communicate and on social relations in general.*

Pattern of organization: *cause/effect*
Supporting points (main ideas):
Paragraph 2: *The fact that cell phones allow us to stay in touch at all time has clearly had an impact on the way we work.*
Paragraph 3: *In daily life, cell phones have also brought about some changes in our habits.*
Paragraph 4: *Furthermore, apart from the users, cell phones can also have an impact on others who happen to be nearby.*

Note: Some paragraphs in a longer passage may have a pattern that is different from the overall pattern of the passage, in which case the paragraphs will include signal words for the different pattern. In long, complex passages, different readers may interpret the thesis statement in slightly different ways. This can lead to their finding different overall patterns (especially when the writer does not use many obvious signal words). Thus, in some of the following exercises, there may be more than one possible answer about the pattern.

A. **Read the passage in Exercise 1 on page 158 again. Working with another student, write the thesis statement, the pattern of organization, and the supporting points. Underline the signal words in the thesis statement.**

Thesis statement: _____

_____

Pattern of organization: _____

Supporting points (main ideas):

_____

_____

_____

_____

_____

_____

_____

_____

_____

B. **Compare your work with that of another pair of students. If you disagree, explain your answers and look back at the passage to check your work.**

EXERCISE 4

A. **Read the passage in Exercise 2 on page 159 again. Working with another student, write the thesis statement, the pattern of organization, and the supporting points. Underline the signal words in the thesis statement.**

Thesis statement: _____

_____

Pattern of organization: _____

Supporting points (main ideas):

_____

_____

_____

_____

_____

_____

_____

_____

B. Compare your work with that of another pair of students. If you disagree, explain your answers and look back at the passage to check your work.

Finding the Thesis Statement in Newspaper and Magazine Articles

Newspaper and magazine articles are structured somewhat differently from most other writing in English. The paragraphs are often shorter, the articles may include many quotations, and they may not have a conclusion. However, these articles always contain a thesis statement. In a short article, it is usually in the first paragraph. In a longer article, the thesis statement may be in the second or third paragraph.

EXERCISE 5

A. Preview and read the newspaper article. Working with another student, write the thesis statement, the pattern of organization, and the supporting points. Underline the signal words for the overall pattern of the article.

Girls Fighting Like Guys

The statistics confirm what teachers and social workers in the United States have been saying for the past decade: Girls are becoming more violent. Not only are they using physical violence more often on other girls and on teachers; they are also getting arrested more often for violent crimes. Some would say simply, "It's about time they fight back." But do we really want our girls to become as violent as the boys? Why are girls fighting more, and what can we do to stop them?

This development relates to more general changes in the roles of men and women in America and the overall trend towards equalization. Girls are clearly demonstrating that they are no different from boys on many levels, including participation in sports, academic accomplishment,[1] and career achievement. Unfortunately, as girls break down the barriers between the sexes, they are also showing that they can be as nasty as boys.

In the 1980s, in speaking about youth violence, psychologist Leonard Eros suggested that one way to curb[2]

the increasing violence of boys would be to "socialize our boys more like we socialize our girls." That is, they should learn to deal with their feelings in ways that do not include violence. However, that has not happened. We have done the opposite. We are socializing girls more like boys, and it is clear from these recent statistics that girls are capable of similar levels of violence.

In this acculturation to violence, the entertainment media has played a key part. Movies, television, music, and video games now depict[3] girls in the kind of superhero roles that used to be exclusively male. From Angelina Jolie in *The Tomb Raider* series to Uma Thurman in *Kill Bill*, women are portrayed as tough and violent. The message they convey to girls is simple: Fighting is an appropriate and acceptable reaction when you are hurt or angry. Not surprisingly, as girls are exposed to these new cultural models, the parameters[4] of their behavior have changed and the repertoire[5] of their responses has expanded.

Some might argue that other factors, including gun availability,

poverty, and a history of abuse, are responsible for the new trend. However, these factors are the same for both boys and girls, and have not changed radically in the past decade. Until recently, girls who were at high risk tended to adopt a very different pattern of behavior, becoming self-destructive, rather than violent against others. Only in recent years have they begun to externalize their negative feelings with aggression and bullying like boys.

As might be expected, school is where girls are most likely to become violent. Here, where the problem is most evident, and the need for a coherent response is most acute, reactions so far have been ineffectual. Standard responses range from disbelief, to uncertainty, to "no tolerance" policies based on the threat of expulsion from school. These policies never worked with boys, and they are not working with girls. Removing the girl (or boy) from school only worsens the impact and extends the problem.

Finding a solution will require a much broader outlook because the problem itself lies not in our schools

---

[1] *accomplishment:* something you can do especially well
[2] *curb:* to control or limit
[3] *depict:* show
[4] *parameters:* agreed limits that control the way something should be done
[5] *repertoire:* possible ways

or their policies, but in the values of American society. We have tolerated the epidemic of violence among boys for too long. Now that it is spreading to the girls, it is time for us to wake up and do something about this toxic environment that is causing so much harm to our young people.

(Source: Adapted from "It's not only guys who fight these days," by Deborah Prothrow-Stith and Howard Spivak, *International Herald Tribune*, November 25, 2005, originally in *The Boston Globe*)

Thesis statement: _____

_____

Pattern of organization: _____

Supporting points (main ideas):

_____

_____

_____

_____

_____

_____

_____

_____

_____

B. *Compare your work with that of another pair of students. If you disagree, explain your answers and look back at the article to check your work.*

EXERCISE 6

A. *Preview and read the magazine article. Working with another student, write the thesis statement, the pattern of organization, and the supporting points. Underline the signal words for the overall pattern of the article.*

Women Show the Ways to Maturity

There's no single way to achieve a well-adjusted life. However, there are at least three different, but equally effective paths that lead to psychological maturity, according to a 39-year study of women who were first contacted as college seniors.

The study, in the *Journal of Personality and Social Psychology*, traced psychological development in 111 graduates of a private women's college. Participants completed questionnaires at five points between ages 21 and 60. Their psychological maturity was rated on a variety of scales.[1]

Some women, dubbed[2] conservers[3] by the researchers, successfully sought the security of marriage, family life, and traditionally female occupations. Conservers reported dealing well with daily situations and with other people, said psychologist Ravenna Helson and graduate student Sanjay Srivastava, both of the University of California, Berkeley. Conservers muted[4] both their positive and

---

[1] *scales:* tests and questionnaires
[2] *dubbed:* called or named
[3] *conserver:* someone who tries to keep things as they are
[4] *mute:* to pay little attention to

negative feelings. They were mostly satisfied with their lives and had little desire to pursue novel challenges.

One such woman, Cathy, became a wife and mother soon after graduation. She worked outside the home when her husband experienced professional difficulties and now helps to run several volunteer groups.

A second group, called achievers, cherished[5] social recognition and career advancement. Achievers reported a sense of mastery of everyday challenges. Over time, they underwent considerable personal growth and developed insight into their lives. They took a creative approach to fulfilling tasks at work. At the same time, achievers' intimate[6] relationships sometimes suffered as a result of their emphasis on professional goals.

One achiever, Andrea, went from college to graduate school to a professional career. She overcame an addiction while ascending the corporate ladder.[7] She married at age 40, when she felt she had her life under control. Andrea and her husband had no children but satisfying careers. Andrea now says she's overcome feelings of worthlessness that began in childhood.

The third group of well-adjusted women, dubbed seekers, valued unconventional[8] pursuits, creativity, and self-discovery. According to the researchers, seekers developed progressively more independence and wisdom in thinking about various life matters. They experienced a lot of emotional highs and lows. A desire to find or accomplish a true calling was uppermost in their minds and often outweighed[9] concerns with daily affairs.

For example, Sara interacted awkwardly with others but shined[10] academically in graduate school. She dropped out and got married after unexpectedly becoming pregnant. Later, she resumed schooling and tried to become more sociable. Sarah wants to leave her current nine-to-five job, which she finds unchallenging, so that she can write "the great American novel."

A roughly equal number of women fell within each category of healthy development. "There are different ways to lead a good life, and each comes with its own trade-offs,"[11] Helson remarked.

(Source: *Science News*, June 30, 2001)

---

[5] *cherish:* to love
[6] *intimate:* close, personal
[7] *ascending the corporate ladder:* moving up in the company
[8] *unconventional:* unusual
[9] *outweigh:* more important
[10] *shine:* to do very, very well
[11] *trade-off:* an acceptable balance between two opposite things

Thesis statement: _____

_____

Pattern of organization: _____

Supporting points (main ideas):

_____

_____

_____

_____

_____

_____

B. Compare your work with those of another pair of students. If you disagree, look back at the passage to check your work.

Focus on Vocabulary

A. Check your understanding of the following target words. Read each word aloud and then write S, M, or N beside it.

S = *you are sure of the meaning of the word*
M = *you think you might know the meaning of the word*
N = *you don't know the meaning of the word at all*

____ involve	____ aware	____ collaborate
____ undergo	____ function	____ consequences
____ circumstances	____ phase	____ abandon
____ ethics	____ focus on	____ adapt to
____ volunteer	____ coordinate	____ community

B. Read the passage from Exercise 1. As you read, look for the target words and circle them. Note that the words in part A are listed in the same order as they appear in the passage but the form may be different.

Human Responses to Disaster

Catastrophic events, such as natural disasters and major terrorist attacks, are extremely traumatic for the people involved. In these situations, where one's own and others' physical safety is threatened, feelings may range from fear, to horror or helplessness. Studies of catastrophe survivors have taught psychologists how individuals who have undergone such traumas and losses respond to these circumstances. Such research is difficult: Ethics prevent psychologists from creating disastrous events in order to study their effects on volunteer subjects. The only way to study these events is to be on the scene after the catastrophe, getting the story from the survivors while it is fresh on their minds. From these stories, psychologists have theorized that responses to extreme natural and human-caused disasters occur in five stages.

The first stage begins immediately after the event and may last for a few moments or several days. During this period, victims experience psychological numbness—a certain inability to think or feel. They may be in a state of shock and confusion, and they have difficulty comprehending what has happened.

This reaction occurs whether or not they have been physically injured themselves during the event.

During the next stage, victims continue to lack awareness of what is going on around them. They appear to function automatically, without conscious control of their thinking or reacting. Later, they may not remember these moments or their actions. When there has been no warning at all of the disaster—as in an earthquake or the September 11, 2001 attacks in New York—this stage lasts longer. While people are in this phase they are also unable to focus their attention on their surroundings or coordinate their actions with other people. This can result in delays in rescue efforts and the loss of lives.

In the third stage after a disaster, victims turn to each other. They pool resources and collaborate in trying to deal with the consequences. At this point, they may experience some pride at having managed to survive, they may be hopeful about the future, and they express their willingness to "roll up their sleeves" and try to rebuild. At the same time, they are physically worn out by the impact of the experience and they may not have much reserve energy.

The fourth stage is when victims are most likely to become depressed or even attempt suicide. They experience a letdown and finally comprehend the full extent of the tragedy. By this time, the public and the media may have lost interest in the disaster and the victims are no longer given special consideration. Though the state of emergency may continue, the survivors feel abandoned and forgotten.

The final period of recovery is the most extended stage, as the survivors struggle to adapt to the changes in their lives. These changes may be personal or they may involve the whole community. In some cases, the victims may have to move elsewhere and start a completely new life. During this phase, survivors feel a basic need to find a meaning in their loss. "Why?" they ask themselves, and they demand answers from those in authority.

C. Working with another student, check to be sure that you have located all of the target words.

EXERCISE 8

A. These sentences are taken from the passage in Exercise 7. Working with another student, read each sentence aloud. Then circle the best meaning or synonym for the underlined word as it is used in the sentence.

1. Catastrophic events, such as natural disasters and major terrorist attacks, are extremely traumatic for the people underlined.

    a. near by   b. left out   c. included

2. Studies of catastrophe survivors have taught psychologists how individuals who have undergone such traumas and losses respond to these circumstances.

    a. experienced   b. seen   c. attempted

3. Studies of catastrophe survivors have taught psychologists how individuals who have undergone such traumas and losses respond to these circumstances.

    a. conditions   b. difficulties   c. memories

4. Ethics prevent psychologists from creating disastrous events in order to study their effects on volunteer subjects.

    a. ordinary customs   b. moral beliefs   c. strong opinions

5. Ethics prevent psychologists from creating disastrous events in order to study their effects on volunteer subjects.

    a. inexperienced   b. professional   c. unpaid

6. During the next stage, victims continue to lack <u>awareness </u>of what is going on around them.

   a. excuses   b. understanding   c. education

7. They appear to <u>function</u> automatically, without conscious control of their thinking or reacting.

   a. behave   b. think   c. understand

8. While people are in this <u>phase</u>, they are also unable to focus their attention on their surroundings or coordinate their actions with other people.

   a. condition   b. age   c. stage

9. While people are in this phase, they are also unable to <u>focus</u> their attention <u>on</u> their surroundings or coordinate their actions with other people.

   a. see clearly   b. take part   c. talk about

10. While people are in this phase, they are also unable to focus their attention on their surroundings or <u>coordinate</u> their actions with other people.

    a. compare   b. organize   c. study

11. They pool resources and <u>collaborate</u> in trying to deal with the consequences.

    a. live together   b. speak together   c. work together

12. They pool resources and collaborate in trying to deal with the <u>consequences</u>.

    a. effects   b. advantages   c. authorities

13. Though the state of emergency may continue, the survivors feel <u>abandoned</u> and forgotten.

    a. left alone   b. unhappy   c. doubtful

14. The final period of recovery is the most extended stage, as the survivors struggle to <u>adapt to</u> the changes in their lives.

    a. learn about   b. describe   c. deal with

15. These changes may be personal or they may involve the whole <u>community</u>.

    a. government   b. town   c. family

B. Compare your answers with those of another pair of students. If you disagree, explain your answers and then use a dictionary to check your work.

A. In this table, write as many different forms of the words as you can thing of without looking in a dictionary.

Noun	Verb	Adjective	Adverb
	abandon	——	——
	adapt		
	——	aware	——
circumstances	——		
	collaborate		
community			
consequences	——		
	coordinate	——	——
ethics	——		
	focus		——
	function		
	involve		——
phase			——
		volunteer	

B. Compare your work with that of another student. Then look in the dictionary for the forms you did not know and write them in the table.

A. Working with another student, write a form of one of the target words in each of the sentences below. Each word may be used only once.

abandon	community	function
adapt to	consequences	involve
aware	coordinate	phase
circumstances	ethics	undergo
collaborate	focus on	volunteer

1. As the disease spread, the patient lost the ability to _____ her movements.

2. Economic _____ were not favorable for a small company in a highly competitive field.

3. In spite of the power shortages, the hospital continued to _____ normally.

4. Proud of the new sports center, the local _____ organized a weekend of activities for young people.

5. The telecommunications industry has _____ enormous changes in the last fifteen years.

6. Since hotels generally do not allow pets, thousands of Italians _____ their pets by the side of the road when they leave for their summer vacations.

7. Relations between the United States and Russia entered into a new _____ with the meeting of the two presidents in Moscow.

8. The movie _____ the many difficulties a foreign worker—even a highly qualified one—faces in England today.

9. The _____ committee of the university has not yet come to a decision about the behavior of Professor Golden.

10. When children enter a new school, they must _____ the new surroundings, the new teacher and the new rules.

11. Dr. Spilotis was well _____ of the fact that some patients had left him for another doctor in town.

12. More than ten hockey players were _____ in the fight that broke out at the end of the first half of the game.

13. Several engineers and architects _____ in the design of the new train station.

14. _____ doctors and nurses who offer their services to an organization called Doctors of the World visit the homeless people living in the streets of Paris.

15. The professor warned her students of the _____ of cheating on a test.

B. Compare your answers with those of another pair of students. If you disagree, explain your answers and look back at the passage to check your work.

EXERCISE 11

A. Make word study cards for the target words that you are still unsure about. Use the cards to study them, first on your own and then with another student. (See Part 2, Unit 1, page 29)

B. 1. Write a sentence for each of the words, leaving a blank instead of the target word. Ask another student to read your sentences and write the target word that should go in each blank.

2. Look at your sentences again. If your classmate wrote a different word, discuss the sentences to find out why. Was your sentence unclear, or did your classmate not know the target word?

UNIT 6 Skimming

Skimming is a form of rapid reading for finding the general idea—or gist—of a passage or a book. In your daily and academic life, you probably skim many things: movie reviews, newspaper articles, and passages and websites that might be useful for a research paper.

When you skim, you have a general question in mind, something you need or want to know about the text, such as:

Skimming Questions

- What is the general meaning?

- Does this agree with what I already know about this subject?

- What is the writer's opinion?

- Will this information be useful to me?

Your eyes should move very quickly as you skim and should focus only on the words or sentences that will answer your questions. Often these are found in the beginning and ending paragraphs, and in the first sentences of the other paragraphs.

Skimming Movie Reviews

Movie reviews in newspapers, magazines, or on the Web usually provide information and the reviewer's opinion about the movie. To get a sense of whether or not you would like to see a movie, you do not have to read the review all the way through—you can skim it.

EXERCISE 1

A. Read the questions and a review of a film called Super Size Me. The review has been edited so you can read only the parts that will help you answer the skimming questions. The first one has been done for you. Work as quickly as you can.

1. What is this movie about?
   The bad effects on the director's health when he ate nothing but food from McDonald's for 30 days.
2. Does this writer have a positive or negative opinion of the movie?

3. Does the writer recommend the movie?

4. In which aspects of the movie is this reviewer most interested?

In this brilliant and innovative documentary, director Morgan Spurlock decided to test McDonald's claim that their food is "good for you." The idea came to him after reading about two fast-food loving, New York teenagers who sued McDonald's

experiment,
30 days
strict diet of fast food.

Before starting his diet, Morgan had a comprehensive medical exam—he was in very

gained 30 pounds (13.5 kg),

the state of his liver.

One could object that no reasonable person would eat all his meals at McDonald's,

Many people eat at fast-food restaurants every week,

almost as many calories as most people should eat in a whole day,

high percentage of saturated fat and very high levels of sodium.

In the movie Spurlock implies that what he undergoes in a month, many Americans experience over a longer period

school lunch programs, schools are promoting the junk food habit from an early age.

At certain points in the film, Spurlock does seem to get carried away with himself.

But on the whole, the movie is fast-paced, laugh-out-loud funny, and very convincing. You'll think twice before you head down the road for your next "Big Mac."

If you do go, however, you may notice one interesting change.

McDonald's eliminated its "Super Size" portions.

B. Compare your answers with those of another student.

C. Now read the entire review on the next page to check the answers to your questions.

SUPER SIZE ME

In this brilliant and innovative documentary, director Morgan Spurlock decided to test McDonald's claim that their food is "good for you." The idea came to him after reading about two fast-food loving, New York teenagers who sued[1] McDonald's as the source of their weight problem. He would film himself as he carried out an experiment, which consisted of living for 30 days on a strict diet of fast food. The rules were simple: he had to eat three meals a day at McDonald's, he had to try everything on the menu at least once, and he always had to "super-size" his meal if asked.

Before starting his diet, Morgan had a comprehensive medical exam—he was in very good shape—and the doctors predicted that the diet would have little effect on his young, healthy body. But check-ups during the experiment proved them wrong: he gained 30 pounds (13.5 kg), his cholesterol soared[2] and after three weeks, one doctor was seriously concerned about the state of his liver.

One could object that no reasonable person would eat all his meals at McDonald's, which is true, of course, but not entirely. Many people eat at fast-food restaurants every week, if not several times a week, since these places offer a quick, relatively cheap meal. Even at that frequency, these meals are far from healthy. The typical order of Big Mac, medium French fries, and strawberry shake includes almost as many calories as most people should eat in a whole day, according to national nutritional guidelines. Furthermore, a meal like that contains a high percentage of saturated fat[3] and very high levels of sodium. True, it might be possible to order a more healthy meal: a small, plain burger, for example, with a diet soda and a small French fries, but how many customers actually choose meals like this?

In the movie Spurlock implies that what he undergoes in a month, many Americans experience over a longer period of regular fast-food consumption. The statistics appear to support his theory that America's waistlines have expanded in direct proportion to the expansion of fast-food chains. Spurlock also backs up his implications with solid reporting about the state of school lunch programs, to show how schools are promoting the junk food habit from an early age.

At certain points in the film, Spurlock does seem to get carried away with himself. We could do without some of the sillier features, such as parodied[4] songs and jokes about the McFish sandwiches. But on the whole, the movie is fast-paced, laugh-out-loud funny, and very convincing. You'll think twice before you head down the road for your next "Big Mac."

If you do go, however, you may notice one interesting change. Just weeks after the movie premiered and won a prize at the Sundance Film Festival, McDonald's eliminated its "Super Size" portions.

---

[1] *sue:* to take legal action against a person or organization
[2] *soar:* to increase quickly to a high level
[3] *saturated fat:* a type of unhealthy fat from meat and dairy products
[4] *parody:* to copy someone's style, especially in an amusing way

EXERCISE 2

A. Read the questions and skim another review of Super Size Me. *This time you must decide which parts to skim. You should skim only those parts of the text that will help you answer the questions. Work as quickly as you can.*

1. Does this writer have a positive or negative opinion of the movie?

2. Does this writer recommend the movie?

3. In which aspect(s) of the movie is this reviewer most interested?

SUPER SIZE ME

This year's most mystifying movie development is just how many otherwise intelligent people have been falling for this steaming pile of junk science and fake journalism from Morgan Spurlock.

Spurlock won Best Director at this year's Sundance Film Festival by videotaping himself eating three meals a day at McDonald's for a month straight, while several outraged doctors charted the inevitable physical damage caused by such a frankly preposterous[1] diet.

I hate to give away "Super Size Me's" ending, but it turns out that if you stop exercising and start stuffing your face with nothing but junk fast food, you're probably going to get very fat and very sick.

No kidding, Spurlock.

"Where does personal responsibility end and corporate responsibility begin?" the director asks at the outset. Not a bad question. Too bad his film has no interest in addressing it. Spurlock throws up a series of irrelevant figures and mean-spirited man-on-the-street interviews, all the while carefully avoiding any serious discussion of the issues.

For example, one short sequence showing the deplorable[2] state of our nation's school lunch programs is quickly taken off the screen to make room for more long segments in which Spurlock dances around in his red-white-and-blue underpants while rubbing his new tummy and complaining about his "Mc-Stomach-ache."

Given the obesity[3] epidemic[4] in this country, we need to start talking frankly about what we're eating—and how little we're exercising—a rather crucial side of the subject that this movie does not address at all. Yet most of "Super Size Me" is a not-so-amusing account of the filmmaker's rapidly declining health (though it should be noted that Spurlock seems to find his own jokes absolutely hilarious).

Abandoning any interesting questions raised in the opening minutes, "Super Size Me" quickly starts accusing the evil fast-food corporations. Here's where Spurlock undermines[5] his own thesis, as I don't recall any McDonald's commercials (or executives for that matter) saying that you should never eat anything besides their food, and I doubt many Americans actually live that way.

So why did Spurlock decide to base his film on such an absurd stunt?[6] Because otherwise "Super Size Me" wouldn't have had as much marketing appeal.

Spurlock touches on serious issues, but his movie is all self-promotion, empty calories, and sugar shock. Ironically enough, he's made the documentary equivalent of fast food. "Super Size Me" is as childish and gimmicky[7] as a Happy Meal, and nearly as indigestible.[8]

(Source: Adapted from a review by Sean Burns in *Philadelphia Weekly*, May 12, 2004)

---

[1] *preposterous:* completely silly and unreasonable
[2] *deplorable:* very bad, shocking, and unacceptable
[3] *obesity:* the state of being extremely overweight
[4] *epidemic:* something bad that develops and spreads quickly
[5] *undermine:* to make something less strong
[6] *absurd stunt:* silly and unreasonable action to get attention
[7] *gimmicky:* tricky and attention-getting
[8] *indigestible:* difficult for the stomach

B. Compare your answers with those of another student. If you disagree, look back at the review to check your work.

C. Look for another review of Super Size Me *or an article about its director, Morgan Spurlock, on the Internet. Skim the review or article and answer the questions in part A. Compare your work with that of another student.*

Skimming for Research

Skimming is especially useful when you need to do research, since it allows you to look quickly through lots of material to get a general idea of the content and to decide if it is relevant for your purposes.

EXERCISE 3

A. Read the research question.

Research question:

In the United States, the infant mortality rate is 7.0 (seven deaths for every thousand babies under the age of one). Though this is lower than the mortality rate in many developing countries (which range up to 287.5 in Angola), it is higher than in all other developed countries. It is higher even than the rate in some developing countries, such as Cuba or Singapore (with the lowest rate of 2.29). What could explain the relatively high infant mortality rate in the United States?

B. Skim the following three articles about infant mortality and write the answers to the skimming questions. Work as quickly as you can.

Article a
Skimming questions:

1. Does this article contain information that is useful for your research?

2. Does it discuss the cause(s) of the high infant mortality rate in the United States?

3. If so, what causes are mentioned?

ABC News: U.S. Babies Die at a Higher Rate

by Marc Lallanilla

What's causing the increased death rate among babies in the United States?

While the health of infants in many countries is improving, babies born in the United States now face an increased risk of dying in the first year of life.

The U.S. infant mortality rate is on the rise for the first time since 1958, according to the Centers for Disease Control and Prevention. In 2001, the infant mortality rate was 6.8 deaths per 1,000 live births—in 2002, the rate rose to 7.0. (2003 data is not yet complete.)

At the same time, other countries are improving their infant mortality rates to the point that they have surpassed[1] the United States. Cuba, for example, reported a lower 2002 rate than the United States at 6.3.

The CIA World Factbook estimates the infant mortality rate in the United States is now comparable to Croatia, Lithuania and Taiwan. Most analysts currently rank the United States 28th in the world in infant mortality, far behind other industrialized nations such as Sweden, France, Japan and Germany.

Premature Births Increase in U.S.

According to health care experts, there is no simple explanation for the increase in U.S. infant mortality.

"But there are a number of factors that could contribute," said Dr. William A. Engle, neonatologist with the Indiana University School of Medicine in Indianapolis. "The number of babies born pre-term[2] has increased in general, and pre-term populations are at a high risk for morbidity and mortality," Engle said.

Births of two or more babies are often associated with prematurity[3], and, Engle said, "The number of multiple births has increased." Some of these multiple births are the result of fertility drugs[4] and in-vitro fertilization procedures[5]. [...]

African-American Rates Alarmingly High

Within the United States, there are important differences in the infant mortality rates between racial groups and across geographic boundaries.

"Infant mortality rates tend to trend with socio-economic status," said Dr. Nancy Green, medical director for the March of Dimes [a charity organization]. "African-Americans have much, much higher rates of infant mortality than other groups."

The rate among African-Americans is nearly double that of the general population: 13.9 versus 7.0. Rates among some other ethnic minorities also tend to be higher: the infant mortality rate among Puerto Ricans is 8.2, and for Native Americans, the rate is 9.1. "Some of that is due to poverty, but it doesn't track perfectly with poverty," said Green. The infant mortality rate among Central and South American immigrants, for example, is only 5.1.

(Source: http://abcnews.go.com/Health)

---

[1] *surpass:* to become better than someone or something
[2] *pre-term:* before time
[3] *prematurity:* born before time
[4] *fertility drugs:* drugs that increase a woman's ability to have a baby
[5] *in-vitro fertilization procedure:* a process in which a doctor places several fertilized eggs in the womb

4. Does this article contain information that is useful for your research?

5. Does it discuss the cause(s) of the high infant mortality rate in the United States?

6. If so, what causes are mentioned?

U.S. Infant Mortality Rate
Up for First Time in Four Decades While Overall
National Health Improvement Slowed

For the first time in 40 years, the infant mortality rate in the U.S. has increased, with seven out of every 1,000 children born in America dying within their first year of life, according to the annual report "America's Health: State Health Rankings," issued by the United Health Foundation, together with the American Public Health Association (APHA) and Partnership for Prevention. The report, available online, was released at the APHA meeting in Washington, D.C., on November 8.

Infant mortality is one of the more sensitive measures of a community's health, since data can be tracked in increments[1] of months as opposed to years, said Georges Benjamin, executive director of APHA at a press conference. He pointed to a number of factors that may be associated with the increase, including women receiving less prenatal[2] care or losing their jobs, cuts to nutrition programs, and climbing poverty rates. A commentary published in the report pointed to an increase in premature births as a culprit,[3] too.

The U.S. infant mortality rate is about double the rate found in Hong Kong (3.1) and Japan (3.4), according to "America's Health." [...] In the National Center for Health Statistics survey, the U.S. ranked 28th among 37 nations. [...]

Reed Tuckson, vice president of United Health Foundation, pointed out that the subtitle of the report is "A Call to Action for People and Their Communities." That may be because there is bad news on other fronts as well. Since 1990, the prevalence of obesity has increased by 97 percent, and the number of uninsured rose by 16 percent, according to the report. Since just last year, there was an 8 percent increase in the number of children living in poverty.

These unsettling statistics emerge against a backdrop in which improvements in the overall health of the nation have slowed dramatically since 2000. During the 1990s, health in the United States advanced by an annual rate of 1.5 percent each year, according to the report. However, during the 2000s, health improvement in the country slowed to an annual rate of only 0.2 percent each year—one eighth the rate of the 1990s.

(Source: *Harvard Public Health Now*, December 10, 2004)

---

[1] *increment:* an amount by which a number or amount increases
[2] *prenatal:* before birth
[3] *culprit:* a reason for or cause of a problem

7. Does this article contain information that is useful for your research?

8. Does it discuss the cause(s) of the high infant mortality rate in the United States?

9. If so, what causes are mentioned?

Eliminate Disparities[1] in Infant Mortality

What is the burden[2] of Infant Mortality?

Infant mortality is used to compare the health and well-being of populations across and within countries. The infant mortality rate, the rate at which babies less than one year of age die, has continued to steadily decline over the past several decades (from 26.0 per 1,000 live births in 1960 to 7.0 per 1,000 live births in 2002). The United States ranked 43rd in the world in 2000. This ranking is due in large part to disparities which continue to exist among various racial and ethnic groups in this country, particularly African Americans.

Examples of Important Disparities

Infant mortality among African Americans in 2000 occurred at a rate of 14.1 deaths per 1,000 live births. This is more than twice the national average of 7.0 deaths per 1,000 live births. The leading causes of infant death include congenital abnormalities[3], pre-term/low birth weight, Sudden Infant Death Syndrome (SIDS), problems related to complications of pregnancy, and respiratory[4] distress syndrome. [...]

Promising Strategies

Focus on modifying the behaviors, lifestyles, and conditions that affect birth outcomes, such as smoking, substance abuse, poor nutrition, lack of prenatal care, medical problems, and chronic[5] illness. Public health agencies, health care providers, and communities of all ethnic groups must partner to lower the infant mortality rate in the United States. This joint approach should address the behaviors, lifestyles, and conditions that affect birth outcomes. Substantial investments have been made in consultation, research, and service delivery to reduce disparities in access to health care and health status. The plan to reduce infant mortality includes:

- A network between health care experts and minority communities to encourage healthy behaviors by pregnant women and parents of infants.

- Research that will determine the cause of SIDS, develop effective strategies to identify at-risk infants more precisely and create effective interventions for high-risk infants.

What Can Healthcare Providers Do to Help Reduce Infant Mortality Rates?

Health care providers should advise their patients about factors that affect birth outcomes, such as maternal smoking, drug and alcohol abuse, poor nutrition, stress, insufficient prenatal care, chronic illness or other medical problems.

What Can Communities and Individuals Do to Help Reduce Infant Mortality Rates?

Communities can play an important role in this effort by encouraging pregnant women to seek

---

[1] *disparities:* unfair differences
[2] *burden:* difficulty
[3] *congenital abnormalities:* conditions that one's born with that are not normal
[4] *respiratory:* relating to breathing
[5] *chronic:* continuing, ongoing

prenatal care in the first trimester,[6] which will ensure a better birth outcome than little or no prenatal care. Parents and caregivers should place sleeping infants on their backs and reduce bed sharing. Research has demonstrated that babies who slept on their stomachs were at a higher risk for SIDS.

(Source: The Office of Minority Health, Centers for Disease Control and Prevention. http://www.cdc.gov)

---

[6] *trimester:* the first three months of a pregnancy

C. Compare your answers with those of another student. If you disagree, refer to the articles to explain your answers.

D. Discuss the following questions with another pair of students.

1. Which article is most helpful in answering the research question? Why?

2. Do all three articles agree on the underlying causes of the poor infant mortality rate in the United States? If not, how do they differ?

Focus on Vocabulary

EXERCISE 4

A. Check your understanding of the following target words. Read each word aloud and then write S, M, or N beside it.

S = *you are sure of the meaning of the word*
M = *you think you might know the meaning of the word*
N = *you don't know the meaning of the word at all*

____ innovative	____ statistics	____ eliminate
____ source	____ promote	____ portion
____ comprehensive	____ feature	
____ guideline	____ convince	

B. *Read the passage from Exercise 1 on page 172. As you read, look for the target words and circle them. Note that the words in Part A are listed in the same order as they appear in the passage but the form may be different.*

SUPER SIZE ME

In this brilliant and innovative documentary, director Morgan Spurlock decided to test McDonald's claim that their food is "good for you." The idea came to him after reading about two fast-food loving New York teenagers who sued McDonald's as the source of their weight problem. He would film himself as he carried out an experiment, which consisted of living for 30 days on a strict diet of fast food. The rules were simple: he had to eat three meals a day at McDonald's, he had to try everything on the menu at least once, and he always had to "super-size" his meal if asked.

Before starting his diet, Morgan had a comprehensive medical exam—he was in very good shape—and the doctors predicted that the diet would have little effect on his young, healthy body. But check-ups during the experiment proved them wrong: he gained 30 pounds (13.5 kg), his cholesterol soared and after three weeks, one doctor was seriously concerned about the state of his liver.

One could object that no reasonable person would eat all his meals at McDonald's, which is true, of course, but not entirely. Many people eat at fast-food restaurants every week, if not several times a week, since these places offer a quick, relatively cheap meal. Even at that frequency, these meals are far from healthy. The typical order of Big Mac, medium French fries, and strawberry shake includes almost as many calories as most people should eat in a whole day, according to national nutritional guidelines. Furthermore, a meal like that contains a high percentage of saturated fat and very high levels of sodium. True, it might be possible to order a more healthy meal: a small, plain burger, for example, with a diet soda and a small French fries, but how many customers actually choose meals like this?

In the movie Spurlock implies that what he undergoes in a month, many Americans experience over a longer period of regular fast-food consumption. The statistics appear to support his theory that America's waistlines have expanded in direct proportion to the expansion of fast-food chains. Spurlock also backs up his implications with solid reporting about the state of school lunch programs, to show how schools are promoting the junk food habit from an early age.

At certain points in the film, Spurlock does seem to get carried away with himself. We could do without some of the sillier features, such as parodied songs and jokes about McFish sandwiches. But on the whole, the movie is fast-paced, laugh-out-loud funny, and very convincing. You'll think twice before you head down the road for your next "Big Mac."

If you do go, however, you may notice one interesting change. Just weeks after the movie premiered and won a prize at the Sundance Film Festival, McDonald's eliminated its "Super Size" portions.

C. *Working with another student, check to be sure that you have located all of the target words.*

A. These sentences are taken from the passage in Exercise 4. Working with another student, read each sentence aloud. Then circle the best meaning or synonym for the underlined word as it is used in the sentence.

1. In this brilliant and <u>innovative</u> documentary, director Morgan Spurlock decided to test McDonald's claim that their food is "good for you."

   a. realistic and true   b. long and interesting   c. new and different

2. The idea came to him after reading about two fast-food loving New York teenagers who sued McDonald's as the <u>source</u> of their weight problem.

   a. cause   b. solution   c. result

3. Before starting his diet, Morgan had a <u>comprehensive</u> medical exam—he was in very good shape—and the doctors predicted that the diet would have little effect on his young, healthy body.

   a. regular   b. special   c. complete

4. The typical order of Big Mac, medium French fries, and strawberry shake includes almost as many calories as most people should eat in a whole day, according to national nutritional <u>guidelines</u>.

   a. habits   b. laws   c. information

5. The <u>statistics</u> appear to support his theory that America's waistlines have expanded in direct proportion to the expansion of fast-food chains.

   a. theories   b. audience   c. facts

6. Spurlock also backs up his implications with solid reporting about the state of school lunch programs, to show how schools are <u>promoting</u> the junk food habit from an early age.

   a. preparing   b. encouraging   c. serving

7. We could do without some of the sillier <u>features</u>, such as parodied songs and jokes about McFish sandwiches.

   a. ideas   b. actors   c. parts

8. But on the whole, the movie is fast-paced, laugh-out-loud funny, and very <u>convincing</u>.

   a. believable   b. boring   c. exciting

9. Just weeks after the movie premiered and won a prize at the Sundance Film Festival, McDonald's <u>eliminated</u> its "Super Size" portions.

   a. made larger   b. ran out of   c. got rid of

10. Just weeks after the movie premiered and won a prize at the Sundance Film Festival, McDonald's eliminated its "Super Size" <u>portions</u>.

    a. servings   b. advertisements   c. customers

B. Compare your answers with those of another pair of students. If you disagree, explain your answers and then use a dictionary to check your work.

A. In this table, write as many different forms of the words as you can think of without looking in a dictionary.

Noun	Verb	Adjective	Adverb
		comprehensive	
	convince		
	eliminate	——	——
feature		——	——
		innovative	
portion		——	——
	promote		
source		——	——
statistic(s)	——		

B. Compare your work with that of another student. Then look in the dictionary for the forms you did not know and write them in the table.

A. Working with another student, write a form of one of the target words in each of the sentences below. Each word may be used only once.

comprehensive	guideline	source
convince	innovative	statistics
eliminate	portion	
feature	promote	

1. With the new evidence, the man was able to _____ the judge that he was innocent.

2. The modern factory farm is a major _____ of pollution.

3. According to recent _____, the population of Japan is the oldest in the world.

4. Many American restaurants serve _____ that are far too large for the average person.

5. One positive _____ of the new airport is the excellent sound system.

6. To be successful in this highly competitive market, companies must _____ constantly.

7. A _____ insurance plan should cover all the possible risks.

8. The American ex-president Jimmy Carter has been a strong _____ of peace around the world.

9. After the football player was found with drugs, he was _____ from the team.

10. According to the new local _____ for water use, families should not wash their cars or water lawns during the day.

B. Compare your answers with those of another pair of students. If you disagree, explain your answers and then use a dictionary to check your work.

EXERCISE 8

A. Make word study cards for the target words that you are still unsure about. Use the cards to study the words, first on your own and then with another student. (See Part 2, Unit 1, page 29)

B. 1. Write a sentence for each of the words, leaving a blank instead of the target word. Ask another student to read your sentences and write the target word that should go in each blank.

2. *Look at your sentences again. If your classmate wrote a different word, discuss the sentences to find out why. Was your sentence unclear, or did your classmate not know the target word?*

UNIT 7 Study Reading

In this unit you will practice three strategies for studying texts so you can make sure that you learn and remember what you have read.

Strategy 1: Text Marking

When you are reading a text that contains many facts and ideas, it is helpful to mark the important facts and ideas so that they stand out and can be used for reviewing and remembering the material.

What to mark in a text

You should select and make visually memorable only the most important information or ideas:

- the topic of the passage
- the thesis statement, if the thesis is directly stated
- signals for the overall pattern of the passage
- the main idea
- the details that support the thesis or main idea, including key dates or names
- ideas that seem to differ from what you already know or have read about
- terms or points that are difficult to understand

How to mark a text

The following is a list of different kinds of marking that good students often use. You should try out all of these techniques and then decide which ones work best for you. Experienced readers develop their own personal style of marking, usually a combination of various techniques.

- Underlining (in pencil)
- Circling or making a box around words or phrases
- Drawing lines or arrows from one part of the text to another
- Writing a key word, date, or name in the margin
- Making a star or arrow in the margin beside an important point
- Making a question mark or exclamation point to express your reaction
- Numbering points in a series

Note: Always preview a text before you read it and mark it. And always mark in pencil so you can make changes if necessary.

Example:

A. Preview the passage on the next page and then read it carefully. Look at the way it has been marked to identify the thesis, the pattern signals, and the supporting points.

The Cultivation of the Pineapple

The pineapple has been cultivated and enjoyed by humans for thousands of years. According to archaeologists, evidence from drawings on ancient Peruvian pottery shows that Native Americans were cultivating the pineapple in about 1,000 A.D. Furthermore, some botanists believe that people in South and Central America began *definition* cultivating it much earlier. Cultivated pineapples do not produce seeds. This fact indicates that the plant has been dependent on humans for its reproduction for such a long time that it no longer can reproduce by itself.

When Europeans discovered the pineapple at the end of the fifteenth century, it was a case of love at first sight. Many of the early explorers reported favorably about this new fruit, saying that it had a delightful smell and a sweet, refreshing taste. In fact, of all the new American fruits that were brought back to Europe, the pineapple was the most successful. While other fruits, such as the tomato, were regarded with great suspicion and believed to be poisonous, the pineapple was accepted relatively quickly.

Throughout the sixteenth century, the ships of the European explorers carried pineapples from Central and South America to other parts of the world. During these voyages, the fruit provided an excellent source of fresh food and vitamins for the ship's crew. Furthermore, when they arrived the travelers found that, if the climate was suitable, it was easy to grow more fruit from the cut-off tops of pineapples. By the end of the sixteenth century pineapples were being cultivated in parts of India, Africa, and China. In Europe, the climate was generally too cold, so the fruit could be grown only by wealthy people with heated greenhouses.

Pineapples remained a luxury food until the early twentieth century, when they became more easily available. Faster shipping and improved rail and road connections made it possible to bring the pineapples to new markets. Then, with the advent[1] of safe industrial canning methods, factories could produce canned pineapple for mass markets. As the fruit became more available and better known, demand rose rapidly for both fresh and canned pineapple. Production quickly expanded to meet that demand, most notably in Hawaii, which dominates the world market. Today, Puerto Rico, the Philippines, Kenya, and Thailand are also important pineapple producers.

———
[1] *advent:* beginning

B. Use the text marking in the passage to help you write the following information.

Overall pattern of organization: _____

Thesis statement: _____

_____

Supporting points (main ideas):

Paragraph 2: _____

Paragraph 3: _____

Paragraph 4: _____

C. Compare your work with that of another student. If you disagree, look back at the text and explain your answers.

A. Preview the passage below and then read it carefully. Mark the text to show the thesis, the pattern signals, and supporting points. Try to use as many different kinds of markings as you can: underlining, marginal notes, circles, numbers, or arrows.

The History of Pizza

One of the most popular foods around the world today is pizza. Pizza restaurants are popular everywhere from Beijing to Moscow to Rio, and even in the United States, the home of the hamburger, there are more pizza restaurants than hamburger places. This worldwide love for pizza is a fairly recent phenomenon. Before the 1950s, pizza was a purely Italian food, with a long history in southern Italy.

The origins of pizza are somewhat uncertain, though they may go back to the Greeks (*pita* bread) or even earlier. Under the Roman Empire, Italians often ate flat circles of bread, which they may have flavored with olive oil, cheese, and herbs. By about the year 1000 A.D. in the area around Naples, this bread had a name: *picea*.

This early kind of pizza lacked one of the main ingredients we associate with pizza: the tomato. In fact, tomatoes did not exist in Europe until the sixteenth century, when Spanish explorers brought them back from South America. The Spanish showed little interest in tomatoes, but southern Italians soon began to cultivate them and use them in cooking. At some point in the 1600s, Neapolitan tomatoes were added to *pizza*, as it was known by then.

The next development in pizza making came about, according to legend, in June 1889, when a Neapolitan pizza maker was asked to make pizza for the king and queen. To show his patriotism, he decided to make it green, white, and red, like the Italian flag, using basil leaves, mozzarella, and tomato. He named his pizza "Margherita," after the queen, and that is what this classic kind of pizza is still called today.

In Italy, pizza remained a specialty of Naples and other areas of the south until well into the twentieth century. Then, in the 1950s and 60s, when many southerners moved to the north to work in the new factories, pizzerias opened up in many northern Italian cities. By the 1980s, they could be found all over the country and pizza had become a part of the Italian way of life.

Today, pizza has become so common in so many countries that its Italian origins are often forgotten. Indeed, the global versions of pizza made with all kinds of ingredients have little in common with the Neapolitan original, as anyone knows who has tasted a pizza in Naples.

B. Use your text marking in the passage to help you write the following information. Change your marking if it does not indicate these points.

Overall pattern of organization: _____

Thesis statement: _____

_____

Supporting points (main ideas):

Paragraph 2: _____

Paragraph 3: _____

Paragraph 4: _____

Paragraph 5: _____

Paragraph 6: _____

C. Compare your work with that of another student. If you disagree, look back at the text and explain your answers.

Strategy 2: Writing Questions for More Effective Reading

In addition to marking a text, write study questions and quiz questions:

- Before you read, use the title, headings and subheadings to form questions about the text. This will help you focus your thinking.

- When you have finished reading and marking the text, write quiz questions about the important facts and ideas to help reinforce your learning.

Example:

A. Read this study question based on the title of the passage below, which is the introduction to a section of a sociology textbook.

Study question: _How is this passage going to analyze urbanization?_

B. Read the passage and look for the answer to the study question. Note facts and ideas that have been marked in the text.

A GLOBAL ANALYSIS OF URBANIZATION[1]

In 1693, William Penn wrote that "the country life is to be preferred for there we see the works of God but in cities little else than the work of man." Most people at the time probably agreed with him. Less than 2 percent of the world's population then were urban dwellers.[2] But in 1998, about 44 percent of the world's population lived in urban areas and more than 50 percent will do so by the end of 2010 (Haub, 1999; Linden, 1993; Fischer, 1984).

While urban populations have grown, cities themselves have changed. We can identify three *** periods in their history: the preindustrial, industrial, and metropolitan-megalopolitan stages.
①   ②   ③

---
[1] *urbanization:* development of cities
[2] *dweller:* resident

C. Working with another student, answer the quiz questions below without looking back at the passage. Then check your answers by reading the passage again.

1. _What percent of the world's population lived in cities in the 1600s?_

2. _How many will live in cities by the end of 2010?_

3. _What are the three different stages of urbanization that occurred over the years?_

A. Preview the next section from the sociology textbook and write a study question from the title.

Study question: _____

B. Now read the section and mark the key facts and ideas in the text.

The Preindustrial City

For more than 99 percent of the time that we humans have been on Earth, our ancestors have roamed about in search of food. They have hunted, fished, and gathered edible plants, but they have never found enough food in more than one place to sustain them for very long. They have had to move on, traveling in small bands from one place to another.

Then, about 10,000 years ago, technological advances allowed people to stop their wandering. This was the dawn of what is called the *Neolithic period*. People now had the simple tools and the know-how to cultivate plants and domesticate animals. They could produce their food supplies in one locale, and they settled down and built villages. The villages were very small—with only about 200 to 400 residents each. For the next 5,000 years, villagers produced just enough food to feed themselves.

About 5,000 years ago, humans developed more powerful technologies. Thanks to innovations like the ox-drawn plow, irrigation, and metallurgy, farmers could produce more food than they needed to sustain themselves and their families. Because of this food surplus, some people abandoned agriculture and made their living by weaving, making pottery, and practicing other specialized crafts. Methods of transporting and storing food were also improved. The result was the emergence of cities.

Cities first arose on the fertile banks of such rivers as the Nile of Egypt, the Euphrates and Tigris in the Middle East, the Indus in Pakistan, and the Yellow River in China. Similar urban settlements later appeared in other parts of the world. The *preindustrial* cities were small compared with the cities of today. Most had populations of 5,000 to 10,000 people. Only a few cities had more than 100,000 and even Rome never had more than several hundred thousand.

Several factors prevented expansion of the preindustrial city. By modern standards, agricultural techniques were still primitive. It took at least 75 farmers to produce enough of a surplus to support just one city dweller. For transportation, people had to depend on their own muscle power or that of animals. It was difficult to carry food supplies from farms to cities, and even more difficult to transport heavy materials for construction in the cities. Poor sanitation, lack of sewer facilities, and ineffective medicine kept the death rate high. Epidemics regularly killed as much as half of a city's population. Moreover, families still had a strong attachment to the land, which discouraged immigration to the cities. All these characteristics of preindustrial society kept the cities small (Davis, 1955).

C. Compare your study question and text markings with those of another student. If you disagree, look back at the text to explain your work. Then write three quiz questions about this section.

1. _____

2. _____

3. _____

D. Ask another pair of students to answer your questions without looking back at the text. Then check the text for the answers.

A. *Preview the next section from the sociology textbook and write a study question from the title.*

Study question: _____

B. *Now read the section and mark the key facts and ideas in the text.*

The Industrial City

For almost 5,000 years, cities changed little. Then their growth, in size and number, was so rapid that it has been called an *urban revolution* or *urban explosion.* In 1700, less than 2 percent of the population of Great Britain lived in cities, but by 1900, the majority of the British did so. Other European countries and the United States soon achieved the same level of urbanization in an even shorter period. Today, these and other Western countries are among the most urbanized in the world, along with many Latin American countries, which have become mostly urbanized in more recent years.

The major stimulus to the urban explosion was the Industrial Revolution. It triggered a series of related events, identified by sociologist Philip Hauser (1981) as population explosion, followed by population displosion and population implosion, and then by technoplosion. Industrialization first causes a rise in production growth, and the mechanization of farming brings about an agricultural surplus. Fewer farmers can support more people—and thus larger urban populations (*population explosion).* Workers no longer needed on the farms move to the city.

There is, then, displacement of people from rural to urban areas (*population displosion)* and a greater concentration of people in a limited area *(population implosion).* The development of other new technologies *(technoplosion)* spurs on urbanization. Improved transportation, for example, speeds the movement of food and other materials to urban centers.

The outcome of these events was the *industrial city.* Compared with the preindustrial city, the industrial city was larger, more densely settled, and more diverse. It was a place where large numbers of people—with a wide range of skills, interests, and cultural backgrounds—could live and work together in a limited space. Also, unlike the preindustrial city, which had served primarily as a religious or governmental center, the industrial city was a commercial hub. In fact, its abundant job opportunities attracted so many rural migrants that migration accounted for the largest share of its population growth. Without these migrants, cities would not have grown at all because of the high mortality rate brought about by extremely poor sanitary conditions.

C. *Compare your study question and text markings with those of another student. If you disagree, look back at the text to explain your work. Then write three quiz questions about this section.*

1. _____

2. _____

3. _____

D. *Ask another pair of students to answer your questions without looking back at the text. Then check the text for the answers.*

A. Preview the next section from the sociology textbook and write a study question from the title.

Study question: _____

B. Now read the section and mark the key facts and ideas in the text.

Metropolis and Megalopolis

Early in this century, the large cities of the industrialized nations began to spread outward. They formed **metropolises**, large urban areas that include a city and its surrounding suburbs. Some of these suburbs are politically separate from their central cities, but socially, economically, and geographically, the suburbs and the city are tied together. The U.S. Census Bureau recognizes this unity by defining what is called a *Standard Metropolitan Statistical Area,* which cuts across political boundaries. Since 1990, most U.S. residents have been living in metropolitan areas with 1 million residents or more (Suro, 1991).

In the United States, the upper and middle classes have usually sparked[1] the expansion of cities outward. Typically, as migrants from rural areas moved into the central city, the wealthier classes moved to the suburbs. The automobile greatly facilitated this development. It encouraged people to leave the crowded inner city for the more comfortable life of the suburbs, if they could afford it. As the number of cars increased, so did the size of suburbs and metropolises. In 1900, there were only 8,000 cars in the United States; by 1930, the number had soared to more than 26 million. Meanwhile, the proportion of the U.S. population living in the suburbs grew from only 15.7 percent in 1910 to 49.6 percent in 1950 (Glaab and Brown, 1983).

Since 1950, virtually all the growth in metropolitan areas has occurred in the suburbs. During the 1960s, U.S. suburbs grew four times faster than inner cities, and stores and entertainment facilities followed the people there. Suburban jobs increased 44 percent, while inner-city employment dropped 7 percent. This pattern of suburban growth at the expense of the urban core continued in the 1970s and 1980s. Today, suburbanites outnumber city residents three to two (U.S. Census Bureau, 2003; Gottdiener, 1983; Jaaret, 1983).

As suburbs expand, they sometimes combine with the suburbs of adjacent metropolitan areas to form a **megalopolis**, a vast area in which many metropolises merge.[2] For hundreds of miles from one major city to the next, suburbs and cities have merged with one another to form a continuous region in which distinctions between suburban, urban, and rural areas are blurred.[3] The hundreds of miles from Boston to Washington, D.C., form one such megalopolis; another stretches from Detroit through Chicago to Milwaukee in the Midwest; and a third goes from San Francisco to San Diego.

---

[1] *spark:* to cause
[2] *merge:* to join together
[3] *blurred:* not clear

C. Compare your study question and text markings with those of another student. If you disagree, look back at the text to explain your work. Then write three quiz questions about this section.

1. _____
2. _____
3. _____

D. Ask another pair of students to answer your questions without looking back at the text. Then check the text for the answers.

A. *Preview the next section from the sociology textbook and write a study question from the title.*

Study question: _____

B. *Now read the section and mark the key facts and ideas in the text.*

The World's Megacities

The world's urban population has grown so fast that today, there are about 40 megacities—cities with populations of 5 million or more. Generally, the poorer the country, the faster its urban growth. Thus, today, only three of the world's megacities are in the United States, and more than half are in developing countries. Many more cities in the developing world will soon become megacities.

Since the emergence of the pre-industrial city 5,000 years ago, great cities have risen and fallen. The same is true today. One city that is collapsing[1] is Kinshasa, the capital of Zaire. Although the country is endowed with[2] abundant natural resources, such as gold, diamonds, copper, and rich agricultural land, Kinshasa has produced massive miseries under the corrupt[3] 30-year-reign of former President Sese Mobutu. Government officials have routinely looted[4] manufactured goods, fuel, food, and medical supplies, even most of the emergency food aid sent by foreign countries. As a result, the annual inflation rate[5] has often soared to more than 3,000 percent and the jobless rate to 80 percent, posing serious threats of starvation and epidemics. In contrast, the city of Curitiba in Brazil is a success story. The city is not rich, but its government makes the most of its resources. One example is

recycling: Parks are lit with lamps made from soda bottles, and some government offices were built in part with old telephone poles. The city also delivers excellent services, including a highly efficient bus system and well-constructed housing projects for the poor (Zwingle, 2002; Linden, 1993).

Most megacities fit between these two contrasting types. They are saddled with[6] serious problems but manage to cope reasonably well, usually in ways that reflect the nature of their societies. Consider Tokyo, for example—the world's most densely populated metropolis. It faces enormous problems, such as overwhelming amounts of waste, traffic-choked streets, and sky-high housing costs. But the technologically advanced Japanese have, among other things, developed an urban heat system that extracts heat from sewage, which is then used to regulate the temperature in several of Tokyo's buildings. To reduce traffic jams, the city has used wireless communication to show drivers whose cars have a computerized navigation system where the congested[7] streets are. And to lower housing costs, Tokyo has started planning to build an underground city (Kuchment, 2003; Wehrfritz and Itoi, 2003; Linden, 1993).

(Source: From Alex Thio, *Sociology: A Brief Introduction*, 6/e. Published by Allyn & Bacon, Boston, MA. © 2005 by Pearson Education. Reprinted by permission of the publisher.)

[1] *collapse:* to fall down in a ruined condition
[2] *to be endowed with:* to naturally have a good quality
[3] *corrupt:* dishonest
[4] *loot:* to steal
[5] *inflation rate:* rise in prices
[6] *to be saddled with:* to struggle with
[7] *congested:* crowded with traffic

C. Compare your study question and text markings with those of another student. If you disagree, look back at the text to explain your work. Then write three quiz questions about this section.

1. _____

2. _____

3. _____

D. Ask another pair of students to answer your questions without looking back at the text. Then check the text for the answers.

Strategy 3: Connecting Graphics and Ideas

Textbooks and newspaper or magazine articles often use graphics to help make a point. These graphics can come in many different forms: graphs, charts, tables and diagrams. Always look at graphics carefully and connect them to specific parts of the text.

Example:

A. Read this passage and study the graph showing the different ethnic backgrounds of millionaires in the United States. The underlined parts of the passage relate to the graph.

The Top Groups of U.S. Millionaires

The economic dominance of English Americans has faced vigorous <u>challenges from other European Americans</u>, who have rapidly moved up the ladder of success in business and other fields. Here is how <u>English Americans</u> compare with Americans of other European ancestries in percentage of <u>households having a net worth of $1 million or more.</u>

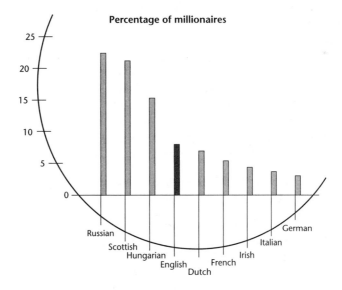

Refer to the graph and the text to answer these questions.

   1. Which ethnic group has produced the fewest millionaires?

   2. Which has produced the most?

   3. Approximately how many millionaires are of Irish ancestry?

   4. Approximately how many are of English ancestry?

C. *Compare your work with that of another student. If you disagree, look back at the text and the graph and explain your work.*

A. *Read this passage and study the graph showing differences in earnings for U.S. workers according to gender and ethnicity. Underline the parts of the passage that relate to the graph.*

Pay Levels for Women

Despite these protections, the earnings gap that many people see between the wages of men and women is only gradually being closed. Historically, this gap has been the result of social conditions for women. [...] Much progress has been made in creating job opportunities for women. Yet some qualified women still find that they cannot advance beyond a certain level in the companies they work for.

Pay Levels for Minorities

Minorities tend to earn lower pay than whites do. Income differences between minority workers and white workers are caused partly by productivity differences. On average, whites historically have had access to more education and work experience, giving them more human capital and hence higher wages. In part, non-discrimination laws are designed to help minority workers get more access to job opportunities where they can improve their skills and build their experience. The goal is that over time these workers will be able to compete equally in the labor market and contribute more to the productive capacity of America.

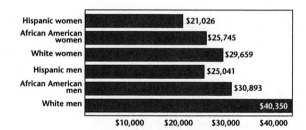

Median[1] Earnings for U.S. Workers, by Gender and Ethnicity, 2000

Source: U.S. Census Bureau

---

[1] *median:* the middle number in a set of numbers arranged in order

(Source: Arthur O'Sullivan and Steven M. Sheffrin *Economics: Principles and Tools,* 2nd Edition. Upper Saddle River, NJ: Prentice Hall, 2003)

B. Refer to the graph and the text to answer these questions.

1. Which group has the lowest median earnings?

2. Which group has the highest median earnings?

3. Which group has higher median earnings—African American women or African American men?

4. Which group has higher median earnings—White women or Hispanic women?

C. Compare your work with that of another student. If you disagree, look back at the text and the graph and explain your work.

Focus on Vocabulary

EXERCISE 7

A. Check your understanding of the following target words. Read each word aloud and then write **S, M,** *or* **N** *beside it.*

S = *you are sure of the meaning of the word*
M = *you think you might know the meaning of the word*
N = *you don't know the meaning of the word at all*

____ facilitate	____ major	____ pose
____ virtually	____ distinction	____ construct
____ core	____ emergence	____ extract
____ adjacent	____ collapse	____ regulate

B. *Read the passages from Exercises 4 and 5. As you read, look for target words and circle them. Note that the words in part A are listed in the same order as they appear in the passage, but the form may be different.*

Metropolis and Megalopolis

In the United States, the upper and middle classes have usually sparked the expansion of cities outward. Typically, as migrants from rural areas moved into the central city, the wealthier classes moved to the suburbs. The automobile greatly facilitated this development. It encouraged people to leave the crowded inner city for the more comfortable life of the suburbs, if they could afford it. As the number of cars increased, so did the size of suburbs and metropolises. In 1900, there were only 8,000 cars in the United States; by 1930, the number had soared to more than 26 million. Meanwhile, the proportion of the U.S. population living in the suburbs grew from only 15.7 percent in 1910 to 49.6 percent in 1950 (Glaab and Brown, 1983).

Since 1950, virtually all the growth in metropolitan areas has occurred in the suburbs. During the 1960s, U.S. suburbs grew four times faster than inner cities, and stores and entertainment facilities followed the people there. Suburban jobs increased 44 percent, while inner-city employment dropped 7 percent. This pattern of suburban growth at the expense of the urban core continued in the 1970s and 1980s. Today, suburbanites outnumber city residents three to two (U.S. Census Bureau, 2003; Gottdiener, 1983; Jaaret, 1983).

As suburbs expand, they sometimes combine with the suburbs of adjacent metropolitan areas to form a megalopolis, a vast area in which many metropolises merge. For hundreds of miles from one major city to the next, suburbs and cities have merged with one another to form a continuous region in which distinctions between suburban, urban, and rural areas are blurred. The hundreds of miles from Boston to Washington, D.C., form one such megalopolis; another stretches from Detroit through Chicago to Milwaukee in the Midwest; and a third goes from San Francisco to San Diego.

The World's Megacities

The world's urban population has grown so fast that today, there are about 40 megacities—cities with populations of 5 million or more. Generally, the poorer the country, the faster its urban growth. Thus, today, only three of the world's megacities are in the United States, and more than half are in developing countries. Many more cities in the developing world will soon become megacities.

Since the emergence of the pre-industrial city 5,000 years ago, great cities have risen and fallen. The same is true today. One city that is collapsing is Kinshasa, the capital of Zaire. Although the country is endowed with abundant natural resources, such as gold, diamonds, copper, and rich agricultural land, Kinshasa has produced massive miseries under the corrupt 30-year-reign of former President Sese Mobutu. Government officials have routinely looted manufactured goods, fuel, food, and medical supplies, even most of the emergency food aid sent by foreign countries. As a result, the annual inflation rate has often soared to more than 3,000 percent and the jobless rate to 80 percent, posing serious threats of starvation and epidemics. In contrast, the city of Curitiba in Brazil is a success story. The city is not rich, but its government makes the most of its resources. One example is recycling: Parks are lit with lamps made from soda bottles, and some government offices were built in part with old telephone poles. The city also delivers excellent services, including a highly efficient bus system and well-constructed housing projects for the poor (Zwingle, 2002; Linden, 1993).

Most megacities fit between these two contrasting types. They are saddled with serious problems but manage to cope reasonably well, usually in ways that reflect the nature of their societies. Consider Tokyo, for example—the world's most densely populated metropolis. It faces enormous problems, such as overwhelming amounts of waste, traffic-choked streets, and sky-high housing costs. But the technologically advanced Japanese have, among other things, developed an urban heat system that extracts heat from sewage, which is then used to regulate the temperature in several of Tokyo's buildings. To reduce traffic jams, the city has used wireless communication to show drivers whose cars have a computerized navigation system where the congested streets are. And to lower housing costs, Tokyo has started planning to build an underground city (Kuchment, 2003; Wehrfritz and Itoi, 2003; Linden, 1993).

(Source: A. Thio, *Sociology: A Brief Introduction,* 6th Edition. Boston: Allyn and Bacon, 2005, p. 406–409)

C. Working with another student, check to be sure that you have located all of the target words.

EXERCISE 8

A. These sentences are taken from the passages in Exercise 7. Working with another student, read each sentence aloud. Then circle the best meaning or synonym for the underlined word as it is used in the sentence.

1. The automobile greatly <u>facilitated</u> this development.

   a. complicated   b. put limits on   c. made easier

2. Since 1950, <u>virtually</u> all the growth in metropolitan areas has occurred in the suburbs.

   a. almost   b. probably   c. entirely

3. This pattern of suburban growth at the expense of the urban <u>core</u> continued in the 1970s and 1980s.

   a. power   b. economy   c. center

4. As suburbs expand, they sometimes combine with the suburbs of <u>adjacent</u> metropolitan areas to form a megalopolis, a vast area in which many metropolises merge.

   a. large   b. nearby   c. distant

5. For hundreds of miles from one <u>major</u> city to the next, suburbs and cities have merged with one another to form a continuous region in which distinctions between suburban, urban, and rural areas are blurred.

   a. large   b. growing   c. wealthy

6. For hundreds of miles from one major city to the next, suburbs and cities have merged with one another to form a continuous region in which <u>distinctions</u> between suburban, urban, and rural areas are blurred.

a. transportation   b. differences   c. similarities

7. Since the <u>emergence</u> of the pre-industrial city 5,000 years ago, great cities have risen and fallen.

a. appearance   b. disappearance   c. end

8. One city that is <u>collapsing</u> is Kinshasa, the capital of Zaire.

a. starving   b. growing   c. failing

9. As a result, the annual inflation rate has often soared to more than 3,000 percent and the jobless rate to 80 percent, <u>posing</u> serious threats of starvation and epidemics.

a. creating   b. limiting   c. avoiding

10. The city also delivers excellent services, including a highly efficient bus system and <u>well-constructed</u> housing projects for the poor.

a. well-regarded   b. well-built   c. well-heated

11. But the technologically advanced Japanese have, among other things, developed an urban heat system that <u>extracts</u> heat from sewage, which is then used to regulate the temperature in several of Tokyo's buildings.

a. removes   b. preserves   c. sends

12. But the technologically advanced Japanese have, among other things, developed an urban heat system that extracts heat from sewage, which is then used to <u>regulate</u> the temperature in several of Tokyo's buildings.

a. support   b. increase   c. control

B. *Compare your answers with those of another pair of students. If you disagree, explain your answer and then use a dictionary to check your work.*

A. In this table, write as many of the missing forms as you can think of without looking in a dictionary.

Noun	Verb	Adjective	Adverb
collapse			——
	construct		
core		——	——
distinction			
emergence			——
	extract		——
	facilitate		——
		major	——
	pose	——	——
	regulate		——
——	——		virtually

B. Compare your work with that of another student. Then look in the dictionary for the forms you did not know and write them in the table.

A. Working with another student, write a form of one of the target words in each of the sentences below. Each word may be used only once.

adjacent	distinction	major
collapse	emergence	pose
construct	extract	regulate
core	facilitate	virtually

1. According to the lawyer, it is necessary to make a _____ between the two cases, even if they seem similar at first glance.

2. The flow of water in the canal was _____ by the new flood gates that were installed before the storm.

3. In the United States and other developed countries, certain diseases like polio have _____ disappeared.

4. The journalist's question about the war _____ a serious political problem for the president.

5. The new traffic rules will _____ the flow of traffic around the city.

6. George Bernard Shaw was a _____ influence on the theater in the twentieth century.

7. Italy _____ from the war with its industry and transportation systems in a very poor state.

8. When the Eiffel Tower was _____ in the late nineteenth century, it was considered a marvel of engineering.

9. Although the acting and the filming is excellent, the real _____ of the film is its political message.

10. The chemistry laboratory is located in the building that is _____ to the library.

11. When the housing market _____ and the prices of houses fell, some people were in serious financial difficulty.

12. Many art museums now have machines that _____ the humidity (water) from the air.

B. *Compare your answers with those of another pair of students. If you disagree, explain your answers and look back at the passage to check your work. You may also use a dictionary to check your work.*

EXERCISE 11

A. *Make study cards for the target words that you are still unsure about. Use the cards to study them, first on your own and then with another student. (See Part 2, Unit 1, page 29)*

B. *1. Write a sentence for each of the words, leaving a blank instead of the target word. Ask another student to read your sentences and write the target word that should go in each blank.*

   2. Look at your sentences again. If your classmate wrote a different word, discuss the sentences to find out why. Was your sentence unclear, or did your classmate not know the target word?

UNIT 8   Summarizing

Another key strategy for learning and remembering the ideas in a text is to summarize what you have read. This means rewriting the important parts in a much shorter form, using some words from the text and some of your own words. Summarizing is especially useful for:

- Reviewing and memorizing information in textbooks for exams;
- Preparing information or ideas from different sources so you can include them in a report or paper.

Summarizing a Passage

When summarizing a passage, the first step is to write a one-sentence summary of each paragraph. Then you can combine the sentences to write a summary of the whole passage.

Step 1. Summarizing a paragraph

- Write a single, complete sentence that is much shorter than the paragraph.
- Include the main idea and supporting facts and ideas.
- In the summary sentence, follow the same pattern of organization as in the paragraph.
- Do not add any facts, ideas, or opinions that are not in the paragraph.

Note: The topic sentence or main idea sentence can sometimes serve as the summary sentence, but it often needs to be changed to include important details found in the paragraph.

Example:

Read the paragraph and mark the text to show the main idea, the pattern of organization, and the supporting facts and ideas. Then read the summary sentence that contains the most important ideas in the paragraph.

In developing countries, poor people have suffered the most from shortages of clean water. There are several reasons for this. First, in many developing countries, the majority of houses in poor villages and urban slums are not yet served by a piped water system. People living in these places often have to walk many miles to find water and carry it home in jugs and plastic containers. Second, these people usually have few alternatives to the piped water supply. There may be water closer by in rivers or lakes, but this is often dangerously polluted. In some areas, street vendors sell water by the liter, but they often charge extremely high prices for water that is not always safe to drink.

Main idea: _Poor people in developing countries have suffered the most from shortages of clean water for several reasons._

Pattern of organization: _Listing_

Supporting facts
and ideas:
People in poor villages and urban slums are usually not served
by a piped water system.

These people have few other sources of fresh water.

Summary sentence: _Poor people in developing countries suffer the most from_
shortages of clean water because their homes do not have
piped in water and they have few other sources of water.

EXERCISE 1

A. Working with another student, read each paragraph and mark the text to show the main idea and the supporting facts and ideas. Then fill in the information below.

Wetlands

1.   Wetlands are areas of land that are covered by water all or part of the year. Throughout history, people have considered wetlands to be land that was wasted and could be put to better use. For this reason, from the time of the Romans, wetlands have been drained and filled so that the land could be used for human activity. Wetlands have been converted into farmland, city neighborhoods, industrial facilities, or garbage dumps. However, in recent years, scientists, environmentalists, and even politicians have begun to realize that wetlands are a valuable part of the environment, as well as a valuable resource for humans.

Main idea: _____

_____

Pattern of organization: _____

Supporting facts
and ideas: _____

_____

_____

Summary sentence: _____

_____

_____

2.   From a biological point of view, wetlands are not wastelands at all, but are among the most productive ecosystems in the world. They contain an immense variety of animal and plant species, which have evolved over millions of years and which depend on wetland ecosystems for their survival. The life cycles of all these species depend on the particular habitat of the wetlands, with its rich mixture of water and organic material from the breakdown of plants in water. The enriched material—known as *detritus*—feeds many small animals living in the water, such as aquatic insects, shell fish, and small fish. These small creatures, in turn, attract larger predatory animals that feed on them, including fish, reptiles, amphibians, birds, and mammals.

Main idea: _____

_____

Pattern of organization: _____

Supporting facts   _____
and ideas:
_____

_____

Summary sentence: _____

_____

_____

3.   In recent years, city planners and politicians are beginning to realize that wetlands are valuable for another reason as well. In 2006, 13.3 inches (about 34 cm) of rain fell on the city of Newburyport in northeastern Massachusetts. In the neighboring city of Haverhill, only about 10 inches of rain fell. However, Haverhill suffered millions of dollars worth of damage from flooding, while Newburyport suffered almost no serious damage. Why such a difference? Both cities are built along the Merrimack River, but in Haverhill the area all along the river has been developed with housing, roads, and commercial buildings. In Newburyport, however, the area along the river has been left in its original state—marshland (wetlands). These wetlands gave the river waters space to spread out when there was a sudden increase in volume due to the rain. The wetland plants and soil also acted like a giant sponge to absorb water. In Haverhill, on the other hand, the water could not spread out, so it rose higher and higher, until it overflowed the banks and flooded areas of the city.

Main idea: _____

_____

Pattern of organization: _____

Supporting facts   _____

and ideas:

Summary sentence: _____

B. Compare your summary sentences with those of another student. Look back at the paragraphs to check your work.

Step 2. Summarizing a whole passage

- Read the passage all the way to the end and mark the overall thesis and the supporting points.
- Determine the overall pattern of organization.
- Write a one-sentence summary of each paragraph.
- Write a short paragraph by combining the summary sentences of the paragraphs (with any necessary changes to connect them).
- The main idea of the summary paragraph should be similar to the thesis of the whole passage and the pattern of organization should be the same as the overall pattern of the passage.

Note: Only the most important ideas and supporting points of the original passage should be included in a summary paragraph. It should not include minor details or your own opinions or ideas. Above all, it should be **much** shorter than the original.

EXERCISE 2

A. Look back at the three paragraphs in Exercise 1. Together they form a longer passage with a thesis statement. Underline the thesis statement. Then write a summary paragraph that includes the thesis statement and your summary sentences.

_____

B. Compare your summary paragraph with that of another student and discuss any differences. Look back at the passage and your summary sentences to check your work.

EXERCISE 3

A. Preview the passage. Then read it carefully and mark the text to show the thesis and supporting facts and ideas. Then fill in the information below.

Persistent Pests

1   In the 1960s, the World Health Organization (WHO) began a campaign to eradicate[1] the mosquitoes that transmit the disease malaria. It was a noble goal, since malaria kills an estimated 3 million people each year in the world's tropical regions, predominantly southern Africa. WHO led an effort to spray the mosquitoes' habitat[2] with a chemical pesticide—a poison used to kill insects—called DDT. Early results were promising, and the mosquito was eliminated from the edge of its native range. The effort soon faltered,[3] however, and the eradication plan was dropped. How could a tiny mosquito thwart[4] the best efforts of a large group of well-funded scientists?

2   Situations like this one have occurred dozens of times in the last several decades. In a common scenario,[5] whenever a new type of pesticide is used to control agricultural pests, the early results are encouraging. A relatively small amount of the poison dusted onto a crop may kill 99% of the insects. However, the relatively few survivors of the first pesticide wave are insects with genes that somehow enable them to resist the chemical attack. [...] The poison kills most members of the insect population, leaving only the resistant individuals to reproduce. And when they do, their offspring[6] inherit the genes for pesticide resistance. In each generation, the proportion of pesticide-resistant individuals in the insect population increases, making subsequent sprayings less and less effective.

3   Since the widespread use of chemical pesticides began in the 1940s, scientists have documented pesticide resistance in more than 500 species of insects. The problems such insects pose—through their impact on agriculture and medicine—are just some of the many ways that evolution has a direct connection to our daily lives. Everywhere, all the time, populations of organisms are fine-tuning adaptations to local environments through the evolutionary process of natural selection. Given the dynamics of Earth and its life, it is not surprising that even the kinds of organisms on the planet—the species—have changed over time.

(Source: Neil S. Campbell, Jane B. Reece, and Eric J. Simon, *Essential Biology with Physiology,* 2nd Edition. San Francisco: Benjamin Cummings, 2004)

_____

[1] *eradicate:* to completely get ride of or destroy something
[2] *habitat:* the natural environment of a plant or animal
[3] *falter:* to become weaker and unable to continue
[4] *thwart:* to prevent something from succeeding
[5] *scenario:* a situation that could possibly happen
[6] *offspring:* children

Thesis: _____

_____

Pattern of organization: _____

Summary of paragraph 1: _____

_____

Summary of paragraph 2: _____

_____

Summary of paragraph 3: _____

_____

Summary paragraph:

_____

_____

_____

_____

_____

_____

_____

_____

B. Compare your summary paragraph with that of another student and discuss any differences. Look back at the passage and your summary sentences to check your work.

Summarizing Long Passages

When you summarize a long passage (more than four or five paragraphs), you need to add an additional step:

- Read the passage all the way to the end and mark the main points (including the thesis and the supporting points).
- Determine the overall pattern of organization.
- Divide the passage into parts. Each part should match a supporting point and may include several paragraphs. (In textbooks, the chapters are usually already divided into subsections or parts.)
- Write a summary sentence for each part.
- Write a paragraph that combines the summary sentences (with any necessary changes to connect them).
- The main idea of the summary paragraph should be the same as the thesis of the original passage, and the pattern of organization should be the same.

A. *Preview the passage. Then read it carefully and mark the thesis statement and important details. Then divide the passage into parts and write the thesis statement, pattern of organization, and a summary sentence for each part.*

The Sunnier, Southern Side of the Street

by Rod Usher

1 In these times of bombs and bio-warfare, it is harder than ever to dance to that old tune, "Just direct your feet to the sunny side of the street." A study published last month in the British *Journal of Psychiatry* found that "depressive disorder is a highly prevalent condition in Europe."
2 The report follows a decision by the European Commission to fund a comparative study of the prevalence[1] of depression in the United Kingdom, Ireland, Norway, Finland and Spain. After questioning 8,850 adults in 1997 and '98, the study concludes that just over 8.5% of them are depressed, always or in episodes[2]. Generalized to the European Union as a whole, this is an epidemic that affects about 30 million people.
3 Women fare worse than men and, predictably, depression is generally less prevalent in rural than urban areas. But the most striking fact revealed by the study is the uneven geographic distribution. The study indicates that depression afflicts[3] 17.1% of the urban population in the U.K. and 12.8% in urban Ireland. In rural parts of these countries and in both urban and rural Finland and Norway, the incidence ranges from 6.1% to 9.3%. But in urban Spain, the percentage drops to a mere 2.6. Why? Spain, where I live, has suffered from violent terrorism for more than 30 years; it has one of the E.U.'s highest unemployment rates, one of the worst records for industrial accidents, and is near the top of the tables for road fatalities,[4] drug abuse and AIDS. It has Europe's highest level of noise pollution.
4 But what Spain has in abundance compared with northern European nations—apart from more sun—is what the researchers in this study call social support structures. These structures have little to do with welfare or the number of doctors or psychiatrists. They are built on *la familia*.

5 One ironic fact about Europe's north-south relative poverty gap is that lack of wealth tends to make families stay together. Offspring remain at home longer, frequently not being able to afford to move out until they are in their late 20s. Old people are not so easily parked in "homes." Generalizing, in Spain, Portugal, Greece and Italy, family life probably runs deeper and longer than in the "better-off" north. Southerners fight and fall out like all families, but they tend to stick together against fate and the outside world. In Spanish hospitals, doctors have to push through ranks[5] of relatives to get near the patient. Old people often die in the house now run by their children; before doing so, they are needed to mind grandchildren while both parents work. If a family member is depressed, he or she can find comfort and care in-house rather than paying a fee to talk to a professional. These qualities add up to a larger sense of *solidaridad*. As organ donors, Spaniards are unsurpassed[6] in Europe; typically they respond generously to fund raisers.
6 Last week, I was in the street having an argument with a Spanish builder. A young mother with a newish baby in a pram happened to pass. The builder, Emilio, instinctively broke off his self-defense to talk to the kid, to feel its fat cheeks. The baby beamed,[7] its mother started talking about how well it was taking the breast, Emilio assured her that the little fellow was a picture of health . . . and my rage fell apart. It was no diversionary[8] tactic—I'd been familied.
7 The depression many Europeans have been suffering since Sept. 11 is no doubt harder to bear in cold Liverpool—where the British urban survey was based—than in the pleasant coastal city of Santander, where the Spanish researchers did their interviews. But a difference of depression of more

---

[1] *prevalence:* how common something is
[2] *episode:* a short period of time
[3] *afflict:* to affect in a harmful way
[4] *fatality:* a death in an accident or violent attack
[5] *ranks:* lines
[6] *unsurpassed:* better than all the others
[7] *beam:* to smile
[8] *diversionary:* intended to take attention away

than 14%? This is not explained by bluer skies or by the Anglo-Latin character divide.

8 A Spanish relative of my wife jokes that two things are best avoided: hot sun and families. But this 86-year-old widow passes hours on the phone with us each week. If we go out, the answering machine is often blinking when we return: "Where are you? Are you all right?" I used to feel harassed[9] by this. Nowadays, the recorded voice makes me smile. A little bit of *familia* can go a long way to brighten this terrorized, often depressing world.

(Source: *Time Magazine*, November 12, 2001)

---

[9] *harassed:* annoyed

Part 1: paragraphs ___1___ through ___3___

Part 2: paragraphs ___4___ through _____

Part 3: paragraphs _____ through _____

Thesis: _____

_____

Pattern of organization: _____

Part 1—Topic: _____

Summary sentence: _____

_____

Part 2—Topic: _____

Summary sentence: _____

_____

Part 3—Topic: _____

Summary sentence: _____

_____

B. Now write a short summary paragraph that combines and connects your summary sentences. The main idea of your summary paragraph should be similar to the overall thesis of the article.

_____

_____

_____

_____

_____

_____

_____

_____

C. Compare your summary paragraph with that of another student and check to see if you have both followed the steps for summarizing a longer passage. Discuss any differences and look back at your part summaries and the passage to check your work.

Summarizing a Textbook Chapter

Summarizing a textbook section or chapter is easier in some ways than summarizing an article or essay because the passages are usually already divided up into sections and subsections.

In a textbook, the introduction to a chapter or chapter section usually contains a statement of purpose that functions like a thesis statement, and explains what the passage will be about and how it will be organized. The headings of the chapter or section usually correspond to the topics mentioned in the statement of purpose.

While textbook sections are often organized in a listing pattern, each subsection can have a different pattern of organization. It is easier to understand and summarize the subsections if you first identify their patterns.

Note: Textbook passages may contain complex ideas that do not fit easily into a one-sentence summary. You should be as concise as possible to aim for one sentence, but may use two sentences if necessary.

A. *Preview the introduction to a section of a sociology textbook. Then read it carefully and look for a sentence that states the purpose of the whole section (what it will be about). Write the statement of purpose on the lines below.*

A GLOBAL ANALYSIS OF URBANIZATION

In 1693, William Penn wrote that "the country life is to be preferred for there we see the works of God, but in cities little else than the work of man." Most people at the time probably agreed with him. Less than 2 percent of the world's population then were urban dwellers. But in 1998, about 44 percent of the world's population lived in urban areas and more than 50 percent will do so by the end of 2010 (Haub, 1999; Linden, 1993; Fischer, 1984).

While urban populations have grown, cities themselves have changed. We can identify three periods in their history: the preindustrial, industrial, and metropolitan-megalopolitan stages.

Statement of purpose: _____

_____

B. *Preview the rest of the section. Then read it carefully and divide the section into parts. Write a number in the margin beside each part and mark the important facts and ideas in the text. Finally, fill in the information at the end of the passage.*

The Preindustrial City

For more than 99 percent of the time that we humans have been on Earth, our ancestors have roamed about in search of food. They have hunted, fished, and gathered edible plants, but they have never found enough food in more than one place to sustain them for very long. They have had to move on, traveling in small bands from one place to another.

Then, about 10,000 years ago, technological advances allowed people to stop their wandering. This was the dawn of what is called the *Neolithic period*. People now had the simple tools and the know-how to cultivate plants and domesticate animals. They could produce their food supplies in one locale, and they settled down and built villages. The villages were very small—with only about 200 to 400 residents each. For the next 5,000 years, villagers produced just enough food to feed themselves.

About 5,000 years ago, humans developed more powerful technologies. Thanks to innovations like the ox-drawn plow, irrigation, and metallurgy, farmers could produce more food than they needed to sustain themselves and their families. Because of this food surplus, some people abandoned agriculture and made their living by weaving, making pottery and practicing other specialized crafts. Methods of transporting and storing food were also improved. The result was the emergence of cities.

Cities first arose on the fertile banks of such rivers as the Nile of Egypt, the Euphrates and Tigris in the Middle East, the Indus in Pakistan, and the Yellow River in China. Similar urban settlements later appeared in other parts of the world. The *preindustrial* cities were small compared with the cities of today. Most had populations of 5,000 to 10,000 people. Only a few cities had more than 100,000 and even Rome never had more than several hundred thousand.

Several factors prevented expansion of the preindustrial city. By modern standards, agricultural techniques were still primitive. It took at least 75 farmers to produce enough of a surplus to support just one city dweller. For transportation, people had to depend on their own muscle power or that of animals. It was difficult to carry food supplies from farms to cities, and even more difficult to transport heavy materials for construction in the cities. Poor sanitation, lack of sewer facilities, and ineffective medicine kept the death rate high. Epidemics regularly killed as much as half of a city's population. Moreover, families still had a strong attachment to the land, which discouraged immigration to the cities. All these characteristics of preindustrial society kept the cities small (Davis, 1955).

The Industrial City

For almost 5,000 years, cities changed little. Then their growth, in size and number, was so rapid that it has been called an *urban revolution* or *urban explosion.* In 1700, less than 2 percent of the population of Great Britain lived in cities, but by 1900, the majority of the British did so. Other European countries and the United States soon achieved the same level of urbanization in an even shorter period. Today, these and other Western countries are among the most urbanized in the world, along with many Latin American countries, which have become mostly urbanized in more recent years.

The major stimulus to the urban explosion was the Industrial Revolution. It triggered a series of related events, identified by sociologist Philip Hauser (1981) as population explosion, followed by population displosion and population implosion, and then by technoplosion. Industrialization first causes a rise in production growth, and the mechanization of farming brings about an agricultural surplus. Fewer farmers can support more people—and thus larger urban populations *(population explosion).* Workers no longer needed on the farms move to the city. There is, then, displacement of people from rural to urban areas *(population displosion)* and a greater concentration of people in a limited area *(population implosion).* The development of other new technologies *(technoplosion)* spurs on urbanization. Improved transportation, for example, speeds the movement of food and other materials to urban centers.

The outcome of these events was the *industrial city.* Compared with the preindustrial city, the industrial city was larger, more densely settled, and more diverse. It was a place where large numbers of people—with a wide range of skills, interests, and cultural backgrounds—could live and work together in a limited space. Also, unlike the preindustrial city, which had served primarily as a religious or governmental center, the industrial city was a commercial hub. In fact, its abundant job opportunities attracted so many rural migrants that migration accounted for the largest share of its population growth. Without these migrants, cities would not have grown at all because of the high mortality rate brought about by extremely poor sanitary conditions.

Metropolis and Megalopolis

Early in this century, the large cities of the industrialized nations began to spread outward. They formed **metropolises**, large urban areas that include a city and its surrounding suburbs. Some of these suburbs are politically separate from their central cities, but socially, economically, and geographically, the suburbs and the city are tied together. The U.S. Census Bureau recognizes this unity by defining what is called a *Standard Metropolitan Statistical Area,* which cuts across political boundaries. Since 1990, most U.S. residents have been living in metropolitan areas with 1 million residents or more (Suro, 1991).

In the United States, the upper and middle classes have usually sparked the expansion of cities outward. Typically, as migrants from rural areas moved into the central city, the wealthier classes moved to the suburbs. The automobile greatly facilitated this development. It encouraged people to leave the crowded inner city for the more comfortable life of the suburbs, if they could afford it. As the number of cars increased, so did the size of suburbs and metropolises. In 1900, there were only 8,000 cars in the United States; by 1930, the number had soared to more than 26 million. Meanwhile, the proportion of the U.S. population living in the suburbs grew from only 15.7 percent in 1910 to 49.6 percent in 1950 (Glaab and Brown, 1983).

Since 1950, virtually all the growth in metropolitan areas has occurred in the suburbs. During the 1960s, U.S. suburbs grew four times faster than inner cities, and stores and entertainment facilities followed the people there. Suburban jobs increased 44 percent, while inner-city employment dropped 7 percent. This pattern of suburban growth at the expense of the urban core continued in the 1970s and 1980s. Today, suburbanites outnumber city residents three to two (U.S. Census Bureau, 2003; Gottdiener, 1983; Jaaret, 1983).

As suburbs expand, they sometimes combine with the suburbs of adjacent metropolitan areas to form a **megalopolis**, a vast area in which many metropolises merge. For hundreds of miles from one major city to the next, suburbs and cities have merged with one another to form a continues region in which distinctions between suburban, urban, and rural areas are blurred. The hundreds of miles from Boston to Washington, D.C., form one such megalopolis; another stretches from Detroit through Chicago to Milwaukee in the Midwest; and a third goes from San Francisco to San Diego.

Part 1—Topic: _____

Pattern of organization: _____

Summary sentence(s): _____

_____

Part 2—Topic: _____

Pattern of organization: _____

Summary sentence(s): _____

_____

Part 3—Topic: _____

Pattern of organization: _____

Summary sentence(s): _____

_____

C. *Now write a short summary paragraph that combines and connects the summary sentences.*

_____

_____

_____

_____

_____

_____

_____

D. *Compare your summary paragraph with that of another student. Discuss any differences and look back at your part summaries and the passage to check your work.*

A. Read the textbook section on "Social Isolation" that you previewed in Unit 1, Exercise 5, page 80. Divide the section into parts and mark the important facts and ideas. Then fill in the following information.

Part 1—Topic: _____

Pattern of organization: _____

Summary sentence(s): _____

_____

Part 2—Topic: _____

Pattern of organization: _____

Summary sentence(s): _____

_____

B. Now write a short summary paragraph that combines the summary sentences.

_____

_____

_____

_____

_____

_____

_____

_____

_____

C. Compare your summary paragraph with that of another student. Discuss any differences and look back at your summaries and the passage to check your work.

Focus on Vocabulary

A. Check your understanding of the following target words. Read each word aloud and then write S, M, or N beside it.

S = *you are sure of the meaning of the word*
M = *you think you might know the meaning of the word*
N = *you don't know the meaning of the word at all*

____ transmit	____ predominant	____ subsequent
____ goal	____ fund	____ document
____ estimate	____ enable	____ dynamics

B. Read the passage from Exercise 3. As you read, look for the target words and circle them. Note that the words in Part A are listed in the same order as they appear in the passage but the form may be different.

Persistent Pests

In the 1960s, the World Health Organization (WHO) began a campaign to eradicate the mosquitoes that transmit the disease malaria. It was a noble goal, since malaria kills an estimated 3 million people each year in the world's tropical regions, predominantly southern Africa. WHO led an effort to spray the mosquitoes' habitat with a chemical pesticide—a poison used to kill insects—called DDT. Early results were promising, and the mosquito was eliminated from the edge of its native range. The effort soon faltered, however, and the eradication plan was dropped. How could a tiny mosquito thwart the best efforts of a large group of well-funded scientists?

Situations like this one have occurred dozens of times in the last several decades. In a common scenario, whenever a new type of pesticide is used to control agricultural pests, the early results are encouraging. A relatively small amount of the poison dusted onto a crop may kill 99% of the insects. However, the relatively few survivors of the first pesticide wave are insects with genes that somehow enable them to resist the chemical attack. [...] The poison kills most members of the insect population, leaving only the resistant individuals to reproduce. And when they do, their offspring inherit the genes for pesticide resistance. In each generation, the proportion of pesticide-resistant individuals in the insect population increases, making subsequent sprayings less and less effective.

Since the widespread use of chemical pesticides began in the 1940s, scientists have documented pesticide resistance in more than 500 species of insects. The problems such insects pose—through their impact on agriculture and medicine—are just some of the many ways that evolution has a direct connection to our daily lives. Everywhere, all the time, populations of organisms are fine-tuning adaptations to local environments through the evolutionary process of natural selection. Given the dynamics of Earth and its life, it is not surprising that even the kinds of organisms on the planet—the species—have changed over time.

(Source: Neil S. Campbell, Jane B Reece, and Eric J. Simon, *Essential Biology with Physiology*, 2d Edition. San Francisco: Benjamin Cummings, 2004)

C. Working with another student, check to be sure that you have located all of the target words.

EXERCISE 8

A. These sentences are taken from the passage in Exercise 7. Working with another student, read each sentence aloud. Then circle the best meaning or synonym for the underlined word as it is used in the sentence.

1. In the 1960s, the World Health Organization (WHO) began a campaign to eradicate the mosquitoes that <u>transmit</u> the disease malaria.

   a. pass on   b. kill off   c. find out

2. It was a noble <u>goal</u>, since malaria kills an estimated 3 million people each year in the world's tropical regions, predominantly southern Africa.

   a. effort   b. idea   c. aim

3. It was a noble goal, since malaria kills <u>an estimated</u> 3 million people each year in the world's tropical regions, predominantly southern Africa.

    a. nearly   b. about   c. over

4. It was a noble goal, since malaria kills an estimated 3 million people each year in the world's tropical regions, <u>predominantly</u> southern Africa.

    a. except   b. mainly   c. only

5. How could a tiny mosquito thwart the best efforts of a large group of <u>well-funded</u> scientists?

    a. with little money   b. with lots of money   c. with lots of experience

6. However, the relatively few survivors of the first pesticide wave are insects with genes that somehow <u>enable</u> them to resist the chemical attack.

    a. allow   b. prevent   c. limit

7. In each generation, the proportion of pesticide-resistant individuals in the insect population increases, making <u>subsequent</u> sprayings less and less effective.

    a. later   b. other   c. earlier

8. Since the widespread use of chemical pesticides began in the 1940s, scientists have <u>documented</u> pesticide resistance in more than 500 species of insects.

    a. viewed   b. noticed   c. recorded

9. Given the <u>dynamics</u> of Earth and its life, it is not surprising that even the kinds of organisms on the planet—the species—have changed over time.

    a. forces   b. difficulties   c. effects

B. Compare your answers with those of another pair of students. If you disagree, explain your answers and then use a dictionary to check your work.

EXERCISE 9

A. In this table, write as many of the missing forms as you can think of without looking in a dictionary.

Noun	Verb	Adjective	Adverb
	document		——
dynamics	——		
	enable		——
	estimate		——
fund			——
		predominant	
——	——	subsequent	
	transmit		——

B. Compare your work with that of another student. Then look in the dictionary for the forms you did not know and write them in the table.

EXERCISE 10

A. Working with another student, write a form of one of the target words in each of the sentences below. Each word may be used only once.

document	estimate	predominant
dynamics	fund	subsequent
enable	goal	transmit

1. Until the middle of the twentieth century, emergency signals from ships at sea were _____ by telegraph.

2. The U.S. government _____ very little research into the treatment of diseases, like malaria, that are common only in developing countries.

3. Though early attempts failed to find a cure for AIDS, _____ attempts have been more successful.

4. The new president stated in her speech that the main _____ of her government is to improve the economic situation in the country.

5. The introduction of computers _____ the company to speed up the production process.

6. Studies of Spanish-speaking Americans show that the _____ group is from Mexico.

7. The _____ among the other family members became clear when the father died.

8. In order to _____ the entire process, they took photographs before, during, and after the destruction of the building.

9. The number of bicycles per 1,000 people in the United States has been _____ at 385, while in the Netherlands, it is 1,000.

B. Compare your work with that of another pair of students. If you disagree, explain your answers and then use a dictionary to check your work.

EXERCISE 11

A. Make study cards for the target words that you are still unsure about. Use the cards to study them, first on your own and then with another student. (See Part 2, Unit 1, page 29)

B. 1. Write a sentence for each of the words, leaving a blank instead of the target word. Ask another student to read your sentences and write the target word that should go in each blank.

2. Look at your sentences again. If your classmate wrote a different word, discuss the sentences to find out why. Was your sentence unclear, or did your classmate not know the target word?

UNIT 9 Critical Reading

With all the information that is available today, you must be on your guard as you read. Nothing is automatically true just because it is in print or on the Web. You need to develop the ability to *read critically*. That is, you need to ask questions like these about the text and about the writer.

- Where is this material from? Is this a valid source of information?
- Who is the writer? Is he or she qualified to write about this topic?
- Can I trust the information here?
- What is the writer's purpose in writing this?
- What is the writer's point of view about the topic?
- How does this information compare to what I already know?
- Based on what I already know and believe, do I agree?

Evaluating Web Sites

It is important to remember that ANYONE can create a web site or put information on the Web. There are no editors to check the reliability of a writer (as in a serious newspaper or magazine). Therefore, when you are reading articles on the Web, you need to be especially critical. Ask yourself:

- Does the writer identify himself/herself? Is he/she qualified to write about this topic?
- Does the web site belong to an organization that you have heard of? If not, use a search engine (Google or others) to look for more information.
- What is the apparent purpose of the web site? Could there be a second, hidden purpose (e.g., it appears to simply offer information about an organization, but actually it aims to convince you to join)?
- Is the information based on reliable, outside sources or the writer's opinions?
- Is this an open-source web site like *Wikipedia,* the online encyclopedia? If it is, anyone can contribute to it, so you should check the information in other sources.

When you are looking for information about a topic on the Web, you may first have to choose among the many sites listed on Google or another search engine. You can tell a lot about a site just from its web address, also known as the URL. Look for the following clues:

1. The name or an abbreviation for an organization that you have heard of.
2. Any indication that it might belong to an organization.
3. A person's name, personal information, or the word "blog"—all of which might indicate that it is a web log or journal created by an individual who wants to express opinions and share experiences with others on the Web.
4. Where the site appears on the list of search results. The sites at the beginning of the list are those that have been linked most by other web sites.

Example:

Look at the following Web addresses. Then read the questions and the answers.

  a. www.daydreamer18.blogspirit.com/archive/2005/05/17/the_piano_man.html

  b. www.cbsnews.com/stories/2005/05/17/world/main695867.shtml

1. Which address do you think is for a web site belonging to an individual? How can you tell?

   Address a seems to be a web site belonging to an individual because it includes the word "blog." Also, the word "daydreamer" seems to refer to personal matters.

2. Which address do you think is a web site belonging to an organization? What kind of organization do you think it is?

   Address b seems to belong to a news organization because it includes the word "news." Also, it includes "CBS," a major U.S. television channel.

3. Which web site do you think provides reliable information?

   Address b probably provides more reliable information since it belongs to a large news organization.

EXERCISE 1

A. The following web addresses are for sites containing information or opinions about the "Piano Man" (see Unit 2, Exercise 3). Study the URLs and answer the questions.

  a. www.mirror.co.uk/news/tm_ojbectid=15882241&method=full&siteid=94762&

  b. www.kentandmedway.nhs.uk/whats_new/piano_man/statement_one.asp

  c. www.jonathan.james.blogspot.com/2005/05/piano man/html

  d. www.edition.cnn.com/2005/WORLD/europe/08/22/uk.pianoman

1. Which URL is for a web site belonging to an individual? How can you tell?

2. Which URL is for a web site belonging to an organization? What kind of organization do you think it is? Circle the name or abbreviation of the organization.

3. Which of the web sites is most likely to provide reliable information?

4. Which web sites would you look up if you wanted to find out what happened to the Piano Man? Why?

B. Compare your answers with those of another student. If you disagree, explain how you decided on your answers.

A. Read these two online articles about the Piano Man and answer the questions.

Online article 1

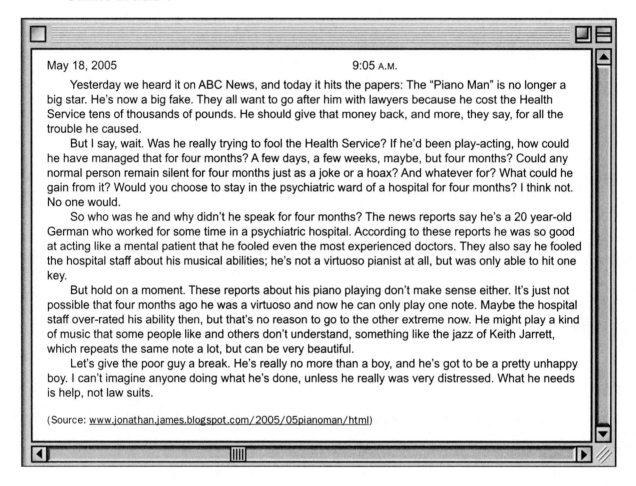

May 18, 2005   9:05 A.M.

Yesterday we heard it on ABC News, and today it hits the papers: The "Piano Man" is no longer a big star. He's now a big fake. They all want to go after him with lawyers because he cost the Health Service tens of thousands of pounds. He should give that money back, and more, they say, for all the trouble he caused.

But I say, wait. Was he really trying to fool the Health Service? If he'd been play-acting, how could he have managed that for four months? A few days, a few weeks, maybe, but four months? Could any normal person remain silent for four months just as a joke or a hoax? And whatever for? What could he gain from it? Would you choose to stay in the psychiatric ward of a hospital for four months? I think not. No one would.

So who was he and why didn't he speak for four months? The news reports say he's a 20 year-old German who worked for some time in a psychiatric hospital. According to these reports he was so good at acting like a mental patient that he fooled even the most experienced doctors. They also say he fooled the hospital staff about his musical abilities; he's not a virtuoso pianist at all, but was only able to hit one key.

But hold on a moment. These reports about his piano playing don't make sense either. It's just not possible that four months ago he was a virtuoso and now he can only play one note. Maybe the hospital staff over-rated his ability then, but that's no reason to go to the other extreme now. He might play a kind of music that some people like and others don't understand, something like the jazz of Keith Jarrett, which repeats the same note a lot, but can be very beautiful.

Let's give the poor guy a break. He's really no more than a boy, and he's got to be a pretty unhappy boy. I can't imagine anyone doing what he's done, unless he really was very distressed. What he needs is help, not law suits.

(Source: www.jonathan.james.blogspot.com/2005/05pianoman/html)

1. Who wrote this article?

2. Does the web site belong to an organization? How can you tell?

3. Do you think this web site is a reliable source of information? Why or why not?

4. Write a question mark in the margin where you have doubts about the information in the text. Underline parts of the text that you think state valid information.

5. Do you think the information or ideas on this site would be useful for a research project about the Piano Man? Why or why not?

Online article 2

22 August 2005

EXCLUSIVE: PIANO MAN SHAM

by Stephen Moyes and Jon Kaila

The mysterious Piano Man has finally broken his silence after more than four months—and has been exposed as a fake.

What is more, the man thought to be a musical genius can hardly play a note on the piano, according to latest reports.

The stranger refused to utter a single word after being found in a soaking wet suit on a beach near Sheerness, Kent.

Now it is claimed that he has confessed to medical staff that he was German. He said he had been working in Paris but had lost his job. He added that his father owned a farm in Germany and he had two sisters.

He made his way to Britain on a Eurostar train and claimed he was trying to commit suicide when the police picked him up on the beach in April.

He flew home to Germany on Saturday. Health chiefs, who have wasted tens of thousands of pounds on treatment, are considering suing him.

The man used to work with mentally ill patients and is thought to have copied some of their characteristics to fool psychiatric doctors about his own imagined illness.

An insider at the Little Brook Hospital in Dartford, Kent, claimed: "A nurse went into his room last Friday and said 'Are you going to speak to us today?' he simply answered, 'Yes, I think I will.' We were stunned. He has been with us for months and we have got nowhere with him. We thought he was going to be with us forever."

The patient was nicknamed Piano Man after reports that he entertained hospital staff with his remarkable talent for classical recitals. When medics gave him a pen and paper, he drew detailed pictures of a grand piano.

Now it is claimed that he could only tap one key continuously on the piano in the hospital chapel. And he said he drew a picture of a piano for therapists because that was the first thing that came into his head.

The hospital insider added. "He claims he was found by police as he was trying to commit suicide. He was obviously in a distressed state and didn't talk to the police. Then it just went on from there." [...]

(Source: http://www.mirror.co.uk)

1. Who wrote the article?

2. Does the web site belong to an organization? How can you tell?

3. This is the web site of *The Daily Mirror*, a newspaper in England. Do you think this web site is a reliable source of information? Why or why not?

4. Write a question mark in the margin where you have doubts about the information in the text. Underline parts of the text that you think state valid information.

5. Do you think the information or ideas on this site would be useful for a research project about the Piano Man? Why or why not?

B. Compare your answers to the questions about the two articles with those of another student. Which article do you think has the most accurate information?

Evaluating Text

In addition to evaluating the sources of reading materials, you need to look closely at the text itself. In the following exercises, you will read a variety of texts to identify and evaluate different aspects.

- Purpose—the reason the writer wrote the text
- Point of view—the writer's position on a particular subject
- Possible bias—how a writer might purposely present ideas or events in ways that favor a particular political or religious belief

Determining the purpose

To evaluate a piece of writing, you need to ask not only who wrote it, but also why it was written—the writer's **purpose**. The three main purposes for writing are:

- To inform—the author presents facts and explains ideas to the reader.
- To persuade—the author uses facts and opinions to argue for or against some idea.
- To entertain—the author tries to amuse or interest the reader with humor, suspense, and stories.

A piece of writing can often fulfill more than one purpose. It can, in fact, be informative, persuasive, and entertaining all at once. However, the writer usually has one primary purpose in writing it.

How can you tell what the writer's purpose is?

- Look at the information in the passage. Does it contain a lot of facts? If it does, the purpose may be to inform or to persuade.

- Look at the language in the passage.

  ➤ If it is neutral and objective, the purpose is probably simply to inform the reader.

  ➤ If it includes terms that are strongly positive, negative, or emotional, the purpose is probably to persuade the reader.

  ➤ If it includes situations or descriptions that are funny, surprising, or intriguing, the writer probably wants to entertain the reader.

Example:

Read the newspaper article. (The facts in the article have been underlined.) As you read ask yourself "What is the writer's main purpose?" Then read the questions and answers below.

Silent Orders on the Left Bank

by Paul Webster

To order a plate of chips at <u>Paris's Café des Signes</u>, interlock your fingers in the form of a steeple, look the waiter in the eye and smile.

France's first <u>silent bistro, where most of the 45-strong staff cannot hear,</u> has <u>been opened officially after a month's trial on the left bank's Avenue Jean-Moulin</u>. During the lunch-time rush, there are none of the usual warning cries of "chaud devant" as waiters and customers exchange extravagant hand signals. A few timid clients point at the menu on the wall, but most people with normal hearing consult charts on every table explaining various signals.

Although the café is open to everyone, <u>it was set up with government backing to train people with hearing impediments for full-time jobs</u>. The "patronne," <u>Martine Lejeau-Perry</u>, said <u>customers with normal hearing quickly learned to "speak"</u> either by imitating the drawings on the charts or making up their own signals. "Perhaps the loudest sound in this café is laughter," she said.

<u>The capital already has a restaurant with blind waiters</u>, where customers eat in the dark.

(Source: *The Guardian Weekly*, June 12–18, 2003)

1. What is the writer's main purpose?
   to inform

2. How can you tell?
   The writer has included a lot of facts, but he has not presented an argument for or against any idea, nor has he used language in an amusing or entertaining way.

A. Read the article. Think about the writer's purpose, and underline the facts. Then answer the questions below.

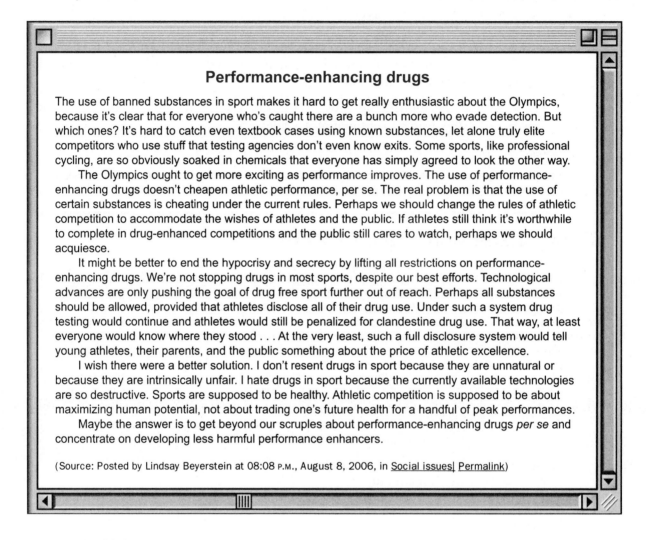

Performance-enhancing drugs

The use of banned substances in sport makes it hard to get really enthusiastic about the Olympics, because it's clear that for everyone who's caught there are a bunch more who evade detection. But which ones? It's hard to catch even textbook cases using known substances, let alone truly elite competitors who use stuff that testing agencies don't even know exits. Some sports, like professional cycling, are so obviously soaked in chemicals that everyone has simply agreed to look the other way.

The Olympics ought to get more exciting as performance improves. The use of performance-enhancing drugs doesn't cheapen athletic performance, per se. The real problem is that the use of certain substances is cheating under the current rules. Perhaps we should change the rules of athletic competition to accommodate the wishes of athletes and the public. If athletes still think it's worthwhile to complete in drug-enhanced competitions and the public still cares to watch, perhaps we should acquiesce.

It might be better to end the hypocrisy and secrecy by lifting all restrictions on performance-enhancing drugs. We're not stopping drugs in most sports, despite our best efforts. Technological advances are only pushing the goal of drug free sport further out of reach. Perhaps all substances should be allowed, provided that athletes disclose all of their drug use. Under such a system drug testing would continue and athletes would still be penalized for clandestine drug use. That way, at least everyone would know where they stood . . . At the very least, such a full disclosure system would tell young athletes, their parents, and the public something about the price of athletic excellence.

I wish there were a better solution. I don't resent drugs in sport because they are unnatural or because they are intrinsically unfair. I hate drugs in sport because the currently available technologies are so destructive. Sports are supposed to be healthy. Athletic competition is supposed to be about maximizing human potential, not about trading one's future health for a handful of peak performances.

Maybe the answer is to get beyond our scruples about performance-enhancing drugs *per se* and concentrate on developing less harmful performance enhancers.

(Source: Posted by Lindsay Beyerstein at 08:08 P.M., August 8, 2006, in Social issues| Permalink)

1. What is the writer's main purpose?

2. How can you tell?

B. Compare your answers with those of another student. If you disagree, explain your answers and look back at the article to check your work.

A. Read the newspaper article. Think about the writer's purpose, and underline the facts. Then answer the questions below.

E-mail Addiction

I recently took a short vacation. The very best thing about it was not the lovely walks, the concerts, the tennis, or just lazing and reading. The best thing was being away from e-mail. (And the worst thing was coming back to 482 messages.)

The stuff is like kudzu.[1] I'm not even talking about spam—the unwanted commercial solicitations for everything from cosmetic surgery to Nigerian banking scams.

Nor am I complaining about reader responses to my column, which I appreciate. If I weren't reading electronic comments, I'd be absorbing old-fashioned letters.

No, I'm referring to everyday e-mail from people I know—co-workers, friends, and acquaintances who assume that e-mail is what we do all day.

I find it appalling to sometimes get responses within a minute or two of sending a message. This suggests that the recipient is compulsively checking e-mail all the time. How can these people get any work done? Don't they have anything better to do?

(Source: Robert Kuttner, *The Boston Globe*, August 24, 2005)

---

[1] *kudzu:* a type of vine that grows very quickly

1. What is the writer's main purpose?

2. How can you tell?

B. Compare your answers with those of another student. If you disagree, explain your answers and look back at the article to check your work.

A. Read the following passages from web sites about coffee. For each passage, write the main purpose and underline the words or phrases that helped you decide.

1. Viennese Blend Coffee is a potent blend of twenty-five percent French Roast and seventy-five percent regular roast coffees that have been blended to complement the dark and smoky flavors of the French Roast. Viennese Blend makes an excellent after-dinner coffee, and its European name suggests its ability to keep the conversation going long into the night. You won't actually find a coffee like this in Vienna anymore, but we're certain that 19th century intellectuals were drinking a similar blend as they discussed their theories of cultural evolution.

(Source: www.peets.com/shop, January 20, 2006)

What is the writer's main purpose?

2. The United States consumes one-fifth of the entire world's coffee, making it the largest consumer in the world. But few Americans realize that agriculture workers in the coffee industry often toil[1] in what can be described as "sweatshops in the fields." Many small coffee farmers receive prices for their coffee that are less than the costs of production, forcing them into a cycle of poverty and debt.

Fair Trade is a viable[2] solution to this crisis, assuring consumers that the coffee we drink was purchased under fair conditions. To become Fair Trade certified, an importer must meet stringent[3] international criteria; paying a minimum price per pound of $1.26, providing much needed credit to farmers, and providing technical assistance such as help transitioning to organic farming. Fair Trade for coffee farmers means community development, health, education, and environmental stewardship[4].

We believe in a total transformation of the coffee industry, so that all coffee sold in this country should be Fair Trade Certified, or if produced on a plantation, that workers' rights should be guaranteed and independently monitored. Our view includes social justice and environmental sustainability[5]: all coffee should be certified organic and shade grown where applicable.

(Source: www.globalexchange.org, January 20, 2006)

---

[1] *toil:* to work very hard
[2] *viable:* possible, doable
[3] *stringent:* strict
[4] *stewardship:* responsibility
[5] *environmental sustainability:* allowing the environment to be maintained unharmed

What is the writer's main purpose?

3. During the past two decades, extensive research has been conducted on the health aspects of caffeine consumption. The U.S. Food and Drug Administration (FDA) classified caffeine as Generally Recognized As Safe (GRAS) in 1958. A more recent review "found no evidence to show that the use of caffeine in carbonated beverages would render[1] these products injurious to health." The American Medical Association (AMA) has a similar position on caffeine's safety, stating that "Moderate tea or coffee drinkers probably need have no concern for their health relative to their caffeine consumption provided other lifestyle habits (diet, alcohol consumption) are moderate, as well."

Most experts agree that moderation and common sense are the keys for consuming caffeine-containing foods and beverages. Moderate caffeine consumption is considered to be about 300 mg which is equal to 3 cups of coffee, but this depends on the individual and can vary from one to several beverages. Consumers with certain health problems may wish to consult with their physician or health care provider about caffeine consumption.

(Source: www.ific.org, July 1998)

---

[1] *render:* to make

What is the writer's main purpose?

B. Compare your answers with those of another student. Then discuss these questions.

1. What sort of web sites do you think these passages come from?

2. Do you think that these web sites are reliable sources of factual information? Why or Why not?

Recognizing point of view

Every writer has a point of view—or way of thinking—about the topic of their writing which has developed out of their particular experiences and background. When you read critically, you need to identify the writer's point of view and consider how it affects the facts or arguments that are presented. You can identify the point of view by looking at the main idea or thesis of a passage and then examining the kind of support that the writer gives for it.

Example:

Read the following passage and ask yourself "What is the writer's point of view about the topic?" (the helpful words or phrases have been underlined for you). Then read questions 1 and 2, and discuss question 3 with another student.

Children and Television

According to recent statistics, the average American, including children, watches four hours of television a day. This <u>cannot be beneficial</u> for the children. Among the many consequences of this situation are the <u>rising levels</u> <u>of obesity</u> among children and the <u>increasing risk of heart disease and diabetes</u>. The fact of spending long hours in front of the television also means that they <u>read less</u> than in the past and this has <u>negatively affected their level of achievement in school</u>. Furthermore, the violence in many programs viewed by children has led to <u>an increase in violent behavior</u> on the part of children.

1. What is the writer's point of view about the topic:

    The writer thinks television is bad for children.

2. How can you tell?

    He/she uses words like "cannot be beneficial," "negatively affected," and lists a series of negative things connected to watching television.

3. Do you agree with the writer? Why or why not?

EXERCISE 6

A. Read the following passages. Identify the writer's point of view about the topic in each passage. Then underline the words or phrases that helped you decide and answer the questions.

Paragraph 1

Smoking in Public Places

In industrialized countries, governments are at last realizing that smoking is harmful to the health of individuals and an intolerable cost to society. With laws that ban smoking in public places and high taxes on cigarettes, they are taking concrete measures to discourage people from this destructive habit. Already there are signs that these measures are having a positive effect, as recent statistics show an overall decline in the number of smokers.

1. What is the writer's point of view about the topic?

2. How can you tell?

3. Do you agree with the writer? Why or why not?

Paragraph 2

Fast Food and Obesity

Can we blame McDonald's and fast food in general for the fact that Americans are overweight? Many people would say yes, and their lawyers are now trying to force changes in the way fast food is made. But let's face it—we can't blame the restaurants. They're just serving what people buy. We should blame ourselves. No one forces us to buy those hamburgers! We would all be much healthier and thinner if we went to the supermarket instead and cooked ourselves a healthy meal at home.

1. What is the writer's point of view about the topic?

2. How can you tell?

3. Do you agree with the writer? Why or why not?

B. Compare your answers with those of another student. If you disagree, explain your answers and look back at the passage to check your work.

Recognizing bias

Bias is similar to point of view but taken a step further. A biased writer expresses a one-sided opinion or prejudice about a person, group, or idea. He or she chooses words that can influence the reader's feelings about the person, group, or idea.

Biased writing may include some of these characteristics:

- It presents only one side of an argument.
- It includes only facts or examples that support the writer's opinion.
- It uses language intended to influence the reader's emotions (fear, anger, pity, outrage).
- It ridicules other opinions or views.

   Bias may be present in many different kinds of writing, including news reporting, political commentary, and even in textbooks. It may involve political or religious opinions, racial or national groups, or other groups, people, or ideas. It is important to recognize bias in writing so that you, the reader, can make a fair judgment about the validity of the writer's ideas.

A. Read each paragraph and decide whether the writer is biased or neutral. Underline the words or phrases that helped you decide. The first one has been done for you.

World Cup Soccer Championships

1. Every four years, ordinary life stops for millions of people in Europe, Asia, Africa, and Latin America—and World Cup soccer begins. In the poorer countries of Africa or South America, this is a rare moment of <u>hope and optimism</u>. If their team wins against a rich country—as Ghana did recently against the United States—the <u>joy is unimaginable, unstoppable</u>. The parties go on for days. In Europe the World Cup matches are a <u>unifying event</u> when the usual political, economic, and cultural <u>differences are set aside</u>. On the night of an important match, hardly a car moves on the streets. The sidewalks are empty. Everyone is watching the game. Then if the home team wins, they all <u>celebrate together</u>. Everyone in the country feels they have <u>gained something vital that makes them stronger and better</u>.

    a. Is the writer biased or neutral? *biased*

    b. If the writer is biased, is the bias in favor of the topic or against it? *in favor*

2. The World Cup soccer championships have opened this week in Germany. Everyone is trying to predict the winner. Some bet on Brazil, which won the last championship, or Argentina, which seems to be in top form. Then there are the usual European top three: France, Germany, and Italy. But there could also be some surprises. At the European championships two years ago, the finals were played between Portugal and Greece, with Greece winning the cup for the first time in its history. For the upcoming matches at the German stadiums, tickets were sold out long ago. There is some concern about the fans becoming overly enthusiastic or even violent. However, the German police say that measures have been taken to prevent any incidents or to contain them quickly.

    a. Is the writer biased or neutral? _____

    b. If the writer is biased, is the bias in favor of the topic or against it? _____

3. It's time for World Cup championship soccer. Once again, if you happen to live in any of the countries where soccer is the national sport, you'll hear about nothing else for a month. People spend hours discussing the physical condition of the players. In the newspapers and on television news programs the journalists are as obsessed as everyone else. People who are normally reasonable become wildly patriotic. If their team is winning, they wave flags, shout, and even sing. You'd think that grown men and women would realize how foolish they look. But no, when those eleven men start running on the field, nothing else seems to matter. The world around them could go up in smoke and they'd never notice. They're totally involved in the primitive ritual of the game.

    a. Is the writer biased or neutral? _____

    b. If the writer is biased, is the bias in favor of the topic or against it? _____

B. Compare your answers with those of another student. If you disagree, explain your answers and look back at the passage to check your work.

EXERCISE 8

A. The articles you will read in this exercise reflect different opinions about banning smokers from the workplace. Read the articles and answer the questions.

Article 1

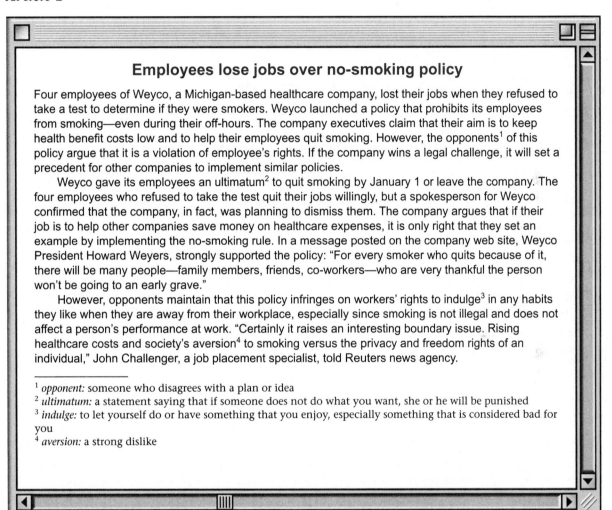

Employees lose jobs over no-smoking policy

Four employees of Weyco, a Michigan-based healthcare company, lost their jobs when they refused to take a test to determine if they were smokers. Weyco launched a policy that prohibits its employees from smoking—even during their off-hours. The company executives claim that their aim is to keep health benefit costs low and to help their employees quit smoking. However, the opponents[1] of this policy argue that it is a violation of employee's rights. If the company wins a legal challenge, it will set a precedent for other companies to implement similar policies.

Weyco gave its employees an ultimatum[2] to quit smoking by January 1 or leave the company. The four employees who refused to take the test quit their jobs willingly, but a spokesperson for Weyco confirmed that the company, in fact, was planning to dismiss them. The company argues that if their job is to help other companies save money on healthcare expenses, it is only right that they set an example by implementing the no-smoking rule. In a message posted on the company web site, Weyco President Howard Weyers, strongly supported the policy: "For every smoker who quits because of it, there will be many people—family members, friends, co-workers—who are very thankful the person won't be going to an early grave."

However, opponents maintain that this policy infringes on workers' rights to indulge[3] in any habits they like when they are away from their workplace, especially since smoking is not illegal and does not affect a person's performance at work. "Certainly it raises an interesting boundary issue. Rising healthcare costs and society's aversion[4] to smoking versus the privacy and freedom rights of an individual," John Challenger, a job placement specialist, told Reuters news agency.

---

[1] *opponent:* someone who disagrees with a plan or idea
[2] *ultimatum:* a statement saying that if someone does not do what you want, she or he will be punished
[3] *indulge:* to let yourself do or have something that you enjoy, especially something that is considered bad for you
[4] *aversion:* a strong dislike

1. What is the writer's purpose—to inform, persuade, or entertain? How can you tell? Mark the words and phrases that helped you to decide.

2. What is the main point of the article?

3. Is the writer for, against, or neutral about the smoking ban? How can you tell?

4. Does the writer seem biased? How can you tell?

Article 2

Trend: You Smoke? You're Fired!

by Stephanie Armour

More companies are taking action against employees who smoke off-duty, and, in an extreme trend that some call troubling, some are now firing or banning the hiring of workers who light up even on their own time.

The outright bans raise new questions about how far companies can go in regulating workers' behavior when they are off the clock. The crackdown is coming in part as a way to curb soaring health care costs, but critics say companies are violating workers' privacy rights. The zero-tolerance policies are coming as more companies adopt smoke-free workplaces.

Weyco, a medical benefits provider based in Okemos, Michigan, this year banned employees from smoking on their own time. Employees must submit to random tests that detect if someone has smoked. They must also agree to searches of briefcases, purses or other belongings if company officials suspect tobacco or other banned substances have been brought on-site. Those who smoke may be suspended or fired.

About 20 employees have quit smoking under the policy, and a handful were fired after they opted out of the testing. "The main goal is to elevate the health status of our employees," says Gary Climes, chief financial officer.

At Investors Property Management in Seattle, smokers are not hired. Employees who smoked before the ban was passed about two years ago are not fired; however, they can't get medical insurance through the company.

Alaska Airlines has a no-smoking policy for employees, and new hires must submit to a urine test to prove they're tobacco-free.

"The debate has gone from where they can smoke to whether they can smoke," says Marshal Tanick, a Minneapolis-based employment lawyer.

Such bans are not legal everywhere: More than 20 states have passed laws that bar companies from discriminating against workers for lifestyle decisions.

There are other ways that companies are taking action against off-duty smoking, such as raising health care premiums for smokers.

Employers say it's about creating a healthy workforce. But it's also a bottom-line issue: Tobacco causes more than 440,000 deaths annually and results in more than $75 billion in direct medical costs a year, according to the Centers for Disease Control and Prevention.

Some smokers' rights groups are vowing legal action. "These matters will be decided in the courts," says Redmond, Washington-based Normon Kjono with Forces, a smokers' rights group. "You're creating a class of unemployable citizens. It won't stand."

And legal experts fear companies will try to control other aspects of employees' off-duty lifestyle, a trend that is already happening. Some companies are firing, suspending or charging higher insurance premiums to workers who are overweight, have high cholesterol or participate in risky activities.

(Source: *USA TODAY*, May 11, 2005)

1. What is the writer's purpose—to inform, persuade, or entertain? How can you tell? Mark the words and phrases that helped you to decide.

2. What is the main point of the article?

3. Is the writer for, against, or neutral about the smoking ban? How can you tell?

4. Does the writer seem biased? How can you tell?

Article 3

Smoke Screen

We support all sorts of policies to combat the use of tobacco. But the World Health Organization's recently announced policy to deny jobs to smokers goes too far.

The organization announced on December 1 that it will no longer hire people who smoke or who won't pledge to stop smoking.

WHO says that its credibility is at stake because it is the world's leading opponent of tobacco use. But there is an important distinction to be made between smoking and smokers. The WHO policy conflates the two in a worrisome way.

Smokers are an easy target. But just as free speech rights must extend to the most unpopular views, so, too, should unsound—but private—activities be protected from raids by the lifestyle police.

(Source: Adapted from *The Boston Globe*, printed in *International Herald Tribune*, January 4, 2006)

1. What is the writer's purpose—to inform, persuade, or entertain? How can you tell? Mark the words or phrases that helped you decide.

2. What is the main point of the article?

3. Is the writer for, against, or neutral about the smoking ban? How can you tell?

4. Does the writer seem biased? How can you tell?

B. Compare your answers with those of another student. If you disagree, explain your answers and look back at the articles to check your work.

Focus on Vocabulary

A. Check your understanding of the following target words. Read each word aloud and then write S, M, or N beside it.

S = *you are sure of the meaning of the word*
M = *you think you might know the meaning of the word*
N = *you don't know the meaning of the word at all*

____ policy	____ confirm	____ site
____ violation	____ issue	____ suspend
____ challenge	____ submit	____ status
____ precedent	____ random	____ discriminate

B. Read two passages from Exercise 8. As you read, look for the target words and circle them. Note that the words in part A are listed in the same order as they appear in the passage but the form may be different.

1. EMPLOYEES LOSE JOBS OVER NO-SMOKING POLICY

Four employees of Weyco, a Michigan-based healthcare company, lost their jobs when they refused to take a test to determine if they were smokers. Weyco launched a policy that prohibits its employees from smoking—even during their off-hours. The company executives claim that their aim is to keep health benefit costs low and to help their employees quit smoking. However, the opponents of this policy argue that it is a violation of employee's rights. If the company wins a legal challenge, it will set a precedent for other companies to implement similar policies.

Weyco gave its employees an ultimatum to quit smoking by January 1 or leave the company. The four employees who refused to take the test quit their jobs willingly, but a spokesperson for Weyco confirmed that the company, in fact, was planning to dismiss them. The company argues that if their job is to help other companies save money on healthcare expenses, it is only right that they set an example by implementing the no-smoking rule. In a message posted on the company web site, Weyco President Howard Weyers, strongly supported the policy: "For every smoker who quits because of it, there will be many people—family members, friends, co-workers—who are very thankful the person won't be going to an early grave."

However, opponents maintain that this policy infringes on workers' rights to indulge in any habits they like when they are away from their workplace, especially since smoking is not illegal and does not affect a person's performance at work. "Certainly it raises an interesting boundary issue. Rising healthcare costs and society's aversion to smoking versus the privacy and freedom rights of an individual," John Challenger, a job placement specialist, told Reuters news agency.

2.   **TREND: YOU SMOKE? YOU'RE FIRED!**
                             by Stephanie Armour

More companies are taking action against employees who smoke off-duty, and, in an extreme trend that some call troubling, some are now firing or banning the hiring of workers who light up even on their own time.

The outright bans raise new questions about how far companies can go in regulating workers behavior when they are off the clock. The crackdown is coming in part as a way to curb soaring health care costs, but critics say companies are violating workers' privacy rights. The zero-tolerance policies are coming as more companies adopt smoke-free workplaces.

Weyco, a medical benefits provider based in Okemos, Michigan, this year banned employees from smoking on their own time. Employees must submit to random tests that detect if someone has smoked. They must also agree to searches of briefcases, purses or other belongings if company officials suspect tobacco or other banned substances have been brought on-site. Those who smoke may be suspended or fired.

About 20 employees have quite smoking under the policy, and a handful were fired after they opted out of the testing. "The main goal is to elevate the health status of our employees," says Gary Climes, chief financial officer.

At Investors Property Management in Seattle, smokers are not hired. Employees who smoked before the ban was passed about two years ago are not fired; however, they can't get medical insurance through the company.

Alaska Airlines has a no-smoking policy for employees, and new hires must submit to a urine test to prove they're tobacco-free.

"The debate has gone from where they can smoke to whether they can smoke," says Marshal Tanick, a Minneapolis-based employment lawyer.

Such bans are not legal everywhere: More than 20 states have passed laws that bar companies from discriminating against workers for lifestyle decisions.

There are other ways that companies are taking action against off-duty smoking, such as raising health care premiums for smokers.

(Source: *USA TODAY*, May 11, 2005)

C. Working with another student, check to be sure that you have located all of the target words.

A. These sentences are taken from the passages in Exercise 9. Working with another student, read each sentence aloud. Then circle the best meaning or synonym for the underlined word as it is used in the sentence.

1. Weyco launched a <u>policy</u> that prohibits its employees from smoking . . .

   a. service   b. group   c. rule

2. However, the opponents of this policy argue that it is <u>a violation of</u> employee's rights.

   a. against   b. proof of   c. an example of

3. If the company wins a legal challenge, it will set a <u>precedent</u> . . .

   a. ideal   b. example   c. goal

4. If the company wins a legal <u>challenge</u>, it will set a precedent . . .

   a. test   b. address   c. account

5. A spokesperson for Weyco <u>confirmed</u> that the company, in fact, was planning to dismiss them.

   a. was angry that   b. could not say   c. said it was true

6. Certainly it raises an interesting boundary <u>issue</u>.

   a. problem   b. service   c. product

7. Employees must <u>submit</u> to random tests that detect if someone has smoked.

   a. agree   b. experience   c. expect

8. Employees must submit to <u>random</u> tests that detect if someone has smoked.

   a. frequent   b. unannounced   c. regular

9. They must also agree to searches of briefcases, purses or other belongings if company officials suspect tobacco or other banned substances have been brought <u>on-site</u>.

   a. into the state   b. to their home   c. to the office.

10. Those who smoke may be <u>suspended</u> or fired.

    a. scolded   b. sent home   c. hired

11. "The main goal is to elevate the health <u>status</u> of our employees," says Gary Climes, chief financial officer.

 a. condition b. insurance c. costs

12. Such bans are not legal everywhere: More than 20 states have passed laws that bar companies from <u>discriminating against</u> workers for lifestyle decisions.

 a. recognizing b. giving favors to c. treating unfairly

B. Compare your answers with those of another pair of students. If you disagree, look back at the sentences and explain your answer and then use a dictionary to check your work.

EXERCISE 11

A. In this table, write as many as possible of the missing forms as you can think of without looking in a dictionary.

Noun	Verb	Adjective	Adverb
challenge			
	confirm		———
	discriminate		———
issue		———	———
precedent			———
		random	
	submit		
	suspend		———
violation		———	———

B. Compare your work with that of another student. Then look in the dictionary for the forms you did not know and write them in the table.

A. Working with another student, write a form of one of the target words in each of the sentences below. Each word may be used only once.

challenge	policy	status
confirm	precedent	submit
discriminate	random	suspend
issue	site	violation

1. The state and local authorities could not come to an agreement about the _____ of the new waste treatment plant.

2. The new president announced some changes in the government's _____ on immigration.

3. The successful legal action by a woman working in the iron mines set an important _____ for the rights of women workers.

4. In the Italian university system, foreign language teachers do not have the same _____ as their Italian colleagues.

5. The prisoner stated that the way he had been treated was a serious _____ of his legal and human rights.

6. The mayor now faces the _____ of improving the city's public transportation system.

7. Certain health _____ such as illness relating to smoking and obesity, should be dealt with in all high school science programs.

8. On weekend nights, the police stop drivers at _____ for a breath test to measure levels of alcohol in the blood.

9. Older workers are often _____ against in favor of younger workers.

10. The student who caused a flood in one of the bathrooms and extensive damage to the school was _____ from school for a month.

11. The police _____ newspaper reports that the thieves had been found, but not the stolen paintings.

12. Though it was against his principles, he decided to _____ to the new rule for the sake of his family.

B. Compare your work with that of another pair of students. If you disagree, explain your answers and then use a dictionary to check your work.

A. *Make study cards for the target words that you are still unsure about. Use the cards to study them, first on your own and then with another student. (See Part 2, Unit 1, page 29)*

B. 1. *Write a sentence for each of the words, leaving a blank instead of the target word. Ask another student to read your sentences and write the target word that should go in each blank.*

2. *Look at your sentences again. If your classmate wrote a different word, discuss the sentences to find out why. Was your sentence unclear, or did your classmate not know the target word?*

PART 4

Reading Faster

Complete the chart and discuss your responses with another student.

How fast do you usually read these?	Very fast	Fast	Moderate	Slow	Very slow
Novel, short story, or detective story			✓		
Newspaper article			✓		
Telephone directory	✓				
New cookbook recipe	✓				
Directions to a friend's house	✓				
Textbook chapter			✓		
Poem				✓	
Letter from a friend			✓		

Many students tend to read everything at the same rate (speed). However, fluent readers adjust their reading speed according to the material that they are reading and their purpose for reading it.

There are three important reasons for learning to read faster:

1. You will get through required reading more efficiently.

2. You will enjoy your extensive reading books more and so you will read more.

3. You will improve your comprehension.

   (See Part 1, Extensive Reading.)

The first two advantages of reading faster are obvious. The connection between reading faster and better comprehension may not be so clear, but it is no less important. When you read slowly, you read one word at a time, like this:

What   really   happens   when   we   read?   Some

people   think   we   read   one   word   at   a   time.

They   think   we   read   a   word,   understand   it

and   then   move   on   to   the   next   word.

Reading separate words this way makes it hard to understand what you read because you must remember each word as a separate piece of information. By the time you get to the end of a sentence you may have forgotten the beginning.

The following five strategies will help you improve your reading rate, that is, the speed at which you read. This is not the same as the "speed reading" sometimes advertised—as in "Learn to read a novel in an hour!" The aim here is to increase your rate gradually, while at the same time building confidence and comprehension.

You should also keep in mind that your goal is not to read everything at maximum speed. Instead, you want to achieve flexibility and the ability to speed up or slow down according to the text and your purpose for reading.

Experts believe that a reading rate of less than 200–250 words per minute (WPM) almost certainly indicates word-by-word reading. Many students who have never worked on increasing their reading rate read at that rate. Others may already read at faster rates. Whatever your rate is now, experience has shown that students who regularly work on their reading rate can double it in one semester. Very often, this also leads to better academic performance.

Strategy 1: Check your reading habits

Certain habits can slow you down. Think about your own reading habits.

a. Do you try to pronounce every word as you read? Pronunciation is not necessary for comprehension. In fact, if you try to say the words, even silently, you will probably understand *less*. The effort of trying to pronounce the words will interfere with your ability to comprehend.

b. Do you usually move your lips while you read silently? Saying the words will prevent you from ever reading faster than about 200 WPM, the fastest speed at which English can be spoken.

c. Do you follow the words you read with your finger or a pencil? Following the words with your finger will also slow you down. The eyes of a good reader do not move line by line through a text. Instead they tend to jump ahead for new information, or back for confirmation of what was read. *Your eyes should be free to follow your thoughts, not your finger!*

d. Do you translate into your native language as you read in English? Or do you often write translations of words in the English text? Translating into your native language takes time and prevents you from concentrating on the ideas. Furthermore, it interferes with your ability to think in English as you read.

Note: If you answered yes to any of the questions, try to change the habits that are slowing you down.

Strategy 2: Read meaningful phrases or "chunks"

Good readers in English "chunk" as they read. That is, they read meaningful groups of words, which are much easier to remember than a lot of separate words. Furthermore, when reading in chunks, they can form connections among the ideas in the text and with information or ideas they know.

What is a meaningful phrase, or chunk?

Good readers in English is a meaningful phrase because it makes sense alone.

English chunk as is not a meaningful phrase because it does not make sense alone.

Readers generally divide up sentences in similar ways, though there may be some differences. Faster readers tend to make longer phrases so they can take in more text at a time. For example:

Each chunk / should be a phrase / that makes sense / by itself. (slower readers)

Each chunk should be a phrase / that makes sense by itself. (faster readers)

EXERCISE 1

A. Read the following paragraph.

Teenagers are not the only ones to be tempted by fast food. Apparently, pigeons also find the salty, fatty meals very attractive. Reports suggest that city pigeons are eating leftovers found in trash cans or outside fast-food restaurants, and as a result they are becoming overweight. Soon they will not be able to sit on power lines without the risk of breaking the lines and causing shortages.

B. Now read the paragraph aloud to another student and listen to the other student read it to you.

C. Read the same paragraph divided into meaningful phrases.

Teenagers are not the only ones   to be tempted   by fast food.
Apparently,   pigeons also find   the salty, fatty meals   very attractive.
Reports suggest   that city pigeons   are eating leftovers   found in trash cans
or outside fast-food restaurants,   and as a result   they are becoming overweight.
Soon they will not be able   to sit on power lines   without the risk
of breaking the lines   and causing shortages.

D. Now read the paragraph aloud to another student, pausing very briefly after each phrase. Was it easier to understand the paragraph with or without the division into phrases?

Note: Students usually find that they understand better when their partners read the paragraph divided into phrases. In listening, as in reading, it is easier for your brain to take in and process information if it is divided into meaningful phrases.

A. Working with another student, read the passage and then divide the sentences into meaningful phrases. The first sentence has been done for you. Note that some phrases may be on two lines of text.

Cat Graves on Cyprus

Archaeologists have found / the earliest known evidence / of a special connection / between humans and cats. Last month in Cyprus they discovered the grave of a 30-year-old villager who died 9,500 years ago. With the body, they found jewelry, sea-shells, and other items. Less than a meter (3 feet) away, in another grave almost certainly made at the same time, lay the bones of a young cat.

Cat bones have been found before near early human settlements, but scientists believe they belonged to wild cats. These cats probably stayed around human villages to catch the mice and rats attracted by the supplies of food. The new find on Cyprus, however, seems to indicate that the cats in this village were tamed and had some special role to play in human activities or a special relationship with certain individuals. These bones showed no signs of having been butchered for eating. And since they were in the right places in the skeleton, the animal must have been buried soon after death; otherwise, the bones would have been taken by other animals.

Other animals were tamed before cats. The first dogs (actually a type of wolf) are known to have lived with humans as early as 15,000 years ago. Their importance in early human settlements is shown by the evidence of dog graves from 12,500 years ago in Israel. The goat was probably the first animal to produce milk for humans, around 10,000 years ago. But until now, the first evidence of household cats came from Egypt only 4,000 years ago. The discovery of the skeleton of this cat, which had clearly been handled with care, is very exciting for archaeologists.

B. Compare your work with that of another pair of students. If you disagree, check with your teacher and correct your phrases. Then read the pasage aloud to each other, pausing briefly after each phrase.

Note: For further practice in dividing text into chunks, you can mark passages in this book or your extensive reading book. Choose one or two paragraphs and divide the sentences into chunks. Then read the paragraphs several times, focusing your eyes on each chunk.

Strategy 3: Skip over unknown words

Do not stop when you come to an unknown word. Skip over the word and continue reading. In some cases, knowing the meaning of the word will not be necessary for understanding the important ideas in the passage. In other cases, you may be able to get a general sense of the word from the context (see Part 2, Unit 2).

A. In this paragraph, every fifth word is missing. Read the paragraph and answer the questions. Do NOT try to guess the missing words.

Anna Polanski, the famous _____ pianist, moved to the _____ States five years ago. _____ year, she plays a free _____ and she invites her _____, friends, fans, and the _____ from a local school. _____ week, her annual concert _____ held at the University _____ Center, and her invited _____ included the children from _____ Park School in Roxbury. _____ this event, Ms. Polanski _____ to play the music _____ Chopin, including his most _____ composition, the Polonaise. _____ her audience enjoyed all _____ the pieces she played, _____ responded most to a _____ of lively marches and _____ that she played at _____ end of the concert. _____ the concert, several children _____ to the stage and _____ Ms. Polanski with bouquets of _____.

1. Was Anna Polanski born in the United States?

2. How often does she give free concerts?

3. Whom does she invite to concerts?

4. What did the audience enjoy most?

5. What did the children give Ms. Polanski?

B. Compare your answers with those of another student. Then discuss the following questions.

1. How many of the questions could you answer?
2. Did you need to know the missing words to understand the passage?

Note: Students usually find that they can read and understand a lot even when many words are missing or unknown.

Strategy 4: Use your extensive reading book

Here are two ways to use your extensive reading book to improve your reading rate.

Reading sprints

Slow reading is often a matter of habit. You read at a certain speed because your eyes are used to moving across the page at that speed. Reading sprints are an effective way to break that habit and force your eyes to move more quickly. Sprints will help you in the same way that running sprints help runners who want to increase their speed. They may seem difficult and tiring at first, and you will probably feel that you are comprehending little of the text. But with practice, they will get easier and your comprehension will improve.

Read the instructions below all the way through before you start so you will be able to concentrate on your reading during the sprint. You will need a reliable clock or watch and your extensive reading book.

Instructions for reading sprints

1. Mark with a pencil where you are now in your book. Make a note of your starting time in the margin and read for five minutes.

2. Write in the margin of your book the number of pages you have read.

3. Count ahead about the same number of pages as those you have just read, and mark the place. (For example, if you read two and a half pages, count ahead two and a half pages.)

4. Try to read those pages in only *four* minutes. If you do not succeed the first time, keep trying until you do, using new pages each time. You will need to force your eyes to move faster along the page, skipping over words or even whole lines of text. Do not worry about your comprehension at this point.

5. Count ahead the same number of pages again, and mark the place as you did before. Try to read that same number of pages in *three* minutes. If you do not succeed, try again with new pages.

6. Now, try to read the same number of pages in *two* minutes. Keep trying until you succeed. You may be able to grab just a few words from the text. This does not matter. The important thing is to make your eyes move quickly and understand *something*.

7. Mark your place in the book again. Make a note of the starting time and read for five minutes without forcing yourself to read fast.

8. Count the number of pages you read this time. Compare this with the number of pages you read the first time.

Note: Many students find that their unforced "normal" speed is faster after the sprints. Regular practice with reading sprints will help you increase your reading rate and become more comfortable reading at faster speeds. (If you feel that you did not understand fully what you read during the sprints, you can read those pages again afterward.)

Rate practice

Follow the instructions below to calculate your reading rate in your extensive reading book. Check your rate regularly (about once a week) and keep track of your progress on the Extensive Reading Rate Progress Charts on the next page.

Calculating extensive reading rate

1. In your extensive reading book, calculate the average number of words per page.

   a. Turn to a full page in your book (preferably without a lot of dialogue unless that is typical of your book).

   b. Count the number of words in three lines and divide by 3 to get the average number of words per line.

   c. Count the number of lines on that page and multiply it by the number of words per line to get the average number of words per page.

   _____ × _____ = _____
      (lines)   (average words per line)   (words on a page)

2. Time your reading.

   a. Open your book and mark your place on the page you are now reading. Before you begin to read, write in the margin the exact time you start reading. Read comfortably for about ten or fifteen minutes. Write the exact time you finished.

   b. Calculate the number of minutes you read:

   _____ min. − _____ min. = _____ min.
      (finishing time)   (starting time)   (reading time)

3. Calculate your reading rate.

   a. Count the number of pages you read, including parts of pages.

   b. Find the total number of words you read by multiplying the number of pages by the number of words per page.

   _____ × _____ = _____
      (pages read)   (words per page)   (words you read)

   c. Calculate your reading rate (words per minute) by dividing the total number of words you read by the number of minutes.

   _____ ÷ _____ = _____
      (words read)   (minutes)   (reading rate — words per minute)

4. Turn to the Extensive Reading Rate Progress Charts on the next page. Write the date and your reading rate.

Book Title _____

Author _____

Book Title _____

Author _____

RATE (words per minute—WPM)

| 520 |
| 500 |
| 480 |
| 460 |
| 440 |
| 420 |
| 400 |
| 380 |
| 360 |
| 340 |
| 320 |
| 300 |
| 280 |
| 260 |
| 240 |
| 220 |
| 200 |
| 180 |
| 160 |
| 140 |
| 120 |
| 100 |
| 80 |

Date

RATE (words per minute—WPM)

| 520 |
| 500 |
| 480 |
| 460 |
| 440 |
| 420 |
| 400 |
| 380 |
| 360 |
| 340 |
| 320 |
| 300 |
| 280 |
| 260 |
| 240 |
| 220 |
| 200 |
| 180 |
| 160 |
| 140 |
| 120 |
| 100 |
| 80 |

Date

Strategy 5: Practice with timed readings

Regular practice in reading against the clock is the best way to increase your reading rate. In the example below, you will time yourself as you read the passage and then answer comprehension questions. These are the same steps you will follow as you read all of the passages in Units 2, 3, and 4. (All of the passages are about 950 words long.)

Example:

A. Write your exact starting time. Preview the passage for a few seconds and then read it all the way through to the end. Push yourself to read a little faster than usual.

Using Cell Phones: Cultural Differences

Starting time $OP.52$

(Write the exact time you begin reading.)

What do you do if your cell phone rings while you are with a group of people? If you are French, you will probably ignore the call. If you are English, you may walk away from the group to answer it. If you are Spanish, you are likely to answer it there in the middle of the group and invite everyone around you to join the conversation.

As many travelers have noticed, there are considerable differences from one country to another in the way people use their cell phones. This has been confirmed by a recent study of cell phone use in three European cities—Madrid, London, and Paris. In spite of the fact that these cities are all in the European Union and share a great deal of history and culture, local customs are still very different. These customs influence the way people in these cities use their phones in public.

According to Amparo Lasén, the Spanish sociologist who conducted the study, there were no real surprises for anyone who is familiar with the customs in these cities. Lasén interviewed people and observed their behavior in three different settings: a major train station, a commercial area, and a business district in each city.

She found that Londoners use their cell phones the least in public. If they are with others, they prefer to let calls be answered by voice mail (a recorded message) and then they check for messages later. If the English do answer a call on the street, they seem to dislike talking with others around. They tend to move away from a crowded sidewalk and seek out a place where they cannot be heard, such as the far side of a subway entrance or even the edge of a street. They seem to feel that the danger of the traffic is preferable to the risk of having their conversation be overheard.

This has led to a behavior that Lasén has called "clustering." At a busy time of day on the streets of London, you may find small crowds of cell phone users grouped together, each one talking into a cell phone. Even when it is raining—as it often is in London—people still prefer not to hold their conversations where others could hear. They talk under their umbrellas or in a doorway.

In Madrid, on the other hand, few people use voice mail because the Spanish dislike talking with machines rather than real voices. If there is no answer, they don't leave a message. They prefer to try again later or wait for a return call. And since the Spanish are not shy about answering their calls in public, the call may come sooner than it would in London or Paris. In fact, in Madrid it is common to hear loud and lively phone conversations on the street, accompanied by shouts, laughter and the waving of hands. In fact, sometimes it happens that a group of friends may be walking down the street together, each talking on their own phone, but smiling and nodding as though it were one large conversation that everyone could hear.

Even when they are not using their phones, the Spanish often hold them in their hands as they walk down the street or put them on the table at a restaurant, so they will not miss any incoming calls. In a movie theater, not only do cell phones occasionally ring, but people sometimes answer them and have brief conversations.

In Paris, however, there are stricter rules about how and when to use cell phones. It is not considered polite to use a phone in a restaurant, for instance, though it might be acceptable in the more informal setting of a café. One special custom that has developed in cafés seems unique to Paris. Young women often place their cell phones on the table beside them to signal that they are expecting someone. When the friend arrives, the phone is put away. In fact, the French are generally very disapproving of phone use in public and are quick to express that disapproval, even to strangers.

In one area, sociologists found that the French and Spanish were similar. Both were quite willing to continue a phone conversation in a romantic situation, even kissing someone present while continuing a conversation on the phone. These people were clearly not using videophones. In London, however, no one was ever observed to be kissing while on the telephone. The English seem to prefer more privacy for their romantic moments.

According to Lasén, cultural stereotypes were supported by yet another difference that she noticed as she conducted her study. In each of the three cities, people reacted to her differently when she was interviewing and observing. In Paris, people frowned at her; in London, they pretended not to notice; in Madrid, however, they did not seem to mind.

Understanding the habits of these European cell phone users has become a lively topic of study for sociologists and psychologists at European universities. But with 1 billion cell phone users around the world, the subject is of interest not only to academic researchers. Habits of cell phone use are also a matter of serious study by telecommunications companies. If they can understand the local customs and customers better, they might be able to change people's behavior and increase cell phone use. For example, if phone companies want to increase their profits in France, they need to convince people that it is acceptable to use their phones in restaurants. The Spanish need to be persuaded that voice mail is not so bad, and the English must learn to leave their phones on all the time.

(Source: Adapted from "A Mobile Tale of Three Cities" by Thomas Crampton. *International Herald Tribune,* June 11–12, 2005)

Finishing time _08: 50_ Reading time __6__

(Write the exact time that you finish reading.)   (Subtract your starting time from your finishing time.)

B. *Write your exact finishing time (minutes and seconds) and reading time. Then turn to the next page and answer the comprehension questions. Do not look back at the passage while you are answering the questions.*

C. Circle the letter of the best answer for each item.

1. Choose the statement that best expresses the thesis (general idea) of this passage.

    a. People in different cities have different social customs.
    b. Londoners do not like to use their cell phones in public.
    c. The way people use cell phones differs in London, Paris, and Madrid.
    d. People in Madrid tend to speak more loudly than in Paris or London.

2. A Spanish sociologist has said that the way people use their cell phones

    a. fits in with their local habits and customs.
    b. is the same in all European countries today.
    c. is related to the person's sex and age.
    d. depends on where they use their phone.

3. Londoners use voice mail a lot because they

    a. enjoy leaving recorded messages.
    b. like to answer calls in crowded places.
    c. do not like to speak with real voices.
    d. prefer not to answer calls in public.

4. In London, people speaking on phones "cluster" together so they can share their conversation with others.

    a. True
    b. False

5. When they are in groups, the people in Madrid

    a. prefer to pay more attention to the people around them.
    b. continue to answer calls and have phone conversations.
    c. stop talking and wait when a cell phone rings.
    d. prefer to leave messages with voice mail.

6. In Paris, a cell phone on a café table beside a young woman means she is expecting someone.

    a. True
    b. False

7. Parisians

    a. do not like it when people use cell phones in public.
    b. use cell phones more than the English or the Spanish.
    c. use their cell phones often in restaurants and movie theaters.
    d. never continue a phone conversation in a romantic moment.

8. You can infer (or conclude) from this passage that

    a. cell phone companies will make less money in the European countries.
    b. sociologists can tell little about people's lives from their phone use.
    c. weather can be an important factor in the way people use cell phones.
    d. technology may be global, but the way people use it is not.

D. Check your answers with your teacher. For any incorrect answers, look back at the passage to understand why they were incorrect.

E. Find your reading rate (WPM) for the example passage on the Reading Rate Table (page 252).

F. Write today's date, your reading rate (WPM), and your comprehension score (the number of correct answers) on the Progress Chart for Timed Readings (page 253).

Guidelines for Timed Reading Practice

- Set a reading rate goal for yourself. If you have a personal goal, you will push yourself more to read faster.

  Your present reading rate: _____ WPM (from the Example above)

  Your personal goal: _____ WPM

- Be sure to record the exact time you start and finish each passage.

- Answer the questions without looking back at the passages.

- Check your answers with your teacher. Then look back at the text to understand any incorrect answers.

- Find your reading rate on the Reading Rate Table on page 252.

- Record your reading rate, comprehension score (the number of correct answers), and the date on the Progress Chart for Timed Readings on page 253.

- After you have read four or five passages, check your progress on the charts for reading rate and comprehension. Your aim should be to increase your reading rate gradually while keeping your comprehension score at six or more correct answers.

  ➤ If your reading rate stays the same, you need to force your eyes to move ahead faster.

  ➤ If you have incorrect answers for more than three questions, you might be reading too fast. Slow down slightly and concentrate more while you read.

Reading Rate Table

All of the passages are about 950 words long. To determine your reading rate in this table, find the time that is closest to your Reading Time. Then look across to find your reading rate. For instance, if you read the example passage in 2:30 (two minutes and thirty seconds) your reading rate would be 380 WPM.

Reading Time (Minutes:Seconds)	Rate (Words per Minute)	Reading Time (Minutes:Seconds)	Rate (Words per Minute)
1:00	950	3:40	260
1:10	815	3:50	248
1:20	714	4:00	238
1:30	633	4:10	228
1:40	572	4:20	219
1:50	518	4:30	211
2:00	475	4:40	204
2:10	439	4:50	197
2:20	408	5:00	190
2:30	380	5:10	184
2:40	357	5:20	178
2:50	335	5:30	173
3:00	317	5:40	168
3:10	300	5:50	163
3:20	285	6:00	158
3:30	271		

Progress Chart for Timed Readings

When you finish a passage, write your reading rate and comprehension score (the number of correct answers). In the "Comments" column write about your reaction to the passage. Was the passage interesting, difficult, etc.?

Passage and Date	Reading Rate (WPM)	Comprehension Score	Comments
Example			
Unit 2			
1			
2			
3			
4			
5			
6			
Unit 3			
1			
2			
3			
4			
5			
6			
Unit 4			
1			
2			
3			
4			
5			
6			

Introduction to Reading Faster Passages

The passages in Units 2, 3, and 4 were researched and drafted by Richard M. Ravin

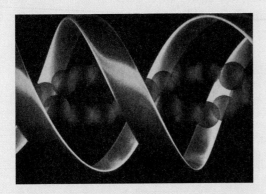

Unit 2—New technology and its impact around the world

Unit 3—People who have made a difference

Unit 4—Inventions that are changing our lives

New Technology and Its Impact Around the World

1. Cell Phones in Africa

Starting time _____

The African continent is home to some of the poorest countries on earth, where people struggle to feed their families on less than $2.00 a day. Nevertheless, Africa is also the world's fastest growing market for cell phones. Cell phones have brought twenty-first century technology to villages where people light their huts with candles and walk hours to find drinking water. Some experts think cell phones will improve life for the 680 million Africans more than any other invention of our time.

Why are cell phones spreading so rapidly in Africa? One reason is simply that other forms of communication are difficult. The roads are terrible in many countries, making travel lengthy and expensive. Regular phones require lines to be laid across Africa's vast jungles and deserts. Cell phones, however, send their signals from towers, which can easily be constructed by hand, sometimes out of leftover pieces of metal.

Furthermore, with the difficult economic situation in many African countries, cell phones can be extremely useful. Many Africans have had to move far from their home villages to look for work. With a cell phone, they can call home regularly and keep in touch or even send money. It is also possible in some countries to make purchases or bank deposits with cell phones. People who run small businesses can use the phones to send in orders or keep in touch with customers. Others can make money selling phone time to those who don't have a cell phone of their own.

Recent studies have shown that where cell phone use has increased in Africa, the economy has been strengthened and the people are better off. In Uganda, for example, a charity group has started a new program with Uganda's largest cell phone company. The program, called villagePhone, helps village women get started as phone owners. The women borrow small amounts of money from banks connected to villagePhone and then use their loan money to buy a phone and some calling minutes. Then they can sell phone time in the village to people without phones. In very little time, these women are usually able to repay the money they have borrowed.

One such woman named Fatima had a small shop in her Ugandan village where she sold household goods and food to support her four children. In the past, Fatima rarely had enough money to buy things to sell in her store and so she made very little money from her business. However, she realized that there was a need for a telephone in her village, since the closest phone was 6.7 miles (4 km) away. She bought a phone with a loan from villagePhone and ran it off an automobile battery. Since starting her villagePhone business, Fatima's income has grown. What's more, her store is now a center of village life.

Fatima's story is like many throughout Uganda. Her villagePhone business is one of about 2,000 such success stories, with more women joining every day. And for each woman with a phone, a whole village has access to new services and new economic possibilities. A similar

program has started in neighboring Rwanda. Soon women there will be using cell phones to raise their income level and improve their lives.

In many parts of Africa, cell phones are also extremely useful in the field of health care. In South Africa, for instance, cell phones help doctors deal with the enormous problem of HIV/AIDS. The rates of infection in South Africa are among the highest in the world and each doctor may have many patients who live in distant villages. Since the doctors cannot visit all the patients themselves, they send specially trained health care workers to see the patients and check that they are following their treatment correctly. Then, using a new cell phone system called Cell-Life, the health-care workers talk to the doctor about any problems and send patients to doctors only if necessary. This allows doctors to use their time more effectively and it saves some patients the cost and difficulty of traveling.

Another advantage of cell phones is that they allow text messaging. This is a system for sending written messages by typing words on the telephone buttons as if they were a computer keyboard. These messages can be sent from one cell phone to another, where they can be read on the phone's small screen. Text messages usually cost less to send than actual phone calls, an important factor for many Africans. They also are useful for people who do not have a computer themselves, but need to send information to someone with a computer.

For example, with Cell-Life, healthcare workers in a village can text-message information about a patient to a city hospital, where the message is stored in a computer with other information about the patient. Before text messaging, health workers had to type and mail all the records themselves, which took much more time, and often resulted in delays in treatment.

Once Africans communicated from one village to another by beating drums, with different drum beats communicating different messages. But since the arrival of inexpensive cell phones in about 1999, new ways of communication have become possible. In 2005, there were 82 million cell phone users on the continent, twice the number of people who owned regular phones, and that number is rising rapidly.

Soon, African cell phone users will be able to connect to the Internet through their phones. Already, many people who may never before have had a bank account or credit card are using cell phones in a mobile banking system. Cell phones are helping Africans to get in touch with each other and to improve their lives.

Finishing time _____   Reading time _____

Now turn to page 264 and answer the questions. Do not look back at the passage.

2. The Three Gorges Dam

After more than fourteen years of work, the world's largest hydroelectric dam will be operating in 2008 or 2009. Built across the Yangtze River in central China, this dam is one of the largest engineering projects in history. The wall of the Three Gorges Dam, which was completed in 2006, is more than a mile and a half wide (2 km), and rises more than 600 feet (183 m) above the river bottom.

The Yangtze, sometimes known in China as "The Dragon," is the world's third longest river. People have lived, fished, and worked along its banks for thousands of years. The area where the dam is being built is among the most beautiful places in China. Towering green mountains sit on both sides of the river, creating narrow passages known as gorges.

But danger lies in the midst of all this beauty. Formerly, the Yangtze rose over its banks once every ten years on average, and this flooding often caused enormous damage and the loss of lives. In the twentieth century, more than 300,000 people died in floods along the river. Since the early 1900s, China's leaders have wanted to build a dam that would control the Yangtze's waters. Reducing the risk of floods is, in fact, the main reason given by the Chinese government for their decision to build the dam.

Another important function of the dam will be to produce electricity. Water from the reservoir will pass through enormous turbines (motors) in the dam before it flows back into the river bed. According to Chinese engineers, this new dam will fill almost one-ninth of China's electricity needs. At present, China depends on burning coal for 75 percent of its power, and this causes severe air pollution in many parts of the country. Hydroelectric power from dams is much cleaner than that produced by coal and less dangerous than that produced by nuclear power. In fact, with its economy expanding rapidly and prices of oil rising, the Chinese government is desperately looking for new sources of energy.

The economic advantages of the new dam, however, do not come without a cost. The lake or reservoir that is formed behind the dam will destroy 395 square miles (632 sq km) of land that for generations has been home to about 1.2 million people and the farms, factories, and towns where they lived. By 2005, over 1 million had already been displaced by the spreading waters; by 2009, whether they want to or not, all of them will have moved.

Many inhabitants of the area have adapted to the new situation with a will to succeed. Huang, a farmer whose house and land vanished under many feet of water, used money he received from the government to buy a small boat. He earns his living now by leading river tours and transporting goods on his boat. While his new land does not grow crops as easily as his old, he likes his new life. He has said that he probably floats right over his old home, but he tries not to think about it.

However, other families have not found it so easy to move their whole lives elsewhere. Many people were not as lucky as Huang to find a new way to make a living. Farmers who were given land often found that the farms were smaller and the land was less productive than their old farms near the river. In fact, the farm land along that part of the Yangtze was some of the most fertile in all of China. Some families also found that the money provided by the government was barely enough to build a very simple house with a concrete floor. For all these reasons, many have found that their economic situation and living conditions are worse than before. So far, the government has not been open to complaints and protests by the citizens who have been badly affected by this situation.

Aside from the social costs of displacing more than a million people, the dam is also causing environmental damage. One problem has already been noticed by environmentalists. Experts say that the reservoir behind the dam is seriously polluted because the area was not cleaned up before it was flooded. The water now contains a combination of human waste, chemicals from now-flooded factories, and very dangerous heavy metals.

A second environmental problem could soon arise, according to environmentalists, as the dam slows the river waters. The Yangtze River has always carried a large amount of silt, or mud, picked up by the strong flow of the water. This silt contains untreated human waste from the towns and cities along the Yangtze. In former times, the flow was powerful enough to wash that waste out to sea. But with the dam blocking the river and slowing the flow of water, some scientists fear that diseases contained in the polluted mud could become a health danger for those who live nearby.

Progress is a complicated thing. The Three Gorges Dam will help satisfy the energy needs of China's 1.2 billion people and it will prevent floods along the Yangtze, bringing a better life to many. But to make such a project happen, more than 1 million people have lost their homes and jobs. Some have already made the change to a new life with ease; others have not, and their lives are worse than before. The Chinese have a saying: Water spilled can never be retrieved. This means that once something has started, there is no going back. In the years ahead, the debate will continue about the Three Gorges Dam and whether or not building it was the right choice for China.

Finishing time _____   Reading time _____

Now turn to page 265 and answer the questions. Do not look back at the passage.

3. Air-Conditioning

Starting time _____

In the United States and other developed countries, air-conditioning is so common that it is difficult to remember what life was like before it existed. First invented in 1902 in Buffalo, New York, air-conditioning keeps homes, cars, offices, and shopping centers cool and dry, all at the push of a button. While many may consider air-conditioning one of life's necessary luxuries, few are aware of how air-conditioning has changed many aspects of the way we now live.

One of the first areas where air-conditioning had an impact was in industry. In the early 1900s factory owners began to use air-conditioning to create better conditions for the storage of supplies. Before long, however, they realized that air-conditioning was also useful on the factory floor, as it resulted in higher production levels. Air-conditioning has undoubtedly been an important factor in the growth of industry, since it allows manufacturing to continue at the same pace year round even in the warmest climates.

Air-conditioning next became common in movie theaters, offices, and stores. Then, after the end of the Second World War, smaller, less expensive air-conditioning units became available, and this made air-conditioning affordable for private homes. Many of the returning soldiers and their new families moved to the suburbs outside America's major cities with a desire to put the war behind them and live the good life. Air-conditioned homes were part of that life, and this led to a number of important changes in American society.

One big change was in architecture. Formerly, homes were built with high ceilings and second stories so that hot air could rise away from main living areas in the summer. With air-conditioning, inexpensive one-level homes could be kept cool in the hottest weather. Additionally, many homes once had front porches where American families gathered in the evening to escape the heat. Family members could talk to each other and to neighbors or passersby. With air-conditioning, however, porches disappeared from new houses and people moved indoors instead. Along with other factors, such as the invention of television, this led to a weakening of Americans' sense of community.

The rise of air-conditioning also allowed the creation of large malls with shops, walkways, movie theaters, and restaurants that are comfortable the year round. In suburban America in the second half of the twentieth century, the air-conditioned mall became the preferred place to go for shopping or for an afternoon's entertainment. Shoppers stopped going to the town and city centers, which led to the closing of many small family-owned businesses, and to the general decline of downtown areas.

With air-conditioning, the architecture of the cities also changed. Builders could now take full advantage of new engineering and materials to create structures that were much larger and taller than ever before. Buildings could take up an entire city block, or rise more than a hundred stories. Furthermore, since the windows did not need to open but were for views alone, buildings could even be covered with glass. Air-conditioning is one of the reasons cities from Shanghai to New York to Berlin have so many shiny skyscrapers.

In the United States, air-conditioning has also influenced the movement of population from the cooler northern states to the southeastern and southwestern states. Before air-conditioning, the hot climate in those regions made them unattractive to northerners. Once air-conditioning made life more pleasant in the summer months, states like Florida and Arizona began to draw people from the north. This population shift has affected regional economies, and also the balance of political power between northern and southern states.

The effects of air-conditioning on society are hardly limited to the United States. Singapore's Senior Minister, Lee Kuan Yew, claims that air-conditioning is one reason for Singapore's rise as an Asian power. In his view, societies in the past progressed most rapidly in countries with cooler climates, but now that countries in tropical zones are using air-conditioning, they can also expand and grow. The use of air-conditioning is seen in some Asian countries as a way to show status. In Hong Kong, for example, office managers tend to keep temperatures extremely cold, sometimes at only 60°F (16°C), 10 to 14°F (6 to 7°C) below the recommended settings. The main reason is simply to show that the company can afford it.

Although air-conditioning has led to economic improvement and has increased daily comfort for people everywhere, its impact on the environment has not been so positive. First, air-conditioning units release polluting chemicals into the air, which contribute to global warming. Furthermore, running air-conditioning on a large scale requires enormous amounts of energy. The burning of coal and oil to produce this energy also contributes to air pollution and thus, to global warming. According to experts, global warming could result in dramatic changes in climate, rising ocean levels, and more violent storms in the years to come.

In some countries, governments and industry are beginning to search for ways to reduce the harm caused by air-conditioning. In Japan, summer temperatures have been raised in office buildings to conserve energy. In the United States, government, industry, and private groups are searching for ways to reduce the amount of dangerous chemicals released by air conditioners, especially those in cars and trucks. Staying cool is important, and many cannot imagine life without air-conditioning. But in the twenty-first century, we will have to find new technologies to make sure that air-conditioning does not create more problems than it solves.

Finishing time _____   Reading time _____

Now turn to page 266 and answer the questions. Do not look back at the passage.

4. DNA Testing

Genetics is one of the most exciting scientific fields of our day. Researchers in many areas of science are finding ways of applying the tools of genetics, and in medicine it has opened doors to dramatic new possibilities for the prevention and treatment of many kinds of disease—from depression to diabetes and Alzheimer's. With the invention of DNA testing, genetics has also had a real impact in a very different field—criminal law.

DNA testing reveals the genes of each individual person. Since the early twentieth century, scientists have known that all human characteristics—from eye color to body height to certain diseases—are contained in a person's genes and are passed from parents to children. Genes work as a chemical instruction manual for each part and each function of the body. Their basic chemical element is called DNA, a copy of which can be found in every cell. The existence of genes and the chemical structure of DNA were understood by the mid-1900s, but scientists have only recently been able to identify a person from just a drop of blood or saliva or a single hair.

One of the most important uses of DNA testing is in criminal investigation, where it provides evidence that helps to prove that some crime suspects are guilty or others are innocent. The very first use of DNA testing in a criminal case was in 1985 in Great Britain, when a man confessed to killing a young woman in the English countryside. Because police had found samples of the killer's DNA at the scene of the crime, a biologist suggested that it might be possible to compare that DNA to some from the confessor's blood. To everyone's surprise, the tests showed that he was not the killer. Nor was he guilty of a similar murder that had happened some time earlier. At that point he admitted that he had confessed to the crimes out of fear and police pressure. The police then asked 5,000 local men for samples of their blood, and DNA testing revealed that one of them was the real murderer, so the first man was set free.

The successful conclusion of this case in England made a big impression on lawyers and police around the globe, especially in the United States. Studies at that time showed that perhaps 5 percent of U.S. prison inmates were in fact innocent of the crimes they had been accused of. That added up to almost 10,000 people. Some, like the man in England, had been pushed to confess to crimes they had not committed. Others had never had a chance to defend themselves in court because of incompetent lawyers. Still others had been convicted on false evidence given by dishonest police officers who wanted to have someone to put in jail.

In 1992, two law professors, Peter Neufeld and Barry Scheck, decided to use DNA evidence to help set free such mistakenly convicted prisoners. With the help of their students, they created a not-for-profit organization called the Innocence Project, which is still operating. Most of their clients are poor men, many from racial and ethnic minorities. In fact, studies have shown that U.S. judges and juries are often influenced by racial and ethnic background, and that people from minority groups are more likely to be convicted. Some of these men had been sentenced to death, a form of punishment used in thirty-eight states out of fifty (as of 2006). For most of these prisoners, their only hope was another trial in which DNA testing could be used to prove their innocence.

Between 1992 and 2006, the Innocence Project helped free 100 men. Some of these prisoners had been in jail for ten, twenty years or more for crimes they did not commit. However, the goal of the Innocence Project is not simply to set free those who are wrongfully in jail. They also hope to bring about real changes in the criminal justice system.

In Illinois in the late 1990s, a group of journalism students at Northwestern University were able to bring about such a change in that state. They began investigating some Illinois prisoners who claimed to be innocent. Through DNA testing, the students were able to prove that in fact the prisoners were not guilty of the crimes they had been accused of. Thirteen of these men were set free, and in 2000, Governor Ryan of Illinois decided to stop carrying out death sentences until further study could be made of the prisoners' cases.

In a study by the Northwestern students and government officials, many serious problems were revealed in the legal system. Police officers had been violent and forced suspects to confess, or they had lied about evidence in court. The reliability of witnesses had not been properly checked, and physical evidence that might have helped the innocent men had been thrown out or not stored properly. As a result of this study, Governor Ryan decided, in 2003, to set free four more prisoners and changed the sentences of 167 others from death to life imprisonment.

The use of DNA in criminal cases is still being debated around the world. Some fear that governments will one day keep records of everyone's DNA, which could put limits on the privacy and freedom of citizens. Other people mistrust the science of DNA testing and think that lawyers use it to get their clients free whether or not they are guilty. But for those whose innocence has been proven and who are now free men, DNA testing has meant nothing less than a return to life. And with the careful use of DNA testing, no innocent person should ever be convicted again.

Finishing time _____   Reading time _____

Now turn to page 267 and answer the questions. Do not look back at the passage.

5. Organ Trafficking

Starting time _____

The successful transplant of human organs is one of modern medicine's most remarkable achievements. In recent years, transplants of hearts and kidneys have saved the lives of thousands of people whose organs were diseased. However, for many more thousands of people organs are desperately needed for a transplant, but none are available for them. This shortage of organs has become a major problem today. Not only do people die who might have been saved, but the enormous demand has encouraged an illegal business in organ sales and transplants around the world.

In an organ transplant, doctors remove the organ from the body of a person (donor), and then place it in the body of another person (recipient). Some organs, such as the heart, come from donors who have died suddenly in accidents. Others, such as a kidney, can be taken from live or dead donors, but are more likely to be accepted by the recipient's body if they come from live donors. These live donors often are family members who wish to help their relative, and whose blood and body features match closely. However, if there is no family member who can donate an organ and who is a good match, the patient is in trouble: only about a third of those needing an organ are likely to find one.

Why are there so few organs available? This is mainly because in the United States, as in all the developed countries, organs can only be removed from a dead body if the person has given written permission. In many cases, people have not done this simply because they did not want to think ahead to a sudden death. In other cases, people do not want to become organ donors for religious reasons. Even if a person has agreed to become a donor, permission from the family is also necessary, and some families do not want doctors to remove organs from their loved ones.

To supply the great need for organs in the developed countries, a highly profitable business has grown. It links wealthy patients who desperately need new organs with people in the developing countries who desperately need money, and with unprincipled doctors who are willing to perform the operations. The business can take many forms. The organs may be removed from donors in their home country and then shipped for sale in the developed countries. Or donors may be brought to the developed country with promises of money and immigration papers and operated on there. Sometimes a third country is used to host the operation. Another kind of business has developed in which wealthy patients travel legally or illegally to another country for a transplant operation. "Transplantation tourism" on the part of wealthy patients has been encouraged by the differences in the costs of transplants in different areas of the world. Whereas in the United States, a kidney transplant can cost $100,000 and a heart transplant $860,000, in China the same operations cost only $70,000 and $120,000. In some countries, such as South Africa, the medical standards and the level of care and cleanliness in the hospitals are high. In other countries, however, patients who travel there for transplants are at risk of complications and infections.

At the other end of the business is the donor who supplies his or her organ. Many of these people live in poor neighborhoods in the Philippines, Brazil, and other countries. They have been promised by a "kidney hunter" that they will earn $10,000 by becoming a donor. In reality, they are often paid less than promised—only around $1,000 to $2,000, while the recipient may have paid $20,000. The money that donors receive usually is quickly spent, and with their weakened body, they are worse off than before. In fact, the removal of a kidney is not a simple operation and many of these donors do not live in conditions that allow them to recover well. Furthermore, they are normally not able to do any hard physical labor for many months and may suffer permanently from ill health.

In other parts of the world, particularly in some eastern European countries, the trade in illegal organs takes a different and even more horrible form. Possible donors are not simply tempted by money and then treated badly. They are promised jobs in Europe or North America, taken away from their villages, and terrified by threats of death. They may be told that the only way for them to return home is to agree to donate their organs. Or they may be killed so the organs can be removed.

Some doctors have argued that the only way to eliminate the illegal trade in organs is to make it legal. This way it would be possible to control the conditions. They also say that if people want to sell parts of their body they should be allowed to do so. But does a desperate, uneducated man who agrees to sell any organ of which he has two, really understand what it would mean to remove an organ from his body?

Most experts in international health care agree that a legal trade in organs could never be truly fair to the donors since it takes advantage of their ignorance and poverty, and almost always leaves them worse off than before. Several things would be necessary before a legal system could ever be adopted: an independent agency would have to check that donors really did agree, a guarantee that they would be paid and treated properly, and above all, medical care for the rest of their life for anything related to the organ removal.

Finishing time _____   Reading time _____

Now turn to page 268 and answer the questions. Do not look back at the passage.

6. Outsourcing in India

Starting time _____

India is a country of many contrasts. In some cities, water buffaloes share the streets with buses and cars. Office workers in business clothes walk past the cooking fires of families who live on the sidewalk. Two hundred and sixty million Indians live on less than one dollar a day, yet India also has one of the world's fastest growing economies.

Behind this growth is the development of fast and cheap telecommunications. Thanks to this, and to the Internet especially, American and European companies can hire workers in India to perform jobs that used to be done by local workers. This process is called outsourcing. For the companies, there are two important advantages to outsourcing. They can pay the Indians far less than they would pay Americans or Europeans. And since India has many English-speaking and highly educated citizens, there is no shortage of qualified people.

It all began in the late 1990s. At that time, Indian technicians were hired by companies in the United States and Europe to fix computer software problems in the coming changeover from the year 1999 to the year 2000. The companies saw how well the Indians carried out their jobs and decided to continue working with them. Other companies followed their example and more jobs were moved to India. Soon outsourcing had become an important part of the global economy.

Today, if you call a company like Dell Computer for customer assistance, you will probably talk to someone working in Bangalore or Hyderabad. Dell's main offices are in Texas, but it hires Indians to supply customer services at 10 percent of an American's salary. Dell has hired more than 10,000 Indians at four different call centers in India, and it is hardly alone. The companies and institutions that outsource work to India include computer and credit card companies, banks, insurance companies, and airlines. Some hospitals have even hired Indian experts to study medical X-rays and e-mail the results back to the United States.

The Indian workers in customer-service jobs receive special training from their American and European supervisors. In addition to learning how to do their jobs, they also learn about the way of life of the westerners with whom they will be talking. Some of these workers have never had a credit card. Some have never seen the kind of business which hired them—a department store, for example. Some had never even left the small towns and villages where they grew up before taking their call center jobs.

These jobs may require the workers to make various changes for their jobs. In order to seem less foreign for the western customers, they usually take names that are common in English, such as Bob or Ann, and they are taught to speak without an Indian accent. Because of time differences with the United States, most Indian call center employees must work all night long instead of during the day.

Few of them complain about these changes, however. Their pay may seem low to westerners, but it is good for Indians. Those who have moved to the city from small towns enjoy the excitement of city life. In addition, many young people see their jobs for western companies as a way to move up in Indian society. American and European-run companies promote workers on the basis of their job performance. This is very different from traditional Indian culture, where promotion often depends on your family and your connections in business and politics.

The economic boom caused by outsourcing has led to big changes in Indian cities. There are many more skyscrapers, hotels, nightclubs, and restaurants with American and European food on the menu. The city of Chennai (formerly known as Madras) has an American-style children's fun park where workers dress up as Hindu gods to entertain the young. Hyderabad has a 1,000-seat movie theater that shows American films the same week they are shown in the United States.

These changes are partly due to the fact that young Indians are learning to enjoy a more western lifestyle. The growing number of foreigners living in India has also had an impact. These westerners go to India to train Indians or to do high-level computer work, and they discover that they like living in India because their money buys more there. In India, they can go to expensive restaurants and have paid help in their homes, luxuries they could never afford at home. Of course, living in India is often a challenge for them. Chennai is known for being the center of technology in India, but it has terrible air pollution and the electricity service often shuts down.

Outsourcing to India has brought change for Americans as well. During the 1980s and 1990s, American industry had already lost many jobs when factories were moved to developing countries. Now jobs are also disappearing in the services (such as call centers) and in areas such as computer programming. By the year 2010, experts believe 3 million jobs will have left the United States for India. This has led some Americans to wonder what jobs will be left for them. In fact, economists are uncertain about the long-term consequences of outsourcing for the United States and Europe.

We now live in what is known as a global economy. Jobs and services move from country to country with the speed of a computer connection. Many countries have seen changes in their economies and culture as a result, some for the better and some for the worse. But outsourcing is now a fact of life. Jobs from the United States and Europe are now traveling beyond India to China, Eastern Europe, the Philippines, Thailand, and many other places.

Finishing time _____   Reading time _____

Now turn to page 269 and answer the questions. Do not look back at the passage.

Questions for Unit 2

After you answer the questions for a passage, follow these steps:

1. Check your answers with your teacher. For any incorrect answers, look back at the passage to understand why they are incorrect.

2. Find your reading rate (page 252) and then fill in the information on the Progress Chart for Timed Readings (page 253).

1. Cell Phones in Africa

1. Choose the statement that best expresses the overall thesis of this passage.

   a. Africans use cell phones only for business purposes.
   b. Cell phones are improving the lives of millions of Africans.
   c. Health-care workers and doctors use cell phones in Africa.
   d. The market for cell phones is growing around the world.

2. Which of the following is NOT mentioned as a reason for the spread of cell phones?

   a. Young Africans like to talk to their friends on cell phones.
   b. Cell phone towers are easy and cheap to build.
   c. The terrible condition of the roads makes travel difficult.
   d. Cell phones do not require putting in phone lines.

3. Cell phones create problems for families with relatives who live far away.

   a. True
   b. False

4. VillagePhone helps village women by

    a. giving them a phone so they can make calls.

    b. putting a telephone in the village so they can make calls.

    c. opening shops where villagers can buy cell phones.

    d. giving them a loan so they can buy a cell phone.

5. When Fatima got a cell phone, she

    a. called her faraway relatives in the city.

    b. was soon able to buy a computer.

    c. began selling phone time to other villagers.

    d. sold it so she could buy food for her children.

6. We can infer from this passage that

    a. women have a strong influence on African village economy.

    b. men do not like to use cell phones as much as women.

    c. women are not able to run businesses in African villages.

    d. village stores are usually not successful in Africa.

7. With cell phones, doctors can care for more patients in less time.

    a. True

    b. False

8. Text messaging allows health-care workers to

    a. talk with patients for a longer time.

    b. keep in touch with their families.

    c. send information to hospital computers.

    d. use a computer in the villages.

2. The Three Gorges Dam

1. Choose the statement that best expresses the overall thesis of this passage

    a. The Three Gorges Dam will provide more energy for the Chinese economy.

    b. The Three Gorges Dam will have a negative effect on the environment.

    c. The Three Gorges Dam will have both positive and negative effects.

    d. The Three Gorges Dam will benefit everyone in China.

2. The Yangtze River

    a. flooded often during the past century.

    b. will flood more often in the future.

    c. hasn't flooded since the early 1900s.

    d. may rise over the dam every ten years.

3. The main reason for building the dam, according to the Chinese government, is to

    a. improve the environment.

    b. improve transportation.

    c. create a freshwater supply.

    d. reduce the risk of floods.

4. The second important reason for building the dam is to

    a. make money for the government.
    b. produce hydroelectric power.
    c. give people in the area more jobs.
    d. improve the local water supply.

5. Some local inhabitants are making a living on the lake formed behind the dam.

    a. True
    b. False

6. Local inhabitants

    a. are not all satisfied with their new lives.
    b. all think the dam is a wonderful opportunity.
    c. are all very unhappy with their situation.
    d. have not noticed any difference in their lives.

7. The lake behind the dam is a good source of drinking water.

    a. True
    b. False

8. You can infer from this passage that the Chinese government is

    a. not at all concerned about the lives of the people displaced by the dam.
    b. very interested in the environmental problems along the Yangtze.
    c. more concerned about the economy than the environment.
    d. unable to successfully carry out large engineering projects.

3. Air-Conditioning

1. Choose the statement that best expresses the overall thesis of this passage.

    a. Air-conditioning has led to economic improvement in the United States.
    b. Air-conditioning has affected the way houses and office buildings are constructed.
    c. Air-conditioning has had both a social and an economic impact in many countries.
    d. Air-conditioning has added to the problem of global warming and climate change.

2. In the United States, air-conditioning was first used in 1902 in factory storage rooms.

    a. True
    b. False

3. Americans began to buy air conditioners for homes after World War II because

    a. industry could now produce at the same level all year.
    b. the climate was changing and becoming warmer.
    c. returning soldiers preferred homes with high ceilings.
    d. smaller, cheaper air-conditioning units were available.

4. As air-conditioning became more common in American homes, families

   a. moved indoors and saw fewer people.
   b. spent more time on their porches.
   c. went to large shopping malls more often.
   d. decided to build large homes with porches.

5. Which of the following is NOT mentioned in the passage as an effect of the use of air-conditioning in the United States?

   a. the rise of large shopping malls
   b. the creation of lively town centers
   c. the construction of tall office buildings
   d. increased production in factories

6. Until recently, according to a government minister in Singapore, the climate prevented economic development in his country.

   a. True
   b. False

7. Which of the following is given as a reason why air-conditioning is environmentally destructive?

   a. It lowers the temperature in cities.
   b. It requires a lot of energy to run.
   c. It costs a lot of money to run.
   d. It leads to economic improvement.

8. We can infer from this passage that most Americans

   a. miss the sense of community before air-conditioning.
   b. would prefer to live in the cooler northern states.
   c. keep their air-conditioning at very low temperatures.
   d. can afford to have air-conditioning in their homes.

4. DNA Testing

1. Choose the statement that best expresses the overall thesis of this passage.

   a. DNA testing has had important effects on the legal system.
   b. DNA testing has helped innocent men go free in Illinois.
   c. DNA testing has shown who was guilty of a crime.
   d. DNA testing uses genetics to identify a person.

2. DNA testing was first used by

   a. a lawyer in New York.
   b. students in Illinois.
   c. doctors in the United States.
   d. police in Great Britain.

3. Before the DNA testing, the suspect in Great Britain said he was innocent.

    a. True

    b. False

4. In the 1980s in the United States

    a. DNA testing was often used in criminal cases.

    b. many people were unfairly sentenced.

    c. some judges refused to give the death sentence.

    d. most prison inmates were innocent of crimes.

5. The Innocence Project uses DNA testing to

    a. help the police put people in prison.

    b. find out which lawyers are incompetent.

    c. prove that suspects are guilty.

    d. set free innocent prisoners.

6. Juries in America are never influenced by the racial or ethnic background of the suspect.

    a. True

    b. False

7. Students in Illinois

    a. proved that some prisoners were not guilty of crimes.

    b. believed that some suspects were from minority backgrounds.

    c. told the governor of Illinois not to set prisoners free.

    d. showed that DNA testing did not always help prisoners.

8. You can infer from this passage that some students in the United States

    a. prefer to study economics or business.

    b. care about social and legal justice.

    c. have been unfairly convicted of crimes.

    d. wish to become famous lawyers.

5. Organ Trafficking

1. Choose the statement that best expresses the overall thesis of this passage.

    a. There is a worldwide shortage of human organs for transplant operations.

    b. Poor people in developing countries are given money to have a kidney removed.

    c. A shortage of human organs for transplants has encouraged illegal trafficking.

    d. Organ transplant operations have saved thousands of lives in recent years.

2. An organ for a transplant operation must come from a donor who

    a. died suddenly in an accident.

    b. is about the same age as the recipient.

    c. is a member of the same family as the recipient.

    d. has the same blood type as the recipient.

3. Various reasons are given to explain why people do not become organ donors. Which of the following is NOT one of these reasons?

   a. Their families refuse to allow organ removal after death.
   b. They are afraid to break laws against donating organs.
   c. They do not want to think about the possibility of dying suddenly.
   d. Their religion is against the removal of organs.

4. We can infer from this passage that

   a. thousands of people die every year because of the lack of organs.
   b. poor people in the United States never sell their organs illegally.
   c. Chinese people are not willing to be organ donors.
   d. an increase in traffic accidents would mean more organ donors.

5. Organ traffickers and the doctors who work for them earn up to $18,000 per kidney transplant.

   a. True
   b. False

6. Kidney donors in developing countries usually

   a. immigrate to wealthy countries with the money they earn.
   b. use the money to improve their lives after the operation.
   c. are given free medical care for a year afterwards.
   d. come from poor families and live in poor conditions.

7. Kidney donors in developing countries are fully informed about the risks of kidney removal.

   a. True
   b. False

8. Most international experts believe the legal sale of organs would not be a good idea because

   a. doctors would make a lot of money from it.
   b. it would never be fair to people who are poor and ignorant.
   c. some countries would get more organs than other countries.
   d. independent agencies would make organs too expensive.

6. Outsourcing in India

1. Choose the statement that best expresses the overall thesis of this passage.

   a. Outsourcing in India allows western companies to pay workers less.
   b. Outsourcing has brought many foreigners to Indian cities.
   c. Outsourcing involves many countries.
   d. Outsourcing has led to change in India and the United States.

2. Outsourcing was made possible by

   a. the changeover from 1999 to 2000.
   b. the development of Indian cities.
   c. fast and cheap telecommunications.
   d. a growing Indian economy.

3. Some jobs in hospitals, such as the analysis of medical X-rays, could never by outsourced to India.

   a. True
   b. False

4. Which of the following is NOT required of Indians working at call centers for western companies?

   a. using names that sound western
   b. shopping in western stores
   c. learning about western ways
   d. working all night long

5. Working for a western company can help young Indians

   a. start a career in Indian politics.
   b. move to a western country.
   c. start a family and a business.
   d. improve their social position.

6. One reason why westerners like living in India is that

   a. they can have a more luxurious life there.
   b. they do not have to work as hard there.
   c. the environment is cleaner there.
   d. the same movies are played there.

7. Experts believe that outsourcing will bring long-term benefits for the United States and Europe.

   a. True
   b. False

8. We can infer from this passage that the Indians who work for western companies

   a. do not work as hard as westerners.
   b. generally work hard and do a good job.
   c. would prefer to work for an Indian company.
   d. have good family connections in business and politics.

1. Dr. Paul Farmer

Starting time _____

In Dr. Paul Farmer's view, health is a fundamental human right. He believes it should not be dependent on income or education, and he has devoted his life to bringing medical care to the poorest people in developing countries. Many doctors assumed that people in these countries were too poor and uneducated to manage complex medical treatments, but Dr. Farmer has demonstrated that this is not true.

Farmer was born in Massachusetts in 1960, and grew up in Florida with his parents and five brothers and sisters. They lived for a while in a converted school bus, and then in a broken-down boat, much of the time without running water. One summer, when the family needed cash, Farmer, his father, and his two brothers got jobs picking oranges and that is where he first heard Haitians speaking Creole, the language that was to become so important to him. In spite of their financial difficulties, the Farmer home was filled with books, and the children were encouraged to pursue their interests and talents.

After graduating from high school at the top of his class, Farmer received a full scholarship to Duke University in North Carolina. As a college student he heard about the terrible conditions for migrant workers on nearby farms. Among these workers were some Haitians whom he got to know. This sparked his interest in Haiti and eventually he took a trip to the small Caribbean island country. While in Haiti he spent time in the central highland region where the people were very poor. They lived in mud huts and had little food and almost no medical care, but he came to admire their spirit and ability to adapt.

Farmer continued his studies at Harvard Medical School, where he earned degrees in both medicine and medical anthropology. He returned to Haiti many times, learning the language and working with local doctors. In 1987, with a few friends, he founded a charity organization, Partners in Health (PIH), based in Boston, Massachusetts. Their first project was to build a small clinic in the village of Cange in central Haiti. Over two decades, the Cange center—Zanmi Lasante—expanded into a large facility. It now cares for more than 220,000 patients a year, with a 104-bed hospital and clinics for women's and children's health, eye care, and surgery.

The Cange center has become a worldwide model for community-based health care. Two principles rule there. First, no patient should ever be turned away. Second, patients should not have to travel long distances to find help. Dr. Farmer says he once met a woman who had carried her child in her arms for three hours to reach the hospital and then three hours more to get home. Afterward, she told him, her arms were so sore she could not use them for weeks. Farmer realized

then that they needed to go out to the people and not make the people come to them. Cange health workers, including Farmer himself, regularly travel to the villages to check on patients.

Farmer has found that traveling to the villages is important for another reason. In a poor country like Haiti, improvements in health are only possible if living conditions also improve. When Farmer visits a village, he looks not only at people with health problems, but also at the houses and the general situation. Over the years, thanks to Partners in Health, the villages around Cange have acquired clean drinking water and the houses have been rebuilt with rainproof roofs and concrete floors.

Farmer spends the greater part of every year in Haiti, which continues to be the main focus of his work, but he is constantly traveling. Through Partners in Health, he has become involved in projects in Peru, Rwanda, Russia, Kazakhstan, Latvia, and Azerbaijan. Having become one of the world's leading specialists in treating HIV/AIDS and tuberculosis, he attends conferences and consults with doctors around the world. His goal is to convince the world's medical experts that even in the most difficult social and economic conditions, it is possible to treat people successfully.

In developing countries, for example, most international health organizations have refused to treat patients with drug-resistant tuberculosis. They claim that the treatment was too expensive, and that the patients would not be capable of following doctors' instructions. Partners in Health has shown, however, that the same treatment that works in the United States can work with patients anywhere. Furthermore, they have shown that it is possible to get the medicines at a lower cost.

For his work among the world's most vulnerable populations, Dr. Farmer has won many important awards. He continues to consult and teach part of the year at some of the world's most famous hospitals and universities. He is also the subject of a best-selling book by Tracy Kidder, *Mountains Beyond Mountain*s: *The Quest of Dr. Paul Farmer, a Man Who Would Cure the World*.

But most of the money Farmer earns from his work or his awards is immediately given to Partners in Health. And despite his fame Dr. Farmer still thinks of himself first and foremost as a doctor. He has not given up a doctor's simplest pleasures and responsibilities, such as walking for hours along dirt tracks to treat sick people in Haitian hill villages. Farmer says it helps remind him why he became a doctor in the first place: to treat the patient at hand. The title of Kidder's book comes from a Haitian saying that Farmer likes to quote: "After mountains there are mountains." In other words, beyond every problem there is another; the best we can do is to solve each problem, one at a time.

Finishing time _____   Reading time _____

Now turn to page 280 and answer the questions. Do not look back at the passage.

2. Christo and Jeanne-Claude

For more than forty years, artists Christo and Jeanne-Claude have been challenging the public's idea of what art can be. Working together, they create pieces known as "installation art" on a giant scale. In these pieces they wrap entire bridges or buildings in fabric, or stretch a nylon fence for miles along country fields. These "gentle disturbances," as the artists call them, temporarily change places that we often take for granted and inspire people to see their world anew.

Christo Javacheff was born in Bulgaria on June 13, 1935, and on the very same day, Jeanne-Claude de Guillebon was born to French parents in Morocco. Christo left Bulgaria in 1958 and settled in Paris. Soon afterward, he took an assignment to paint a portrait of Jeanne-Claude's mother, who had moved to Paris, and he fell in love with the daughter. Christo and Jeanne-Claude were married and began collaborating on art, though in the first years only Christo took credit for their work. In 1964, they moved to New York City where they still live. In a custom they began as young artists, Christo and Jeanne-Claude go by their first names only.

At the start of their career, their works of installation art were small. Using the technique they became famous for, they covered motorcycles, trees, and open spaces with cloth or sheets of plastic. By hiding the small details and decoration, they hoped the true beauty of an object or space would be more evident. As interest in their work grew, they went on to larger installations. In 1968, they wrapped entire art museums in Switzerland and the United States. Over the next thirty years, Christo and Jeanne-Claude completed nearly twenty major projects. They wrapped the Pont Neuf, a bridge in Paris, they surrounded eleven Florida islands with pink skirts, and they constructed 3,100 20-foot-tall blue and yellow umbrellas in California and Japan.

The project that made them most famous, however, was in New York City. In February 2005, they designed and organized the installation of 7,500 tall black metal "gates" hung with orange-colored fabric along 23 miles of walkways in Central Park. For the two weeks that the gates were up, the park was filled with thousands of people. Both New Yorkers and visitors from out of town wanted to see this transformation of the park. Just to keep going through the gates, people walked to corners of the park where they had never been before. Under the gates, the walkers felt as though they were strolling under saffron-colored sails. The bright fabric fluttering in the wind created a whole new dimension to the normally black and white winter scenery. Observed from one of New York City's skyscrapers, the gates looked like a river of bright color flowing through the park. They created a feeling of joyful celebration and brought New Yorkers together.

The inspiration for The Gates, as the installation was informally called, came from the initial 1854 design for Central Park. The original designers had planned for gates along the park's surrounding walls, but those gates were never built. Christo and Jeanne-Claude focused on the fact that New Yorkers love walking, and that Central Park is one of their favorite places for walking and for meeting. The gate structures were designed to mirror the grid of the city streets near the park. Tall and narrow, they seemed to invite people to walk through them. The fabric was chosen carefully and cut in such a way that it could swing freely in the wind and seem to follow the curving paths on which the gates were built.

Christo and Jeanne-Claude first proposed the idea for The Gates twenty-six years earlier, but New York officials at that time did not welcome the project. In the course of trying to get permission from the city offices in charge of the park, the artists received a vast collection of documents. These include a 245-page book published in 1981, which explained why the project could not be completed. Christo and Jeanne-Claude have kept all these documents, along with all the drawings and papers regarding the design, which they consider to be part of the artwork itself. No matter how long and frustrating it was, getting permission was part of the process of creating The Gates. Christo and Jeanne-Claude recognize that their artwork, in this case, was not made *about* Central Park; it was made *out of* Central Park.

In spite of all the delays and objections, the artists persisted. They received building permits for The Gates in 2003, by order of Mayor Michael Bloomberg. Several more years were required for the design and the construction of the 7,500 structures with their pieces of orange fabric. And finally, on February 13, 2005, The Gates were open. For the actual installation and removal of the gates, 900 workers were required. It is important to note that no public money was used for The Gates. As for all of their installations, Christo and Jeanne-Claude raised the money privately by selling drawings, artwork, and models to collectors. When The Gates came down, Christo and Jeanne-Claude gave away or recycled all the materials used in the project. This is an important part of their artistic philosophy. Nothing they make is permanent, and what they make should not harm the environment in any way.

When asked about the meaning of The Gates, Jeanne-Claude said, "We do not build meanings, we do not build messages, we do not build symbols . . . we only build art." Some art critics have said that their work is not serious or is unattractive. However, the crowds in Central Park seemed to feel otherwise.

Finishing time _____   Reading time _____

Now turn to page 281 and answer the questions. Do not look back at the passage.

3. Wangari Maathai

Starting time _____

Wangari Maathai is one of the world's most honored environmentalists. For nearly thirty years, she has fought to protect the fragile landscape of her native Kenya. The Green Belt Movement she founded in 1977 has established over 6,000 tree nurseries and planted more than 20 million trees across Kenya. For her remarkable successes, Wangari Maathai was awarded the Nobel Peace Prize in 2004. She was only the twelfth woman to receive it in the century-long history of Nobel prizes.

Born in 1940, Wangari Maathai grew up on a farm in Nyeri, Kenya. She traveled to the United States to earn a master's degree in science, and then to Germany and back to Kenya for a Ph.D. The first woman in eastern and central Africa to earn a Ph.D. degree, she then became the first woman to be the head of a university department in Kenya. She was director of the Kenya Red Cross in the 1980s and was elected to Parliament (with 98 percent of the vote) in 2002. A woman of many firsts, she then became the first African woman to win a Nobel Prize.

Maathai's commitment to the environment began when she returned to Kenya from her studies abroad and saw how the landscape was being destroyed by uncontrolled tree cutting. The trees were being cut down by poor families who needed firewood for cooking. However, cutting down the trees only made the situation worse for these families in the long run. With the trees gone, the fertile topsoil blew away with the wind or was washed away by rainstorms. The land became dusty, stony, and unproductive. Families were no longer able to grow enough food, and since the cattle and goats could no longer find enough grass, there was also less milk or meat. In general, families in the area became poorer. Furthermore, the soil that ended up in rivers contained human and animal waste that polluted the water supplies and led to greater risk of diseases.

Maathai knew that this environmental problem was not going to be resolved by the Kenyan government. She had to find a way to change the situation on her own. To save the topsoil, it was necessary to plant more trees. But unless people were educated about the importance of trees, the new ones would be cut down like the old ones. Maathai decided to turn to the women of Kenya. She felt that since the women often suffered the most from environmental destruction they would be the most willing to work for change. Others told her that poor and uneducated women would not be capable of understanding environmental problems, but she did not believe this was true.

The idea of a widespread tree-planting program came to her in 1976. At the time she was an active member of the National Council of Women in Kenya (of which she later became chairwoman). Maathai began with a small group of women and the planting of seven trees in a park in Nairobi. Then she went out into the countryside to teach ordinary women in villages how to plant trees on their small farms and in school and church yards. At first, she had no tree nurseries, no staff, and no money, but other women joined her and the movement started to grow. Small grants of money arrived from international environmental organizations and the program developed into the "Green Belt Movement." Run for and by women, it provides paid work and thus financial stability to hundreds of thousands of Kenyan women.

After establishing the tree-planting program, Maathai turned to other aspects of Kenyan society. She challenged the government to improve education, food distribution, and other areas of concern to women. As a well-known voice against the corrupt government of Daniel arap Moi she was often a target for threats and violence. She was put in prison several times, and after one arrest in 1991, she was freed only through pressure from international human rights organizations. In 1992 she was beaten by the police for participating in a hunger strike to protest government torture. Finally, in 2002 change came to Kenya with the fall of arap Moi. Maathai was elected to Parliament, and soon after, the new government appointed her Assistant Minister for the Environment, Natural Resources and Wildlife.

In the years since the beginning of the Green Belt Movement, Wangari Maathai has expanded her interests beyond Kenya. Under her guidance, at least six other African countries have developed tree-planting programs like the Green Belt Movement with similar success. In 1995, Maathai joined forces with other women leaders at the Fourth World Conference on Women in Beijing, China. Dressed in bright yellow, she marched with a thousand others to protest violence against women worldwide. In the late 1990s, Maathai led the Jubilee 2000 Coalition in Africa. This organization works to convince world leaders and banks to cancel the debts of the world's poorest countries.

Dozens of international organizations have honored Maathai for her efforts to protect the environment and improve the lives of the poor in Africa. In deciding to give her the Peace Prize in 2004, the Nobel Committee changed its definition of peace for the first time since the Prize was founded in 1901. In fact, the award to Maathai was the first to be given to someone in the environmental field. Maathai has said she understands why the Nobel Committee chose to offer an environmentalist an award normally given to politicians or human rights leaders.

"People are fighting over water, over food and over other natural resources. When our resources become scarce, we fight over them. In managing our resources and in sustainable development, we plant the seeds of peace."

Finishing time _____   Reading time _____

Now turn to page 282 and answer the questions. Do not look back at the passage.

4. Rosa Parks

On December 1, 1955, Rosa Parks became the inspiring public face of the civil rights struggle in the United States. On that day, in Montgomery, Alabama, she refused to obey a bus driver and give up her seat in the front of the bus to a white man. In Alabama, as in many other states, laws required that blacks could only travel at the back of the bus. Parks was arrested by the police for not giving up her seat, but her action was the turning point in the fight to make every American an equal citizen under the law.

Rosa Parks was forty-two when this happened and had lived in a world defined by race. She was the daughter of a carpenter and a teacher, James and Leona McCauley, who separated when she was young. Raised by her maternal grandparents, Parks and her younger brother grew up on a farm outside Montgomery, the capital of Alabama.

In Alabama, as in all the former slave-holding states, the black slaves had been freed at the end of the Civil War in 1865. But freedom did not mean equality. Many states, particularly in the south, had laws to segregate blacks (keep them separate) from whites, and to deny them an equal position in society. Blacks could not eat at the same restaurants, attend the same schools, or worship at the same churches. Furthermore, blacks were often the victims of racial violence; house burnings and murders of blacks were common. As a child, Parks would lie awake at night, frightened that the Ku Klux Klan, a white extremist society, might come and burn down the house. Parks once said: "Back then we didn't have any civil rights. It was just a matter of survival, of existing from one day to the next."

After studying at a private school for black girls and at the High School of the Alabama State Teachers College, Rosa married a barber, Raymond Parks. He was already active in the civil rights movement and was the first activist she had ever encountered. Because of the dangers of violence or arrest, it was not usual for women to get involved in the struggle for civil rights, but Rosa was determined to lend her hand. Despite her husband's worries, she became an active member of the National Association for the Advancement of Colored People (NAACP) and other civil rights groups.

In 1955, the nation's civil rights leaders wanted to challenge the segregation laws that kept blacks separate from whites. They needed a case that could test the legality of these laws under the United States Constitution. Looking for a person of moral strength and courage, they chose Rosa Parks. As they had expected, she was arrested when she refused to give up her seat and in response, the black leaders in Montgomery formed the Montgomery Improvement Association (MIA). As president, they elected a minister who was new to town, the twenty-six-year-old Reverend Martin Luther King, Jr.

The next year was difficult for blacks in Montgomery. To call attention to their fight for civil rights, MIA organized a boycott of the city buses. Because they refused to ride the buses, some people had to walk as many as 20 miles to work. Blacks were arrested for no reason, and violence against black families increased, with bombings of homes and churches. At the same time, Reverend King's leadership and inspiring speaking style captured the nation's attention. The court case brought by MIA went ahead to the Supreme Court, which on November 13, 1956, ruled that the separation of blacks and whites on buses was illegal. Access to public services had to be open to all on a first-come, first-served basis, with no discrimination on the basis of race.

The day after the ruling became final, Rosa Parks took her seat on a Montgomery bus with a white man sitting behind her. She and all the blacks of Montgomery could now ride the bus freely. But the struggle for equality for blacks was not over. The Reverend Martin Luther King Jr., who had made a name for himself in Montgomery, continued to fight for civil rights—in the schools and at the workplace—becoming the greatest civil rights leader America has known.

In Montgomery, both Rosa and Raymond Parks lost their jobs because of their activism. Following the court ruling, they received threats to their lives and safety, so they decided to move out of the South, settling in Detroit, Michigan, in 1957, where they lived out the rest of their days. From the 1960s until she retired in the late 1980s, Rosa Parks worked as a staff member for John Conyers, U.S. Representative. Colleagues and friends remember her as a quiet and modest woman, who never wished to be the center of attention, even when Nelson Mandela, president of South Africa, called her onstage during a Detroit visit in the 1990s.

After her husband's death in 1987, Rosa Parks cofounded the Rosa and Raymond Parks Institute for Self-Development, an organization that sponsors programs to help teenagers travel the country and learn of its civil rights history. President Bill Clinton awarded Rosa the Presidential Medal of Freedom in 1996, and in 1999 the U.S. Congress gave her a Congressional Gold Medal.

When she died at age ninety-two, the U.S. Senate passed a resolution allowing her body to lie in honor in the U.S. Capitol Building. Rosa Parks was the first woman in history to be given this honor. Speaking after her death, the civil rights leader Reverend Jesse Jackson summed up why Rosa Parks was so important to America's struggle for civil rights: "She sat down in order that we might stand up."

Finishing time _____   Reading time _____

Now turn to page 283 and answer the questions. Do not look back at the passage.

5. Tim Berners-Lee

Starting time _____

I f it weren't for Tim Berners-Lee, we would not have the World Wide Web. Before his invention, computer users could transfer information only within local networks of computers, such as those used by companies or universities. Because of his work, we now have the whole vast universe of information, commerce, and communication that is the World Wide Web.

Growing up in Great Britain, Tim Berners-Lee was born to work in computers. His parents met on a project to build an early computer at the University of Manchester. As a child in the 1960s, Berners-Lee played math games at the dining table and built make-believe computers out of cardboard boxes. While he was a student at Oxford University, he was caught breaking into computer files, and was banned from using the university computer. He then decided to build his own computer out of extra electronic parts and an old TV set. After graduation, he worked for a few years as a computer programmer and then, in 1980, was hired for six months to work at CERN, the European nuclear research center in Switzerland.

During these six months, he began the project that made him famous. Like many great inventors, Berners-Lee started out wanting to solve a simple problem for himself. Many files in his computer contained data that was related to other data in his system, but he could not always remember how all the data was connected. He decided to create a computer program that would help him keep track of these connections.

To do this, Berners-Lee made use of a technique already known to computer programmers called "hypertext." These are specially chosen words in a document that can serve as links to text in other files. He gave a number to each piece of hypertext so that he could refer to it. This was in the days before the invention of the computer mouse, so it was not possible to "click and go." When he came upon hypertext in one of his documents and typed its link number, his computer connected him to the related document. This system, which he developed with the help of a colleague, Robert Cailliau, was named Enquire, after a British encyclopedia that he had loved as a boy.

At first, Enquire was designed to work on Berners-Lee's computer alone. However, the many scientists at CERN were eager to have access to the large stores of information on other computers at the lab, so he expanded it to work with any computer at CERN. But Enquire could not reach beyond the lab. This was his next ambition, to expand his network at CERN and create a worldwide system of information sharing.

In 1984, Berners-Lee returned to work at CERN. As the largest Internet center in Europe it was a good place for him to work toward his vision. His first step was to create a common set of rules and regulations. He began by inventing HTML, the simple computer language that programmers still use to write pages with links. Next, he devised URLs, a way of giving web pages an address, and HTTP, a set of common rules that control the way web pages are sent and received. He then invented the first web browser program to move from web page to web page. Finally, after thinking long and hard, Berners-Lee decided to give a name to this new, expanded Internet system. He called it the World Wide Web.

The first Web site, which belonged to CERN, went online on August 6, 1991. It provided an explanation of the World Wide Web, how to obtain a browser, and how to set up a Web server. Basically, Berners-Lee (with CERN's approval) was announcing his invention to the world and sharing it with anyone interested. Enthusiasm for the new system was immediate. Computer experts around the world began working on further inventions for the Web. Some programmers who developed ways to use pictures and graphics on the Web earned millions of dollars from their inventions. Berners-Lee, however, never patented his inventions and never made any money from them.

Berners-Lee has always seen the Internet as a means for people around the world to share knowledge, and he believes it is important to keep the Internet open to everyone. Some people have wondered whether we are paying too high a price for this universal access, since it also allows access to Web sites that are dangerous for society, such as those that promote child pornography or terrorism. For Berners-Lee, though, the problems with the Internet are no different from the general problems in our society. In his view, we need to encourage the good things and try to keep out the bad things, but we must keep the Web open and neutral. A neutral communications medium is essential to our society; he says, "It is the basis of democracy."

The world has hardly ignored Tim Berners-Lee's contribution to technology. He has won dozens of prizes, honorary degrees, and other honors, including in 2004, the European Millennium Technology Prize worth $1.2 million. Also in that year, Britain's Queen Elizabeth made Berners-Lee a Knight Commander of the British Empire.

In his typically modest fashion, Berners-Lee insisted on sharing the credit with others. "This is an honor which applies to the whole Web development community, and to the inventors and developers of the Internet, whose work made the Web possible," he said. Tim Berners-Lee still drives a small car to his office at the Massachusetts Institute of Technology. There he oversees the international organization called WC3 that fights to keep the World Wide Web working for everyone no matter their age, country, or income level.

Finishing time _____   Reading time _____

Now turn to page 284 and answer the questions. Do not look back at the passage.

6. José Antonio Abreu

Starting time _____

Thirty years ago, José Antonio Abreu dreamed that music could improve the lives of the poorest children and teenagers in Venezuela. He began by teaching eleven children in the capitol city of Caracas and from there, created a nationwide program of classical music study and performance. Even today, his students come from communities where drug abuse, violence, and hunger are a daily fact of life. But in the National System of Children and Youth Orchestras of Venezuela (FESNOJIV), they become a part of a community and begin a path to a productive future. They also make music that is praised around the world.

Born in 1939, José Antonio Abreu studied economics at the Universidad Andrès Bello and received an advanced degree in petroleum economics in 1961. For a while, he taught economics at the university level and was a member of the Venezuelan Congress. However, his love of music led him to get a second degree in music composition and organ from Venezuela's national music academy. In time, he gave up economics and focused entirely on classical music.

Abreu's first move was to found a National Youth Symphony Orchestra. His immediate aim was to give young musicians the opportunity to play regularly and train under good conductors. The two symphonic orchestras in Venezuela at the time were both filled mainly by Europeans and North Americans. Abreu wanted to see more Venezuelans in the orchestras, but young musicians in Venezuela had few opportunities to gain musical experience.

Beyond simple music training, however, Abreu had a larger social vision. He saw music as a weapon against poverty. His hope was that music might rescue some of his country's most at-risk children from the desperate conditions of their lives. As he has said, "Poverty generates anonymity, loneliness. Music creates happiness and hope in a community, and the triumph of a child as a musician helps him aspire to even higher things."

Over the years this hope has been fulfilled. Abreu has seen his students cut ties with the criminal gangs they used to belong to. Many have become music teachers themselves, becoming a source of pride for their families and inspiring others to give up their destructive behavior. One student came to music at the age of fifteen after nine arrests for robbery and drugs. He said that the first person who really understood him and had confidence in him was his music teacher. He credits his orchestra experience with literally saving his life.

The success of the first youth orchestra attracted immediate attention from government officials. In a short time, the Venezuelan government started four more youth orchestras in other parts of the country. They recognized FESNOJIV as an important social force and supported it financially from the beginning. Before long the program had become part of official government social and educational policy.

Financial support from the Venezuelan government has been an important part of the success of Abreu's music program. Before this program, there was no public music education at all in Venezuela and private music lessons were too expensive for the great majority of its citizens. The students in Abreu's program begin learning their instruments at the age of four. They pay nothing for their lessons or their instruments. From their very first day, each student also becomes a member of an orchestra, starting with one of the country's 60 children's orchestras and moving on to one of the 120 youth orchestras.

Children in the program study music for several hours on weekday afternoons at neighborhood music centers. On weekends, the older students practice all day long. Being part of a group inspires all the students to work hard and achieve their best. This positive attitude affects the students' work in school and their lives in general. The children's total involvement and desire to excel helps them quickly gain technical ability. Because they are playing in an orchestra, they also learn about making music together and many other aspects of musical performance.

The Venezuelan youth orchestras have toured abroad and have joined with youth orchestras from other countries in international music festivals. People who hear them for the first time are amazed at the quality of their playing, often far beyond that of other youth orchestras. They find it hard to believe that many of these teenagers come from the poorest families. Musicians and educators from other countries have traveled to Venezuela to see how the music program works. Many of the world's top musicians—from Sir Simon Rattle to Claudio Abbado—have praised Abreu and Venezuela's program as the most important and innovative development in music anywhere.

For his work, José Antonio Abreu has received multiple honors, including serving for five years in the 1980s as Venezuela's Minister of Culture. In 1998, he was named as a United Nations cultural Ambassador for Peace. In 2000 he received Sweden's Right Livelihood Award, known as the Alternative Nobel Prize, given to people who have made important contributions to the betterment of humanity.

In his own country, Abreu and his youth symphonies have established a minor cultural revolution. While many countries honor young athletes or pop stars, Venezuelan society embraces its young classical musicians. The country now hosts twenty-eight professional orchestras and whereas in the past, Venezuelan musicians had trouble finding jobs even in their own country, now they are also playing in American and European orchestras. The Berlin Philharmonic, one of the top orchestras in the world, recently hired a seventeen-year-old Venezuelan bass player.

How has all this come about? "El Maestro," as Abreu is called by the thousands and thousands of students who love him, has always kept to his simple view: "Music makes our children better human beings."

Finishing time _____   Reading time _____

Now turn to page 285 and answer the questions. Do not look back at the passage.

Questions for Unit 3

After you answer the questions for a passage, follow these steps:

1. Check your answers with your teacher. For any incorrect answers, look back at the passage to understand why they are incorrect.

2. Find your reading rate (page 252) and then fill in the information on the Progress Chart for Timed Readings (page 253).

1. Dr. Paul Farmer

1. Choose the statement that best expresses the overall thesis of the passage.

   a. Dr. Paul Farmer runs a large health clinic in Haiti.

   b. Dr. Paul Farmer treat patients with HIV/AIDS and tuberculosis.

   c. Dr. Paul Farmer is a famous doctor who went to Harvard.

   d. Dr. Paul Farmer works to bring better health care to poor people.

2. Farmer's parents

    a. were much like other middle-class American families.
    b. had lots of money and were not interested in books.
    c. had little money, but encouraged the children to read.
    d. were interested mainly in sports and farming.

3. When Farmer went to Haiti, he worked on a farm picking oranges.

    a. True
    b. False

4. The Cange center—Zanmi Lasante—is a

    a. large community health facility in central Haiti.
    b. charity organization in Boston, Massachusetts.
    c. center for medical anthropology at Harvard University.
    d. project for the treatment of HIV/AIDS and tuberculosis.

5. According to this passage, Farmer believes that

    a. people should not be kept in the hospital for long.
    b. patients should not have to travel far to get medical help.
    c. doctors should not have to travel far for their jobs.
    d. health workers should not have to carry patients.

6. Cange health workers check the patients and the living conditions in the villages.

    a. True
    b. False

7. Farmer has shown that poor people in developing countries

    a. need stronger medicines than people in wealthy countries.
    b. must be treated differently from people in wealthy countries.
    c. cannot follow the same treatment as people in wealthy countries.
    d. can manage the same treatments as people in wealthy countries.

8. You can infer from this passage that Farmer

    a. cares a lot about the patients he treats.
    b. would like to dedicate more time to research.
    c. enjoys earning lots of money and getting awards.
    d. wants to write a book about his experiences in Haiti.

2. Christo and Jeanne-Claude

1. Choose the statement that best expresses the overall thesis of the passage.

    a. Christo and Jeanne-Claude build works of art in American parks.
    b. Christo and Jeanne-Claude believe that art should be serious and unattractive.
    c. Christo and Jeanne-Claude make art that allows people to see places in a new way.
    d. Christo and Jeanne-Claude are famous for wrapping buildings and bridges.

2. The two artists sometimes work on separate art projects.

   a. True
   b. False

3. Christo and Jeanne-Claude wrapped objects

   a. so they could be unwrapped later.
   b. in order to get the attention of the public.
   c. because they liked wrapping things.
   d. so that the real shape could be seen.

4. The Gates were installed

   a. along the streets of New York.
   b. in New York's Central Park.
   c. on a skyscraper in New York.
   d. in an art museum in New York.

5. The Gates

   a. made many New Yorkers feel angry.
   b. made no difference to people in New York.
   c. had a positive effect on people walking among them.
   d. affected most the visitors from out of town.

6. When Christo and Jeanne-Claude first proposed The Gates twenty-six years earlier

   a. the city of New York refused permission.
   b. Mayor Bloomberg of New York refused permission.
   c. the artists did not have enough money.
   d. the drawings and plans were not yet ready.

7. All the art projects done by Christo and Jeanne-Claude are paid for by the artists.

   a. True
   b. False

8. We can infer from this passage that

   a. there is a lot of public art in the parks of New York.
   b. Christo and Jeanne Claude are not able to sell much of their artwork.
   c. people in New York are not very interested in public art.
   d. Christo and Jeanne-Claude want to keep their artistic independence.

3. Wangari Maathai

1. Choose the statement that best expresses the overall thesis of the passage.

   a. Maathai was the first African woman to win a Nobel Peace Prize in 2004.
   b. Maathai has worked to improve the environment and the lives of poor Africans.
   c. Maathai started the Greenbelt Movement by planting trees in Kenya in 1976.
   d. Maathai is a member of Parliament and an important politician in Kenya.

2. Maathai studied at universities in the United States, Germany and Kenya.

   a. True
   b. False

3. When Maathai returned to Kenya, she realized that

   a. tree cutting was the answer to environmental problems.
   b. Kenya had many environmental problems.
   c. tree cutting was destroying the environment.
   d. Kenya's landscape was very special.

4. When poor people cut down the trees around them,

   a. they become even poorer.
   b. the grass will grow better.
   c. the government punishes them.
   d. families can grow more food.

5. We can infer from this passage that in the 1970s

   a. women were especially interested in health problems.
   b. most men in Kenyan villages were corrupt.
   c. most women in Kenyan villages were not educated.
   d. the Kenyan government was worried about the environment.

6. The Greenbelt Movement

   a. helps villagers plant and grow food for their families.
   b. plants trees in parks in Nairobi and other cities in Africa.
   c. teaches children in schools about the environment.
   d. teaches women to plant trees in their villages.

7. Maathai was beaten and put in prison by the government of Daniel arap Moi.

   a. True
   b. False

8. Maathai believes that environmental destruction

   a. can lead to fighting over water, food, and resources.
   b. is less important than human rights problems.
   c. cannot be avoided in poor African countries.
   d. is one result of economic development in Africa.

4. Rosa Parks

1. Choose the statement that best expresses the overall thesis of the passage.

   a. Rosa Parks refused to give up her seat to a white man on a bus in Alabama.
   b. Rosa Parks was a member of several civil rights groups in Alabama.
   c. Rosa Parks was awarded the Presidential Medal of Freedom in 1996.
   d. Rosa Parks played a key role in black Americans' fight for civil rights.

2. In the 1950s in Alabama and other states,

    a. there were still black slaves in many cities.

    b. laws kept blacks and whites separate.

    c. laws gave blacks the same rights as whites.

    d. blacks were free to go anywhere they wanted.

3. When Rosa Parks was a child, white people sometimes burned down the houses of black families.

    a. True

    b. False

4. You can infer from this passage that in the mid-twentieth century

    a. there was probably very little violence of any kind in American society.

    b. black people who were violent against whites were probably not severely punished.

    c. white people who were violent against blacks were not severely punished.

    d. violent actions were probably always severely punished by American courts.

5. The Montgomery Improvement Association

    a. worked for civil rights for blacks.

    b. was a religious association.

    c. aimed to improve life in the city.

    d. organized activities for black women.

6. Reverend Martin Luther King Jr.

    a. was arrested for his work on Park's case.

    b. worked as a lawyer on Park's case.

    c. brought Park's case to national attention.

    d. was the first activist in Montgomery.

7. Rosa and Raymond Parks got their jobs back after the boycott in Montgomery.

    a. True

    b. False

8. Rosa Parks was the first woman in American history to

    a. start an organization helping teenagers learn about civil rights.

    b. be arrested for refusing to give up her seat on a bus.

    c. meet Nelson Mandela, the president of South Africa.

    d. lie in the U.S. Capitol Building after her death.

5. Tim Berners-Lee

1. Choose the statement that best expresses the overall thesis of the passage.

    a. Berners-Lee is a famous computer programmer from Great Britain.

    b. Berners-Lee invented the World Wide Web so people could share information.

    c. Berners-Lee has become rich and famous because of the World Wide Web.

    d. Berners-Lee believes that the Internet should remain open and neutral.

2. Berners-Lee made his first computer

   a. at the Massachusetts Institute of Technology.

   b. when he was working at CERN.

   c. as a child in Manchester.

   d. when he was a student at Oxford.

3. Berners-Lee began working on his invention because

   a. he wanted to solve a problem he was having on his computer.

   b. his colleagues at CERN wanted a better way to share information.

   c. he wanted to remember information from a British encyclopedia.

   d. a colleague gave him the idea for a new computer system.

4. Enquire could work only with the computers at CERN.

   a. True

   b. False

5. In the process of developing the World Wide Web, Berners-Lee

   a. learned many languages.

   b. built a new kind of computer.

   c. created HTML, URLs, and HTTP.

   d. invented the computer mouse.

6. The first Web site provided information about

   a. CERN.

   b. Berners-Lee.

   c. the World Wide Web.

   d. the Enquire program.

7. The Web has made it possible for some programmers to earn millions of dollars.

   a. True

   b. False

8. You can infer from this passage that

   a. some people would like to limit access to the Web.

   b. Berners-Lee would like to limit access to the Web.

   c. Berners-Lee wishes he had made more money from his invention.

   d. many people think the World Wide Web should be closed down.

6. José Antonio Abreu

1. Choose the statement that best expresses the overall thesis of the passage.

   a. Abreu's music program has helped many young Venezuelans.

   b. Venezuela has hundreds of children's and youth symphony orchestras.

   c. Learning to play an instrument can help young people gain a positive attitude.

   d. The National Youth Orchestra of Venezuela has been praised around the world.

2. When Abreu founded the National Youth Symphony Orchestra, he

    a. hoped to attract more foreign musicians to Venezuelan orchestras.
    b. wanted to practice conducting a large symphony orchestra.
    c. wanted to give young Venezuelans a chance to play in an orchestra.
    d. believed that young Venezuelans should go to other countries to study music.

3. Abreu believes that music can

    a. improve the economy of a poor country.
    b. encourage young people to become involved in drugs.
    c. encourage young people to leave their families.
    d. help a child stop destructive social behavior.

4. Some students in Abreu's music program used to have ties with criminal gangs.

    a. True
    b. False

5. Abreu's music program is

    a. fully supported financially by the Venezuelan government.
    b. supported mostly by international charity organizations.
    c. paid for by the families of the students in the program.
    d. supported financially by Abreu himself and other famous musicians.

6. The children in the music program have to pay for their instruments and lessons.

    a. True
    b. False

7. People who hear the Venezuelan youth orchestras are surprised

    a. about the size of the orchestra.
    b. by the kind of music they play.
    c. to see such young musicians.
    d. by the high-quality playing.

8. You can infer from this passage that in the past

    a. Venezuelans were more interested in art than music.
    b. not many Venezuelans were interested in classical music.
    c. young Venezuelans went to the United States to study music.
    d. many Venezuelans were interested in classical music.

UNIT 4

Inventions That Are Changing Our Lives

1. Robots

Since our earliest days, humans have used tools to improve their lives. At first, these tools were simple and handheld, such as knives or hammers, and they were used to perform basic tasks that were necessary for survival. Over time, the tools and the technology for using them became more complicated. First they were mechanical, then electrical, and finally electronic. One of the most recent developments in tools is the robot. The latest robots can be taught to perform complex tasks that require an almost humanlike ability to process information and make decisions.

The word *robot* first appeared in a 1921 stage play by Czech writer Karel Capek. In the play, a man makes a machine that can think, which he calls a robot and which ends up killing its owner. In the 1940s, the American science fiction writer Isaac Asimov wrote a series of stories about robots and invented the term *robotics*, the science of robots.

Meanwhile, in the real world, the first robots were developed by an engineer, Joseph F. Engelberger, and an inventor, George C. Devol. Together they started Unimation, a manufacturing company that produced the first real robot in 1961, called the Unimate. Robots of this type were installed at a General Motors automobile plant and proved to be a success. They worked reliably and saved money for General Motors, so other companies were soon acquiring robots as well.

These industrial robots were nothing like the terrifying creatures that can often be seen in science fiction films. In fact, these robots looked and behaved nothing like humans. They were simply pieces of computer-controlled machinery, with metal "arms" or "hands." Since they were made of metal, they could perform certain jobs that were difficult or dangerous for humans, particularly jobs that involve high heat. And since robots were tireless and never got hungry, sleepy, or distracted, they were useful for tasks that would be tiring or boring for humans. Industrial robots have been improved over the years, and today they are used in many factories around the world. Though the use of robots has meant the loss of some jobs, at the same time other jobs have been created in the design, development, and production of the robots.

Outside of industry, robots have also been developed and put to use by governments and scientists in situations where humans might be in danger. For example, they can be sent in to investigate an unexploded bomb or an accident at a nuclear power plant. Researchers also use robots to collect samples of hot rocks or gases in active volcanoes. In space exploration, robots have performed many key tasks where humans could not be present, such as on the surface of Mars. In 2004, two robotic Rovers—small six-wheeled computerized cars—were sent to Mars. The Rovers had lasers that functioned as eyes and software that was designed to help them travel around holes or rocks. While on Mars, they performed many scientific experiments and took thousands of photographs, sending all the results back to Earth. Among other things, the Rovers discovered that Mars probably once had water on its surface just like Earth.

As robots were developed for industry and science, some inventors also found uses for smaller and less expensive robots. The first of these appeared in the 1980s, as an educational tool for learning about computers. Then in the 1990s, further technological improvements led to the invention of robot toys. The most famous of these was AIBO, a robotic dog produced by Sony. It could run around a room and chase a ball like a real dog. However, in spite of great enthusiasm for AIBO when it first appeared, it was too expensive ($2,000) to be successful in the long run.

Inventors have been more successful with robots that can help with housework. The Roomba, for example, is a robotic vacuum cleaner. Made of lightweight plastic, it is low and round, with wheels. Before it begins cleaning a room, Roomba first moves all around it to "learn" about the shape of the room and the furniture in it. Then it starts vacuuming, avoiding the walls and furniture. When it begins to run out of power, it returns to a base to recharge. It does all of this without any human direction. With a price tag of only about $200, the Roomba has sold well— about 2 million Roombas were sold in its first four years. The same company that makes Roomba has now developed a floor-washing robot called the Scooba.

What is the future for robots? One likely use of robots was demonstrated in a race for robot-controlled cars held in 2005 by the United States Defense Department. The winner of this race across the Nevada desert—and the winner of $2 million—was a Volkswagen Tuareg model called Stanley, designed by robot specialists at Stanford University in California. Stanley arrived at the finish line 170 miles (273.5 km) away, after traveling over the rough land in a little less than seven hours—without a human behind the steering wheel. This was possible because its computer "brain" was able to deal with the various tasks required along the trip. It could read a map, find its location, judge what was ahead, and make decisions based on all this information.

Robots have come a long way. Once story writers and movie makers imagined them as dangerous humanlike machines that could take over the Earth. Now robots help people at home, in factories, and in scientific research. In the next decade many new uses will be found for robots, especially in cars. As one designer said, "A person's role in the car is changing. People will become more planners than drivers." Robots will do the rest.

Finishing time _____   Reading time _____

Now turn to page 296 and answer the questions. Do not look back at the passage.

2. Lasers in Modern Medicine

Starting time _____

A laser is a device that makes a beam of light so narrow and strong that it can cut like a knife. (LASER stands for Light Amplification by the Stimulated Emission of Radiation.) When it was invented, no one knew that it would change modern medicine. But now, with this wonderful tool, doctors can safely perform operations and treatments that were once very dangerous or painful, or simply impossible with regular surgical instruments.

The first person to imagine something like a laser was Albert Einstein in 1917. He realized that it might be possible to create a very strong, bright beam of light by changing the way light acted. However, he never investigated this idea any further and neither he nor anyone else tried to produce a laser beam for many years.

Finally, in the late 1950s, scientists began experimenting with light and figured out how to create the strong beams we now know as laser beams. In these first experiments, they used mirrors and artificial gem stones to change the light. Other scientists soon were producing the same results by sending light through special gases. The light created by either of these methods was very different from normal light. The beams from lasers remain narrow and do not spread out as light normally does, even over great distance. Furthermore, laser beams can be created entirely of one color, while normal light, such as that from a lightbulb, contains a combination of all the colors.

In the early years after the invention of lasers, scientists called them "a solution looking for a problem." It was obvious that lasers were very special, but it took scientists a while to find practical applications for them. Over time, hundreds of uses have been found for lasers in many areas of science and technology. They are used in the newest telecommunication systems, in computer printers, and in compact disc players. They are also used in show business to create special lighting effects. But where lasers have made the most difference is undoubtedly in the world of medicine, where they can be used for many tasks that require fine precision.

First, doctors can use lasers as cutting tools. Surgeons prefer lasers to surgical knives for certain operations because laser beams can be made much narrower than a knife blade. Also, with lasers, doctors can work more quickly than with metal tools, and so there is less risk of infection. Furthermore, a laser beam produces heat, which helps to close off the skin or tissue being cut into and reduces bleeding. Thus, lasers have proved extremely useful in the fine surgery required to reconstruct veins and arteries. They are also used in surgery to remove certain kinds of brain or liver cancers. Doctors are experimenting with ways to find cancer in various parts of the body through the use of a colored liquid that colors only the cancerous areas. Then they can use lasers designed for that color to find the cancer and burn it away. This removes the disease from the body but damages nothing else.

Lasers have also dramatically changed the work of eye doctors. Poor vision is one of the most common medical problems in the world, and until recently the only way to correct it was with eyeglasses or contact lenses. Now many vision problems can be corrected permanently with laser surgery. This surgery has made an enormous difference for people who were practically blind without their glasses or contact lenses. After a lifetime of worrying about breaking or losing their glasses or lenses, they can see normally without them.

For eye surgery, doctors need to be extremely precise and extremely quick. They use what is known as a cool laser, which produces beams that can cut out 39 millionths of an inch of tissue in 12 billionths of a second. In other words, this kind of laser is so precise it could cut into a strand of hair without cutting all the way through. In vision surgery, these lasers are used on a part of the eye called the cornea, which is the transparent covering on the outside. When the cornea is not perfectly round, we cannot see clearly. To improve vision, the doctor shapes the cornea with a laser until it is more round. The process takes only a few minutes and because the laser is cool, there is little pain.

Another use of lasers in medicine is for the removal of marks on the skin. In the case of cancerous growths, laser beams can be used with far more precision than knives or other tools. A laser beam with its one color of light can be directed to find one color within the skin and destroy only the skin of that color. Some people are born with large dark red marks on their face, for example, which can cause embarrassment and psychological problems. With a dark red laser beam, doctors can remove that mark. In recent years, doctors have also developed ways to use laser beams to make people look younger by removing wrinkles around the mouth and eyes. In all of these skin operations, the laser is able to work on just the top layers of skin, causing much less pain and skin damage and with less risk of infection or damage than what would be caused by other kind of tools.

It has been fifty years since lasers were first invented and were seen as a solution looking for a problem. Now they are solving many problems in the world around us, in technology and above all, in medicine. They have become essential tools for scientists and doctors as they perform lifesaving operations and improve the quality of our lives.

Finishing time _____   Reading time _____

Now turn to page 297 and answer the questions. Do not look back at the passage.

3. Leeches as Medical Treatment   Starting time _____

Leeches are small wormlike creatures that live in water and suck the blood of animals and humans. Mention leeches and most people today show signs of disgust or fear. In the past, though, leeches were commonly used in medicine to drain blood from people. Then advances in science led to other kinds of treatments, and leeches disappeared from the sick room. Now, however, they are making a comeback. Leeches are being used after operations for the reattachment of body parts, in the prevention of pain from arthritis, and in the treatment of heart disease.

The use of leeches in medicine goes back at least 2,500 years. Doctors used them to treat the sick in ancient Egypt, India, Persia, and Greece. It was believed in those days that taking blood from patients helped to bring their bodies back into balance. This belief and the practice of draining blood with leeches continued through the ages, reaching a high point in early nineteenth century France. There, a leading physician promoted the idea that all illness resulted from having too much blood in the body. At that time, Parisian hospitals required as many as 6 million leeches a year for their patients. Young French women made their living by wading into ponds to capture the leeches that stuck to their legs.

By the middle of the nineteenth century, however, the practice of draining blood from patients was becoming less popular. With a better understanding of diseases and of the human body, doctors realized that taking blood from the patient (with or without leeches) was not helpful in many cases. Thanks to the work of various scientists, including Frenchman Louis Pasteur, doctors gradually came to accept that many diseases are caused by germs. They realized that other approaches—and particularly limiting the spread of germs—were more effective in treating illness, and that in fact, leeches made no real difference in many cases.

By the twentieth century, doctors had completely abandoned the use of leeches to drain blood. But in 1985 Dr. Joseph Upton, a surgeon in Boston, Massachusetts, discovered a new use for them. Faced with a young patient whose ear had been bitten off by a dog, Upton successfully reattached the ear in a twelve-hour operation. However, within three days, the ear had turned black because blood could not move through it properly. During the operation, it had been fairly easy for Upton to reattach the arteries that brought blood to his patient's ear, since artery walls are thick and easy to see. However, since the veins that carry blood away from the ear are much smaller and hard to find, Upton had not been able to reattach enough of them. If something wasn't done quickly, the ear would not survive.

Luckily, Dr. Upton remembered an article he had read about research into the properties of leeches. Though the results of the research were still uncertain, Upton decided to take a chance. He bought some leeches from a laboratory and placed them on the boy's ear and they began to feed. The boy felt no pain because the mouths of leeches contain a natural painkiller. As the leeches sucked some of the extra blood out of the boy's ear, they added a special chemical to the blood so it would not harden and form clots and it would flow more easily.

Within a few minutes, the boy's ear began to lose the terrible black color. The leeches had soon eaten enough and fell off. At that point, they looked dramatically different. While at the start, they had been small and thin, now they looked like long, fat black cigars. Several days later, after applying more leeches, the boy's ear was entirely pink and healthy. Thanks to leeches, Dr. Upton had performed the first successful reattachment of a child's ear. Other doctors then began to experiment with the use of leeches in the reattachment of other body parts, and finally, in 2004, the United States Food and Drug Administration approved the use of medicinal leeches in reconstructive surgery.

Another use of leeches has been investigated by a team of German doctors who study the ability of leeches to reduce pain. Their patients suffer from arthritis, a painful joint disease that often affects knees, elbows, shoulders, hips, or fingers. When the German doctors put leeches on the arthritic knees of their patients, almost all of them felt immediate relief from the pain. Most of the patients continued to be pain-free for over a month and some for as long as six months. Furthermore, unlike many drugs that are effective pain killers, there were no side effects from applying the leeches.

Leeches have also proved indirectly useful in treating patients with heart and blood diseases. Since the 1880s, researchers have understood that certain chemicals in leeches prevent blood from clotting or becoming hard. Many people with heart or blood problems live with a serious risk of the formation of blood clots, which can travel through the blood to the heart or brain and cause death. In the 1950s, a scientist identified the chemical in a leech that prevents clotting and called it *hirudin.* Later studies led to experiments with hirudin and the development of a drug that thins the blood of patients who are at risk for blood clots. Now researchers are also investigating the giant Amazonian leech of South America. This 18-inch (45 cm) leech produces a chemical that attacks and dissolves clots already in the blood. This chemical could prove to be extremely useful in medicine.

Though doctors today do not view the use of leeches as the all-purpose treatment it once was, they now see that for certain problems, this ancient remedy may be valid after all.

Finishing time _____   Reading time _____

Now turn to page 298 and answer the questions. Do not look back at the passage.

4. GPS (Global Positioning System)

Starting time _____

With a GPS receiver, you need never be lost again. Whether you are driving in a new city or climbing a mountain path, you can use GPS (Global Positioning System) to find out exactly where you are. How is this possible? A system of twenty-four satellites sends continuous signals from 12,000 miles above the Earth. Based on the location of the satellites, GPS receivers on the earth can use these signals to find their own location.

GPS had its beginnings in the 1940s when the United States military developed a navigation system using radio signals from different ground locations. However, because the signals were easily interrupted or lost, the system did not always work. American scientists realized they might be able to use satellites to send signals after 1957, when the Soviet Union launched *Sputnik I*, the first man-made satellite. Since the scientists could follow the satellite's path and track its radio beams, it occurred to them that they could calculate the exact position of the satellite, using their exact location on the Earth. Using the same logic, they also realized that if they knew the exact location of the satellite, they could calculate their own position on the Earth. A system using signals sent from satellites was clearly the solution for global navigation.

The first such system was developed by the U.S. Navy in the 1960s. It sent signals from five satellites and was used mainly by military ships and airplanes. However, with only five satellites, it was not always possible to get a signal everywhere on the globe. This meant ships or planes could not depend on the system in emergency situations—in war or in bad weather. More satellites and better signals were needed. After years of research, the first GPS satellite was launched in 1978, ten more had been launched by 1989, and a complete set of twenty-four satellites were in orbit by 1994.

Though it was originally created for military uses, GPS has by now become an essential global navigating tool. Around the world, ships depend on GPS, as do airports and airplanes. In recent years, the development of very small and inexpensive receivers has made possible all kinds of other uses. Many cars now come equipped with GPS receivers and computerized maps to show where you are. Farmers put GPS receivers on tractors to help them find their way at night over dark fields. Emergency telephone operators use GPS to locate people who have called in for help. And parents or pet owners put receivers on their children or their dogs so they cannot be lost.

However, what makes GPS so useful—the way it allows us to keep track of people and things—could also make it dangerous if it is used for the wrong purposes. Some organizations that are concerned about rights to privacy have argued that there should be limits to who can use GPS and for what purpose. In the United States, several cases have been brought to court to question the right of the government or private companies to track people without their knowledge.

One important case came up in 2003 before the Supreme Court in the state of Washington. Under American laws protecting the right to privacy, the government or the police are not allowed to investigate a person's private life if there is no evidence that he or she has committed a crime. In the Washington case, the police had wanted to learn more about the habits of a man they suspected, so they hid a GPS receiver in his car. Lawyers for the suspect argued that this was illegal because it went against his right to privacy. The Washington Supreme Court agreed. In their view, hiding a GPS receiver in a car was like putting an invisible police officer in the back seat. This was acceptable practice only if the police already had evidence that the suspect had been involved in a crime and if they had permission from a judge. Otherwise, it could not be used.

In 2005, another interesting case involving GPS was brought before the Supreme Court in Connecticut. This case involved a rental car company that decided to use GPS technology to prevent customers from driving their cars too fast. They hid GPS receivers in all their rental cars, which allowed them to know where each car was at any time. The receivers could also be used to calculate the speed at which a car moved from one place to another. If the car was driven faster than 80 miles per hour (120 km/hour), the driver was charged an extra $150. Though the rental contract did mention GPS in very small print, customers were not told about it or about the extra charge.

One customer who was charged $450 for speeding three times became very angry, and he decided to bring the rental company to court. In his view, the rental company had used GPS to spy on him illegally and the charges were unfair. The Connecticut Supreme Court agreed that this use of GPS was not acceptable and told the rental company to return the $450. According to the judges, the rental company should have informed the driver about the existence of a GPS receiver in the car and about the speeding charge.

As a technology for finding location, GPS is the latest in a long series of technological developments. Travelers once looked for patterns in the stars to find their way through unknown lands. Then, they began to use maps, which were first drawn in Turkey in about 6200 B.C.E. and became more and more accurate over the centuries. But the remarkable precision of GPS raises many new questions today about how and when this technology should be used.

Finishing time _____   Reading time _____

Now turn to page 299 and answer the questions. Do not look back at the passage.

5. Green Buildings

Starting time _____

The green building movement is changing the way buildings are constructed. This movement started in the 1970s, as people began to see that modern life was destroying the environment we all share. Natural resources were being destroyed, energy and water consumption was rising, and so was pollution of all kinds. This environmental destruction has continued, and one important factor has been the way that buildings are constructed. In fact, energy use in buildings represents about 32 percent of all energy use in the United States.

In the early years, green builders were a small minority, and their goals of reducing the environmental impact of buildings were considered unrealistic. Now, however, the green building movement is growing, as builders have been able to take advantage of new technology and as the costs of this technology have gone down. Environmental building methods are now practical enough to save money for builders and for building owners, even as they reduce damage to the environment.

First, green builders try to make use of recycled materials as much as possible. In fact, vast amounts of materials such as steel, cement, and wood are used in construction. Now there are companies that specialize in gathering old materials, processing them, and selling them to builders for new buildings. States and cities are encouraging these companies, as the reuse of materials also means less waste in dumps. For larger builders or individual homeowners, it is possible to find everything from steel and cement to doors, windows, sinks, tubs, brick, and hardware.

Another way that builders can reduce environmental impact is to reduce the energy requirements of a building. This can be done in several ways. One is to provide an alternative, nonpolluting source of energy. The first alternative energy source to be developed was solar power. With solar panels—wide, flat sheets of special material—it is possible to produce electricity from the rays of the sun. Builders can install solar panels on the roofs of buildings and connect them to cooling or lighting systems. Once the panels are installed, they provide energy at no cost and with no pollution.

Another, nonpolluting solution for reducing energy use is a technology known as geothermal heating. To obtain geothermal heat, builders place special pipes below ground, where temperatures remain constant all year. In the winter, the earth's natural heat can be collected in these pipes, and then transferred into the building's heating system. In the summer, heat in the building can be collected and sent to the pipes underground.

A different kind of solution to the energy problem is for builders to reduce the amount of energy required in a building. For example, it is possible to cut electricity use noticeably just by improving natural lighting and installing low-energy lightbulbs. To reduce the amount of fuel that is needed for heating or cooling, builders can also add insulation to the walls so that the building stays warmer in winter and cooler in summer. They can also consider the position of the building to take advantage of natural heating and cooling effects of the sun, the wind, and other buildings nearby. Furthermore, builders can plant trees that help reduce energy use by providing shade in sunny weather and protection from cold wind.

One of the best examples of advanced green building design in the United States is the Genzyme Center of Cambridge, Massachusetts. In 2000, the Genzyme Company decided to build the most environmentally responsible office building ever made in America. Every aspect of the design and building had to take into account two things: the need for a safe and pleasant workplace for employees and the need to lessen the negative environmental impact.

First, in constructing the building, 75 percent of the building materials were recycled materials. Furthermore, at least half of all the building materials came from nearby (less than 500 miles away) to use less energy in transporting them. Now, special mirrors on the roof bring the sunlight into the center of the building so that most of the employees can work under natural light. The windows in the building can be opened—unlike windows in many American office buildings—so that people can get fresh air. Indoor gardens make the place more pleasant and also help clean the air of pollutants. Above all, the energy use has been reduced by 43 percent and water use by 32 percent, compared with other buildings of the same size.

In other parts of the world, several large-scale projects have recently been developed according to green building principles. One of these is in the town of Vauban, Germany, in an area that was once the site of army housing. This site has been completely rebuilt with houses that require 30 percent less energy than conventional houses. These houses are also heated by special nonpolluting systems that run on wood chips, and they are equipped with solar energy panels.

An even larger project is under way in China. The first phase of this project, in a small farming village, will include houses for 400 families built with solar power, nonpolluting bricks, and recycled wall insulation. In a second phase, entire neighborhoods in six cities will be built according to green building principles. And if all goes well, the Chinese government plans to copy these ideas in new neighborhoods all across China.

Whether on a small scale or large scale, green building ideas are spreading. For many years, they were viewed as a costly option for the wealthy, but now individuals, companies, and governments are beginning to see their benefits. In addition to the fact that they are environmentally friendly, green buildings improve living and working conditions and also save money in the long run.

Finishing time _____   Reading time _____

Now turn to page 300 and answer the questions. Do not look back at the passage.

6. Wikipedia

Starting time _____

The goal of Internet-based encyclopedia Wikipedia (www.wikipedia.org) is to give everyone on the planet free access to information. Like other encyclopedias, Wikipedia contains lots of information: more than 2.5 million articles in 200 different languages covering just about every subject. Unlike other encyclopedias, however, Wikipedia is not written by experts, but by ordinary people. These writers are not paid and their names are not published. They contribute to Wikipedia simply because they want to share their knowledge.

Encyclopedias began in ancient times as collections of writings about all aspects of human knowledge. The word itself comes from ancient Greek, and means "a complete general education." In fact, early encyclopedias were not used as reference books as they are today, but served as textbooks for learning. Nothing has survived of the very first Greek or Roman encyclopedias. The oldest encyclopedia still in existence is a collection of thirty-seven volumes on the natural sciences, written by the Roman scholar, Pliny the Elder, in the first century B.C.E.

By the 1600s, many huge encyclopedias had been produced in Europe, in the Middle East, and also in China. These encyclopedias were all handwritten and handcopied, so they were expensive and rare. The invention of the printing press and a more systematic approach to organizing the information (in alphabetical order) allowed encyclopedias to become more accessible, but they were still aimed at scholarly readers. This was the case with the first Encyclopedia Britannica in Edinburgh, Scotland, from 1768 to 1771, which included long technical articles.

Real popularity for encyclopedias came in the nineteenth century in Europe and the United States, with the publication of encyclopedias written for ordinary readers. By the twentieth century, it was common for middle-class families to buy a multivolume encyclopedia to keep in their home. With the invention of the CD-ROM, the same amount of information could be put on a few computer discs. Then with the Internet, it became possible to create an online encyclopedia that could be constantly updated, like Microsoft's Encarta.

However, even Internet-based encyclopedias like Encarta were written by paid experts. At first, Wikipedia, the brainchild of Jimmy Wales, a businessman in Chicago, was not so different from these. In 2001, he had the idea for an Internet-based encyclopedia that would provide information quickly and easily to everyone. Furthermore, that information would be available free, unlike other Internet encyclopedias at the time.

But Wales, like everyone else, believed that people with special knowledge were needed to write the articles, and so he began by hiring experts. He soon changed his approach, however, as it took them a long time to finish their work. He decided to open up the encyclopedia in a radical new way, so that everyone would have access not only to the information, but also to the process of putting this information online.

To do this, he used what is known as "Wiki" software (from the Hawaiian word for "fast"), which allows users to create or alter content on a web page. The system is very simple: When you open the web site, you can simply search for information or you can log on to become a writer or editor of articles. If you find an article that interests you—about your hometown, for example—you can correct it or expand it. Someone else may do the same. This process goes on until no one is interested in making any more changes. The success of this method can be measured by Wikipedia's extraordinary growth. By September 2006, there were 1 million Wikipedia articles in the English version alone, compared with 65,000 in the latest edition of the Encyclopedia Britannica.

Ideally, with this system of multiple editing, errors are found and corrected, and the final result is an accurate and interesting article. In reality, however, there can be problems. First, errors may not be detected and so articles may contain inaccurate information. Second, Wikipedia depends on the good intentions of its users and there is no way to prevent jokers or evil doers from using it for their own purposes. In a recent case, someone added false and harmful information to the biography of a retired American newspaper editor. That information was eventually found and deleted, but not before it had been online for months. No one ever discovered who had written it.

Wales himself has said that though Wikipedia is very useful for many purposes, it should never be used for serious research, since the facts have not been checked by experts. In a recent British study, however, Wikipedia was rated quite highly when compared to the Encyclopedia Britannica. The editors of a scientific journal asked scientists to look for factual errors in forty-two different articles in the two encyclopedias. They found four mistakes on average in each of the Wikipedia articles, and three mistakes in each of the Britannica articles. Thus, error is apparently always possible, even when articles are written by experts.

Wikipedia serves as a good example of the best and worst of the Internet. It is the creation of people who wish to share their knowledge with others, and the information is free. On the other hand, it can be used by people to cause harm, and the information cannot be fully trusted. Most college professors for example do not allow students to use Wikipedia as their only source in writing research papers.

Will Wikipedia change the world as Jimmy Wales dreams? If he and his followers find a way to make Wikipedia error-free, maybe it will. They know their encyclopedia has mistakes, but, as Wales has said, "There are many more good people than bad in the world and in this project."

Finishing time _____   Reading time _____

Now turn to page 301 and answer the questions. Do not look back at the passage.

Questions for Unit 4

After you answer the questions for a passage, follow these steps:

1. Check your answers with your teacher. For any incorrect answers, look back at the passage to understand why they are incorrect.
2. Find your reading rate (page 252) and then fill in the information on the Progress Chart for Timed Readings (page 253).

1. Robots

1. Choose the statement that best expresses the overall thesis of the passage.

   a. The word *robot* was invented by a Czech writer in 1921.
   b. Some kinds of robots are used in industry and scientific research.
   c. Robots can be used to perform many complex tasks these days.
   d. In the future, people won't drive cars—robots will.

2. The first real robot was

   a. installed in an automobile plant.
   b. a machine that could think like a person.
   c. invented by a science fiction writer.
   d. looked and behaved like a human.

3. Industrial robots cannot do jobs that require high heat.

   a. True
   b. False

4. In industry, robots

   a. have taken away some jobs and created others.
   b. have caused many factories to close.
   c. look and behave a lot like human beings.
   d. are used instead of computer programmers and engineers.

5. Robots are useful in space exploration because they

   a. travel much faster and farther than humans.
   b. can go places where people cannot go.
   c. take better photographs than humans.
   d. have eyes and ears and a brain just like humans.

6. The Roomba can vacuum a room all by itself.

   a. True
   b. False

7. The robot-controlled car, Stanley,

   a. was designed by the United States government.
   b. could travel long distances without a driver.
   c. required a robot specialist in the back seat.
   d. cost $2 million to design and build.

8. You can infer from this passage that

   a. scientists do not see much future need for robots.
   b. the toy industry will probably create many more robots.
   c. the robots of the future will not look like humans.
   d. robots could be dangerous to humans in the future.

2. Lasers in Modern Medicine

1. Choose the statement that best expresses the overall thesis of the passage.

   a. Lasers are used in many kinds of medical operations.
   b. Scientists have found many uses for lasers in technology.
   c. Eye surgery has changed dramatically with the use of lasers.
   d. Laser light beams were first produced in the 1950s.

2. Albert Einstein

    a. believed it was not possible to produce a laser beam.

    b. was the first person to produce a laser beam.

    c. imagined a laser beam, but never produced one.

    d. experimented with laser beams as early as 1917.

3. Laser beams always contain all the colors, like normal beams of light.

    a. True

    b. False

4. Scientists realized that laser beams were special, but

    a. Einstein thought it was not possible to use them.

    b. they also thought they might be dangerous.

    c. they did not know what to do with them at first.

    d. doctors did not want to use them at first.

5. One reason why doctors use lasers in surgery is because they

    a. allow doctors to see what they are doing.

    b. create interesting lighting effects.

    c. cost less than metal tools.

    d. are more precise than metal tools.

6. Poor vision

    a. improves only temporarily with laser surgery.

    b. can be corrected permanently with laser surgery.

    c. must be corrected by glasses and lenses.

    d. can be corrected only in young people.

7. Doctors use laser beams to make people look younger.

    a. True

    b. False

8. You can infer from this passage that compared with the past more

    a. people are having surgery to change the way they look.

    b. people are getting cancer of the brain or the liver.

    c. doctors are specializing in eye surgery and vision problems.

    d. doctors are using traditional methods to correct vision problems.

3. Leeches as Medical Treatment

1. Choose the statement that best expresses the overall thesis of the passage.

    a. The germ theory of disease was an important discovery.

    b. Doctors once used leeches as an all-purpose treatment.

    c. Leeches are an ancient form of medical treatment.

    d. Leeches are once again being used in medicine.

2. In the past, doctors treated patients with leeches because they believed that

    a. people had too much blood in their bodies.
    b. draining blood from patients was good for them.
    c. young women needed to earn a living from leeches.
    d. ancient treatments were the best kind of treatment.

3. Doctors stopped using leeches when

    a. they learned about germs and disease.
    b. patients showed signs of disgust and fear.
    c. leeches became more difficult to find.
    d. scientists discovered the chemical called hirudin.

4. The boy's ear was in danger because he had been bitten by a leech.

    a. True
    b. False

5. Dr. Upton had

    a. seen other doctors use leeches after surgery.
    b. to go and get the leeches from a pond himself.
    c. often used leeches in experiments with dogs.
    d. never used leeches on people before.

6. After the leeches were applied to the boy's ear, it

    a. turned black from too much blood.
    b. became healthy and normal.
    c. became unhealthy and fell off.
    d. it could hear sounds better than before.

7. When leeches bite they add a chemical to the blood that prevents clotting.

    a. True
    b. False

8. You can infer from this passage that

    a. researchers believe that leeches may harm people.
    b. ancient remedies are never useful in our modern age.
    c. there may be some valid medical use for ancient remedies.
    d. leeches may also be useful against cancer and diabetes.

4. GPS (Global Positioning System)

1. Choose the statement that best expresses the overall thesis of the passage.

    a. GPS has made it possible to keep precise track of a lost person or stolen car.
    b. GPS receivers capture continuous signals from twenty-four satellites.
    c. GPS began as a tool for the military but now has many nonmilitary uses.
    d. GPS may not be used secretly by the police in the United States.

2. The first radio navigation system

    a. was developed by the Soviet Union.

    b. followed the path of a man-made satellite.

    c. was used to follow a suspected criminal.

    d. depended on signals sent from the ground.

3. *Sputnik I*, the satellite launched by the Soviet Union,

    a. was developed by the Soviet military.

    b. sent GPS signals to Soviet scientists.

    c. helped American scientists develop GPS.

    d. was captured by the American military.

4. Having twenty-four satellites in the system means that

    a. it is possible to get a signal from any place on earth.

    b. it may not be possible to get a signal in some places.

    c. signals are easily interrupted or lost in some places.

    d. only military ships and airplanes can use GPS.

5. The twenty-four GPS satellites were launched between 1978 and 1994.

    a. True

    b. False

6. The Supreme Court in Washington decided that the police

    a. can put an invisible police officer in the back seat of someone's car.

    b. have to ask a judge before they can use GPS to follow someone.

    c. should not use rental cars when they are following a criminal.

    d. may investigate people's private lives whenever they want to.

7. A rental company used GPS to find out if its customers were criminals.

    a. True

    b. False

8. You can infer from this passage that in the United States

    a. private companies are allowed to use GPS to locate customers.

    b. the use of GPS has reduced the number of airplane accidents.

    c. the police can use any means to find out about a suspected criminal.

    d. the decisions of the Supreme Court are very important legally.

5. Green Buildings

1. Choose the statement that best expresses the overall thesis of the passage.

    a. The green building movement began because people were worried about pollution.

    b. All buildings are generally made so that they will be environmentally friendly.

    c. Environmental problems are causing serious damage to the world we live in.

    d. Green buildings are friendlier to the environment than ordinary buildings.

2. Environmental building methods

    a. now save money for building owners.

    b. are now very expensive for building owners.

    c. are not practical for building owners now.

    d. are now considered unrealistic.

3. Recycled building materials cannot be used by homeowners.

    a. True

    b. False

4. Geothermal heating

    a. works through solar panels.

    b. uses the natural heat of the earth.

    c. requires a lot of fuel.

    d. does not work in the summer.

5. Which of the following is NOT a way to reduce energy use?

    a. Use low-energy lightbulbs.

    b. Add insulation to the walls.

    c. Make the building larger.

    d. Position the building carefully.

6. The Genzyme Center was designed specially to be

    a. the most beautiful building in Cambridge.

    b. an environmentally responsible office building.

    c. an example of how to use recycled building materials.

    d. convenient for using public transportation.

7. China is planning several large green building projects in the country and in cities.

    a. True

    b. False

8. You can infer from this passage that green builders

    a. have been more successful with private homes.

    b. are particularly concerned with lowering energy use.

    c. have not been successful outside the United States.

    d. have planted lots of gardens in their buildings.

6. Wikipedia

1. Choose the statement that best expresses the overall thesis of the passage.

    a. Wikipedia was founded by Jimmy Wales, an American businessman, in 2001.

    b. Wikipedia is a free online encyclopedia that is written and edited by its users.

    c. Wikipedia contains 2.5 million articles in 200 different languages.

    d. Encyclopedias are large collections of general knowledge.

2. The oldest encyclopedia to survive until today was written

    a. by a Roman scholar named Pliny the Elder.

    b. for ancient Greek readers in Athens, Greece.

    c. in Edinburgh, Scotland, in the eighteenth century.

    d. about literature and the arts in ancient Rome.

3. Until the nineteenth century, encyclopedias were very popular with ordinary readers.

    a. True

    b. False

4. Wales decided not to use paid experts to write articles for Wikipedia because

    a. Encarta did not use them either.

    b. it cost too much to pay them.

    c. they took too long to produce articles.

    d. he disagreed with what they wrote.

5. "Wiki" software makes it possible

    a. for experts to check the facts in a web article.

    b. to find out if facts are accurate in a web article.

    c. to write long articles for a web encyclopedia.

    d. for users to add or change information on a Web page.

6. In Wikipedia articles, errors are

    a. found and corrected by paid experts.

    b. corrected by the founder, Jimmy Wales.

    c. found and corrected by ordinary readers.

    d. not possible because of the "Wiki" software.

7. According to a study, Wikipedia has fewer factual errors than the Encyclopedia Brittanica.

    a. True

    b. False

8. You can infer from this passage that

    a. students know they shouldn't use Wikipedia as the only source.

    b. most college professors do not think that Wikipedia can be trusted.

    c. Wales does not trust people to find or correct errors in the articles.

    d. Wales believes it will be possible to make Wikipedia error free.

Appendix 1

2,000 Most Frequent Words in English Language Texts

Source: Adapted from Michael West, *A General Service List of English Words*. London: Longman. 1936/1953. Available at http://www.lextutor.ca

First Thousand

able	ask	call	crowd	eat	figure
about	associate	can	crown	effect	fill
above	at	capital	cry	efficient	find
accept	attack	captain	current	effort	fine
accord	attempt	car	cut	egg	finish
account	average	care	danger	eight	fire
accountable	away	carry	dark	either	first
across	back	case	date	elect	fish
act	bad	castle	daughter	eleven	fit
active	ball	catch	day	else	five
actor	bank	cause	dead	empire	fix
actress	bar	center	deal	employ	floor
actual	base	certain	dear	end	flow
add	battle	chance	decide	enemy	flower
address	be	change	declare	English	fly
admit	bear	character	deep	enjoy	follow
adopt	beauty	charge	defeat	enough	food
advance	because	chief	degree	enter	for
advantage	become	child	demand	equal	force
adventure	bed	choose	department	escape	foreign
affair	before	church	depend	even	forest
after	begin	circle	describe	evening	forget
again	behind	city	desert	event	form
against	believe	claim	desire	ever	former
age	belong	class	destroy	every	forth
agent	below	clear	detail	example	fortune
ago	beneath	close	determine	except	four
agree	beside	cloud	develop	exchange	free
air	best	coal	die	exercise	fresh
all	between	coast	difference	exist	Friday
allow	beyond	coin	difficult	expect	friend
almost	big	cold	direct	expense	from
alone	bill	college	discover	experience	front
along	bird	colony	distance	experiment	full
already	black	color	distinguish	explain	furnish
also	blood	come	district	express	future
although	blow	command	divide	extend	gain
always	blue	committee	do	eye	game
among	board	common	doctor	face	garden
amount	boat	company	dog	fact	gas
ancient	body	complete	dollar	factory	gate
and	book	concern	door	fail	gather
animal	both	condition	doubt	fair	general
another	box	consider	down	faith	gentle
answer	boy	contain	draw	fall	get
any	branch	content	dream	familiar	gift
appear	bread	continue	dress	family	girl
apply	break	control	drink	famous	give
appoint	bridge	corn	drive	far	glad
arise	bright	cost	drop	farm	glass
arm	bring	cotton	dry	fast	go
army	broad	could	due	father	god
around	brother	council	duty	favor	gold
arrive	build	count	each	fear	good
art	burn	country	ear	feel	great
article	business	course	early	fellow	green
as	but	court	earth	few	ground
	buy	cover	east	field	group
	by	cross	easy	fight	grow

half	language	million	old	profit	rough
hand	large	mind	on	progress	round
hang	last	miner	once	promise	royal
happen	late	minister	one	proof	rule
happy	latter	minute	only	proper	run
hard	laugh	miss	open	property	safe
hardly	laughter	mister	operate	propose	sail
have	law	modern	opinion	protect	sale
he	lay	moment	opportunity	prove	salt
head	lead	Monday	or	provide	same
hear	learn	money	order	provision	Saturday
heart	leave	month	ordinary	public	save
heat	left	moon	organize	pull	say
heaven	length	moral	other	purpose	scarce
heavy	less	more	otherwise	put	scene
help	let	moreover	ought	quality	school
here	letter	morning	out	quantity	science
high	level	most	over	quarter	sea
hill	library	mother	owe	queen	season
history	lie	motor	own	question	seat
hold	life	mountain	page	quite	second
home	lift	mouth	paint	race	secret
honor	light	move	paper	raise	secretary
hope	like	Mrs.	part	rank	see
horse	likely	much	particular	rate	seem
hot	limit	music	party	rather	sell
hour	line	must	pass	reach	send
house	lip	name	past	read	sense
how	listen	nation	pay	ready	sensitive
however	literature	native	peace	real	separate
human	little	nature	people	realize	serious
hundred	live	near	per	really	serve
husband	local	necessary	perhaps	reason	service
idea	long	necessity	permit	receipt	set
if	look	need	person	receive	settle
ill	lord	neighbor	picture	recent	seven
important	lose	neither	piece	recognize	several
in	loss	never	place	record	shadow
inch	love	new	plain	red	shake
include	low	news	plan	reduce	shall
increase	machine	newspaper	plant	refuse	shape
indeed	main	next	play	regard	share
independent	make	night	please	relation	she
industry	man	nine	point	relative	shine
influence	manner	no	political	religion	ship
instead	manufacture	noble	poor	remain	shoot
interest	many	none	popular	remark	shore
into	mark	nor	population	remember	short
introduce	market	north	position	reply	should
iron	marry	not	possess	report	shoulder
it	mass	note	possible	represent	show
join	master	notice	post	republic	side
joint	material	now	pound	reserve	sight
jointed	matter	number	poverty	respect	sign
joy	maybe	numerical	power	rest	silence
judge	mean	numerous	prepare	result	silver
just	measure	object	present	return	simple
justice	meet	observe	president	rich	since
keep	member	occasion	press	ride	sing
kill	memory	of	pressure	right	single
kind	mention	off	pretty	ring	sir
king	mere	offer	prevent	rise	sister
know	metal	office	price	river	sit
lack	middle	official	private	road	situation
lady	might	often	problem	rock	six
lake	mile	oh	produce	roll	size
land	milk	oil	product	room	sky

sleep
small
smile
snow
so
social
society
soft
soldier
some
son
soon
sort
soul
sound
south
space
speak
special
speed
spend
spirit
spite
spot
spread
spring
square
stage
stand
standard
star
start
state
station
stay
steel
step
still
stock
stone
stop
store
story
strange
stream
street
strength
strike
strong
struggle
student
study
subject
substance
succeed
such
suffer
suggest
summer
sun
Sunday
supply
support
suppose
sure
surface
surprise

surround
sweet
sword
system
table
take
talk
tax
teach
tear
tell
temple
ten
term
test
than
the
then
there
therefore
they
thing
think
thirteen
thirty
this
though
thousand
three
through
throw
thursday
thus
till
time
to
today
together
ton
too
top
total
touch
toward
town
trade
train
travel
tree
trouble
true
trust
try
Tuesday
turn
twelve
twenty
two
type
under
understand
union
unite
university
unless
until
up

upon
use
usual
valley
value
variety
various
very
vessel
victory
view
village
virtue
visit
voice
vote
wage
wait
walk
wall
want
war
watch
water
wave
way
we
wealth
wear
Wednesday
week
welcome
well
west
western
what
when
where
whether
which
while
white
who
whole
why
wide
wife
wild
will
win
wind
window
winter
wise
wish
with
within
without
woman
wonder
wood
word
work
world
worth
would
wound

write
wrong
year
yes
yesterday
yet
yield
you
young
youth

Second Thousand

abroad
absence
absent
absolute
absolutely
accident
accuse
accustom
ache
admire
advertise
advice
afford
afraid
afternoon
agriculture
ahead
aim
airplane
alike
alive
aloud
altogether
ambition
amuse
anger
angle
annoy
anxiety
apart
apologize
apology
applaud
applause
apple
approve
arch
argue
arrange
arrest
arrow
artificial
ash
ashamed
aside
asleep
astonish
attend
attention
attract
audience
aunt
autumn
avenue

avoid
awake
awkward
axe
baby
bag
baggage
bake
balance
band
barber
bare
barely
bargain
barrel
basin
basket
bath
bathe
bay
beak
beam
bean
beard
beast
beat
beg
behave
behaviour
bell
belt
bend
berry
bicycle
billion
bind
birth
bit
bite
bitter
blade
blame
bless
blind
block
boast
boil
bold
bone
border
borrow
bottle
bottom
bound
boundary
bow
bowl
brain
brass
brave
breakfast
breath
breathe
bribe
brick
broadcast
brown

brush
bucket
bunch
bundle
burial
burst
bury
bus
bush
busy
butter
button
cage
cake
calculate
calm
camera
camp
canal
cap
cape
card
carriage
cart
cat
cattle
caution
cave
cent
century
ceremony
chain
chair
chalk
charm
cheap
cheat
check (verb)
check (noun)
cheer
cheese
chest
chicken
chimney
christmas
civilize
clay
clean
clerk
clever
cliff
climb
clock
cloth
club
coarse
coat
coffee
collar
collect
comb
combine
comfort
commerce
companion
compare
compete

competition
complain
complicate
compose
confess
confidence
confuse
congratulate
connect
conquer
conscience
conscious
convenience
conversation
cook
cool
copper
copy
cork
corner
correct
cottage
cough
courage
cousin
cow
coward
crack
crash
cream
creature
creep
crime
criminal
critic
crop
cruel
crush
cultivate
cup
cupboards
cure
curious
curl
curse
curtain
curve
cushion
custom
customer
damage
damp
dance
dare
deaf
debt
decay
deceive
decrease
deed
deer
defend
delay
delicate
delight
deliver
descend

deserve
desk
despair
devil
diamond
dictionary
dig
dinner
dip
dirt
disappoint
discipline
discuss
disease
disgust
dish
dismiss
disturb
ditch
dive
donkey
dot
double
dozen
drag
drawer
drown
drum
duck
dull
during
dust
eager
earn
earnest
ease
edge
educate
elastic
elder
electric
elephant
empty
enclose
encourage
engine
entertain
entire
envelope
envy
especial
essence
essential
evil
exact
examining
excellent
excess
excite
excuse
explode
explore
extra
extraordinary
extreme
fade
faint

false
fan
fancy
fashion
fasten
fat
fate
fault
feast
feather
female
fence
fever
fierce
film
finger
firm
flag
flame
flash
flat
flavor
flesh
float
flood
flour
fold
fond
fool
foot
forbid
forgive
fork
formal
forward
frame
freeze
frequent
fright
fruit
fry
fun
funeral
fur
gallon
gap
garage
gay
generous
glory
goat
govern
grace
gradual
grain
gram
grammar
grand
grass
grateful
grave
gray
grease
greed
greet
grind
guard

guess
guest
guide
guilty
gun
habit
hair
hall
hammer
handkerchief
handle
harbor
harm
harvest
haste
hat
hate
hay
heal
health
heap
hello
hesitate
hide
hinder
hire
hit
hole
holiday
hollow
holy
honest
hook
horizon
hospital
host
hotel
humble
hunger
hunt
hurray
hurry
hurt
hut
ice
ideal
idle
imagine
imitate
immediate
immense
improve
inform
informal
informally
inn
inquire
insect
inside
instant
instrument
insult
insure
intend
interfere
international
interrupt

invent
invite
inward
island
jaw
jealous
jewel
joke
journey
juice
jump
key
kick
kiss
kitchen
knee
kneel
knife
knock
knot
ladder
lamp
lazy
leaf
lean
leather
leg
lend
lesson
liberty
lid
limb
liquid
list
liter
load
loaf
loan
lock
lodging
log
lone
loose
lot
loud
loyal
luck
lump
lunch
lung
mad
mail
male
manage
map
mat
match
meal
meantime
meanwhile
meat
mechanic
medicine
melt
mend
merchant
mercy

merry
message
messenger
meter
mild
mill
mineral
miserable
mistake
mix
model
moderate
modest
monkey
motion
mouse
mud
multiply
murder
mystery
nail
narrow
neat
neck
needle
neglect
nephew
nest
net
nice
niece
noise
nonsense
noon
nose
noun
nuisance
nurse
nut
oar
obey
ocean
offend
omit
onward
oppose
opposite
orange
organ
origin
ornament
outline
overcome
pack
pad
pain
pair
pale
pan
parcel
pardon
parent
park
passage
passenger
paste
path

patient	pump	rub	slide	suspicion	treat
patriotic	punctual	rubber	slight	swallow	tremble
pattern	punish	rubbish	slip	swear	tribe
pause	pupil	rude	slope	sweat	trick
paw	pure	rug	slow	sweep	trip
pearl	purple	ruin	smell	swell	trunk
peculiar	push	rush	smoke	swim	tube
pen	puzzle	rust	smooth	swing	tune
pencil	qualify	sacred	snake	sympathy	twist
penny	quarrel	sacrifice	soap	tail	typical
perfect	quart	sad	sock	tailor	ugly
perform	quick	saddle	soil	tall	umbrella
permanent	quiet	sake	solemn	tame	uncle
persuade	rabbit	salary	solid	tap	universe
pet	radio	sample	solve	taste	upper
photograph	rail	sand	sore	taxi	upright
pick	rain	satisfy	sorry	tea	upset
pig	rake	sauce	soup	telegraph	upward
pigeon	rapid	saucer	sour	telephone	urge
pile	rare	saws	sow	temper	vain
pin	rat	scale	spade	temperature	veil
pinch	raw	scatter	spare	tempt	verb
pink	ray	scent	spell	tend	verse
pint	razor	scissors	spill	tender	violent
pipe	recommend	scold	spin	tent	vowel
pity	refer	scorn	spit	terrible	voyage
plane	reflect	scrape	splendid	thank	waist
plaster	refresh	scratch	split	theater	wake
plate	regret	screen	spoil	thick	wander
plenty	regular	screw	spoon	thief	warm
plough	rejoice	search	sport	thin	warn
plural	relieve	seed	staff	thirst	wash
pocket	remedy	seize	stain	thorn	waste
poem	remind	seldom	stairs	thorough	wax
poison	rent	self	stamp	thread	weak
police	repair	sentence	steady	threat	weapon
polish	repeat	severe	steal	throat	weather
polite	replace	sew	steam	thumb	weave
pool	reproduce	shade	steep	thunder	weed
postpone	reputation	shallow	steer	ticket	weigh
pot	request	shame	stem	tide	wet
pour	rescue	sharp	stick	tidy	wheat
powder	resign	shave	stiff	tie	wheel
practical	resist	sheep	sting	tight	whip
practise	responsible	sheet	stir	tin	whisper
praise	restaurant	shelf	stocking	tip	whistle
pray	retire	shell	stomach	tire	wicked
preach	revenge	shelter	storm	title	widow
precious	review	shield	stove	tobacco	wine
prefer	reward	shirt	straight	toe	wing
prejudice	ribbon	shock	strap	tomorrow	wipe
preserve	rice	shoe	straw	tongue	wire
pretend	rid	shop	stretch	tonight	witness
pride	ripe	shout	strict	tool	wool
priest	risk	shower	string	tooth	worm
print	rival	shut	strip	tough	worry
prison	roar	sick	stripe	tour	worse
prize	roast	signal	stuff	towel	worship
probable	rob	silk	stupid	tower	wrap
procession	rod	sincere	suck	toy	wreck
profession	roof	sink	sudden	track	wrist
program	root	skill	sugar	translate	yard
prompt	rope	skin	suit	trap	yellow
pronounce	rot	skirt	supper	tray	zero
proud	row	slave	suspect	treasure	

Appendix 2

Academic Word List

This is a list of the 570 words most frequently encountered in academic texts such as textbooks and professional journals.

Source: A. Coxhead, *Academic Word List*, 1998, Victoria University of Wellington, New Zealand. More information available at http://language.massey.ac.nz/staff/awl/index.shtml

abandon	bias	constitute	distinct	fee	inhibit
abstract	bond	constrain	distort	file	initial
academy	brief	construct	distribute	final	initiate
access	bulk	consult	diverse	finance	injure
accommodate	capable	consume	document	finite	innovate
accompany	capacity	contact	domain	flexible	input
accumulate	category	contemporary	domestic	fluctuate	insert
accurate	cease	context	dominate	focus	insight
achieve	challenge	contract	draft	format	inspect
acknowledge	channel	contradict	drama	formula	instance
acquire	chapter	contrary	duration	forthcoming	institute
adapt	chart	contrast	dynamic	foundation	instruct
adequate	chemical	contribute	economy	founded	integral
adjacent	circumstance	controversy	edit	framework	integrate
adjust	cite	convene	element	function	integrity
administrate	civil	converse	eliminate	fund	intelligence
adult	clarify	convert	emerge	fundamental	intense
advocate	classic	convince	emphasis	furthermore	interact
affect	clause	cooperate	empirical	gender	intermediate
aggregate	code	coordinate	enable	generate	internal
aid	coherent	core	encounter	generation	interpret
albeit	coincide	corporate	energy	globe	interval
allocate	collapse	correspond	enforce	goal	intervene
alter	colleague	couple	enhance	grade	intrinsic
alternative	commence	create	enormous	grant	invest
ambiguous	comment	credit	ensure	guarantee	investigate
amend	commission	criteria	entity	guideline	invoke
analogy	commit	crucial	environment	hence	involve
analyze	commodity	culture	equate	hierarchy	isolate
annual	communicate	currency	equip	highlight	issue
anticipate	community	cycle	equivalent	hypothesis	item
apparent	compatible	data	erode	identical	job
append	compensate	debate	error	identify	journal
appreciate	compile	decade	establish	ideology	justify
approach	complement	decline	estate	ignorant	label
appropriate	complex	deduce	estimate	illustrate	labor
approximate	component	define	ethic	image	layer
arbitrary	compound	definite	ethnic	immigrate	lecture
area	comprehensive	demonstrate	evaluate	impact	legal
aspect	comprise	denote	eventual	implement	legislate
assemble	compute	deny	evident	implicate	levy
assess	conceive	depress	evolve	implicit	liberal
assign	concentrate	derive	exceed	imply	license
assist	concept	design	exclude	impose	likewise
assume	conclude	despite	exhibit	incentive	link
assure	concurrent	detect	expand	incidence	locate
attach	conduct	deviate	expert	incline	logic
attain	confer	device	explicit	income	maintain
attitude	confine	devote	exploit	incorporate	major
attribute	confirm	differentiate	export	index	manipulate
author	conflict	dimension	expose	indicate	manual
authority	conform	diminish	external	individual	margin
automate	consent	discrete	extract	induce	mature
available	consequent	discriminate	facilitate	inevitable	maximize
aware	considerable	displace	factor	infer	mechanism
behalf	consist	display	feature	infrastructure	media
benefit	constant	dispose	federal	inherent	mediate

medical	overall	prior	require	source	theme
medium	overlap	priority	research	specific	theory
mental	overseas	proceed	reside	specify	thereby
method	panel	process	resolve	sphere	thesis
migrate	paradigm	professional	resource	stable	topic
military	paragraph	prohibit	respond	statistic	trace
minimal	parallel	project	restore	status	tradition
minimize	parameter	promote	restrain	straightforward	transfer
minimum	participate	proportion	restrict	strategy	transform
ministry	partner	prospect	retain	stress	transit
minor	passive	protocol	reveal	structure	transmit
mode	perceive	psychology	revenue	style	transport
modify	percent	publication	reverse	submit	trend
monitor	period	publish	revise	subordinate	trigger
motive	persist	purchase	revolution	subsequent	ultimate
mutual	perspective	pursue	rigid	subsidy	undergo
negate	phase	qualitative	role	substitute	underlie
network	phenomenon	quote	route	successor	undertake
neutral	philosophy	radical	scenario	sufficient	uniform
nevertheless	physical	random	schedule	sum	unify
nonetheless	plus	range	scheme	summary	unique
norm	policy	ratio	scope	supplement	utilize
normal	portion	rational	section	survey	valid
notion	pose	react	sector	survive	vary
notwithstanding	positive	recover	secure	suspend	vehicle
nuclear	potential	refine	seek	sustain	version
objective	practitioner	regime	select	symbol	via
obtain	precede	region	sequence	tape	violate
obvious	precise	register	series	target	virtual
occupy	predict	regulate	sex	task	visible
occur	predominant	reinforce	shift	team	vision
odd	preliminary	reject	significant	technical	visual
offset	presume	relax	similar	technique	volume
ongoing	previous	release	simulate	technology	voluntary
option	primary	relevant	site	temporary	welfare
orient	prime	reluctance	so-called	tense	whereas
outcome	principal	rely	sole	terminate	whereby
output	principle	remove	somewhat	text	widespread

Appendix 3

Record of Books Read

Title	Author	Date begun	Date finished	Number of pages